Karl Marx

KARL MARX
An Intellectual Biography

Rolf Hosfeld

Translated by
Bernard Heise

Berghahn Books
New York • Oxford

Published by
Berghahn Books
www.berghahnbooks.com

English-language edition
©2013 Berghahn Books

German-language edition
© Piper Verlag GmbH, München, 2009
Die Geister, die er rief. Eine neue Karl-Marx-Biografie
By Rolf Hosfeld

Library of Congress Cataloging-in-Publication Data

Hosfeld, Rolf.
[Geister, die er rief. English]
Karl Marx: an intellectual biography/Rolf Hosfeld; translated from the German
by Bernard Heise.
    p. cm.
Translation of: *Die Geister, die er rief.*
Includes bibliographical references and index.
ISBN 978-0-85745-742-4 (hardback: alk. paper)
1. Marx, Karl, 1818–1883. 2. Communists—Germany—Biography. I. Title.
HX39.5.H634713 2012
335.4092—dc23
[B]

2012001693

British Library Cataloguing in Publication Data

A catalogue record for this book is available from the British Library

Printed in the United States on acid-free paper

ISBN 978-0-85745-742-4 (hardback)

Failed prophecies
often make invaluable inspirational
reading.

RICHARD RORTY

CONTENTS

ACKNOWLEDGMENTS

Sometimes one has one's own ideas; sometimes they are provided by others. In this case it was Ulrich Wank of the Piper publishing house who suggested during a conversation in Munich that I contemplate a short, essayistic intellectual biography of Marx from a new perspective. Like many of my generation, I had read Marx's writings fairly extensively during my university studies, but more than three decades had passed since then; thus I agreed only after some hesitation. Having completed the manuscript, I am very thankful to Ulrich Wank, for without him I would certainly never have devoted myself again so fully to this subject. Gerd Koenen, Michael Jäger, and Jutta Lukas took upon themselves the friendly effort to critically review the text and thereby very much helped me to avoid unsustainable theses and obvious mistakes. My readers Renate Dörner and Kristen Rotter accompanied the product through all its stages with a watchful eye and constructive understanding, as did my wife Elke, who at appropriate and inappropriate times was always a patient listener.

Note on the Text

The author has used italics in the text to denote a quote from Marx's writings. These quotes may be only one word or a short phrase. It is the author's intention to infuse the text with Marx's voice and perspective in a seamless manner. Longer quotes from Marx and other outside sources appear in quotation marks or as indented text. The source for the italic quotes may be found in the attributed note, or in the case where several quotes appear in the paragraph, the attributed note will appear at the end of the paragraph.

IDEAS

World Spirit

"The weapon of criticism cannot, of course, replace criticism by weapons," Karl Marx wrote from Parisian exile in 1844.[1] Apart from any broader meaning, this was also a summary of his personal experience. This sentence by the then 26-year-old can thus be regarded as primarily an autobiographical statement.

Conditions of censorship had prompted Marx to resign as the editor in chief of the liberal *Rheinische Zeitung* on 18 March 1843.[2] The year had started under *gloomy prospects*,[3] and now the weapon of criticism was also knocked out of his hands. Quite a few people were frustrated with Prussian censorship, which had radicalized many. This experience played no small part in turning Marx into the radical remembered by posterity. He, too, was a child of his times.

Czar Nicholas I was to some extent personally responsible for this turn of events, for the decision against the Cologne paper came about under pressure from Russia. Anti-Russian articles criticizing Berlin's dependency on St. Petersburg displeased the czar, who lodged a determined protest against them. The Prussian ambassador was taken to task at a court ball, and a sharply formulated letter was subsequently sent from the Winter Palace to Potsdam. The *Rheinische Zeitung* was banned. Marx had to go. "I can do nothing more in Germany," he wrote at the beginning of 1843. "Here one makes a counterfeit of oneself."[4] A right life amidst the wrong? No, that was impossible. He went to Paris, the cosmopolitan European city that years earlier had also attracted the poet Heinrich Heine, for the same reasons.

Back then Heine had been pursuing the promises of the July Revolution in Paris. "Sunbeams wrapped up in printing paper" was what he called the first newspaper reports of the struggles for freedom in the French capital when they reached him.[5] For him the experience was like a journey from Hades into life. Indeed, July 1830 marked a caesura for the entire century. "These combats in the streets of Paris," wrote Benedetto Croce in the *History of Europe in the Nineteenth Century*, "attained to the significance of a world-battle; it seemed to the anxious watchers that the thick black clouds which were lowering at the horizon of European political life had suddenly been scattered by the 'July sun.'"[6] And Hegel laconically told his students in 1831 that after the downfall of Napoleon, the reestablishment of Bourbon government at the Congress of Vienna was not much more than the staging of a fifteen-year farce.[7]

A creature of the Holy Alliance had suddenly collapsed and provided contemporaries with a theatrical spectacle of a shattered eternity. It did not make world history, yet as Hegel's student Eduard Gans reported, the long-awaited defeat of the French Restoration was a great European event.[8] It revealed that the principle of revolution, not that of restoration, would determine the further course of the nineteenth century. The first consequence was the independence of Belgium. England underwent electoral reform in 1832; in 1834 Spain obtained a constitutional charter. In Germany in 1832, Liberals and Democrats gathered at the Hambach Palace for a celebration of brotherhood among nations. In the same year, Giuseppe Mazzini founded the freedom movement La Giovine Italia and made it receptive to European ideals.

The July victory in Paris, however, had already foreshadowed the beginning of a new division between the *bourgeoisie* and the *people*. Eugène Delacroix captured it with an image in his famous painting *Freedom at the Barricades*, which was the surprise of the 1831 annual Parisian Art Salon. An allegory of freedom? Yes—but only with difficulty could it maintain a balance between the bourgeoisie and the proletarian figures from the Faubourgs surging forward to the barricades. "All being leads to sorrow," the painter noted in a brief note entitled "Metaphysics."[9] Something uncertain and almost melancholic hung over this bare-breasted apotheosis of freedom from the heroic days of July. In the same year, Karl Marx entered his third year at Trier's Friedrich-Wilhelm-Gymnasium. In certain respects, Marx belonged to his century's generation marked by revolution. In Lyon in 1831 and 1834, the silk weavers staged an uprising with the battle cry "Vivre en travaillant ou mourir en combattant" (Live working or die fighting). In 1835, three years after the Hambach celebration, Marx became a university student. During the Rhine crisis in 1840 he experienced a highly emotional upsurge of Germanic feeling and hatred of the French, but this left no traces upon him. In any event, as a baptized Jew from Trier, he could hardly comprehend the nationalism that, having arisen in the wake of the Wars of Liberation against Napoleon, was receiving fresh impetus from the French call for the annexation of the territories on the left bank of the Rhine. That was not his world. He had problems with the Prussians, but his memories of the French were marked more by nostalgia. Those were the good years when the Civil Code was introduced to the Mosel region and the emancipation of the Jews was proclaimed. Also in 1840, Justus Liebig published his *Organic Chemistry in Its Application to Agriculture and Physiology*, a milestone on the way to rational agricultural practice and the modern world.

For his first semester, Marx completed the journey from Koblenz to Bonn by steamship. Since 1827 there had been a regular link between Mainz and Cologne, and it abruptly changed all conceptions of space and time. "The Rhine steamers go too fast," the heroine Wally complains in an 1835 novel by Karl Gutzkow.[10] The break from the Age of Slowness occurred at a new tempo and provoked irritation. Progress, the magic word of the eighteenth century, became manifest in the landscape. The first industrial settlements were created, steamships suddenly became a part of the romantic Rhine's silhouette, and soon the railway would slice through arcadian Nature like a sickle. The upheaval was tremendous. The future became the new slogan in a world that for hundreds of years had been based on tradition. This, too, shaped the "revolutionary generation."

In October 1836, Marx still had to use a mail coach to make his way to Berlin, his second place of study. The first railway—between Berlin and Potsdam—would not exist until two years later. Thus the journey from the Mosel to the Spree was familiarly slow, taking just over a week. Industrialization was then only taking its first tentative steps in the Prussian capital, which, despite gas lighting, still largely preserved its rural character. At the time of Marx's arrival, the future railway magnate August Borsig employed barely fifty workers.

The transfer to Berlin was his father's wish. The university there had a reputation as a demanding school far more conducive to a son's advancement than the university in Bonn, which was dominated by rakish fraternities. Marx himself, however, may have been more attracted by its reputation for academic freedom. Minister of Culture Stein zum Altenstein was still in charge there, and he cultivated Wilhelm von Humboldt's ideal—an academic space predominantly free from the state—as a political program. The university "Unter den Linden" was considered the only public space in Prussia that was more or less free of censorship, and the atmosphere in Berlin was characterized by an almost feverish intellectual curiosity. Here over the next few years Marx would be introduced to the weapons of criticism.

His first idea developed out of an intense engagement with Hegel's philosophy during a convalescent stay on the peninsula between the Spree and Lake Rummelsburger. At the beginning of 1837, the student attracted the attention of the doctor because of a *weakness in his chest and the periodic spitting up of blood,* and a little later he was declared an invalid *because of an irritability of the lungs.* That summer Marx began the first of the many spa treatments he would undergo throughout life. Illness was almost fashionable during the overly sensitive Biedermeier period in which he grew up. With his dispositions, he could easily have dedicated himself to the widespread cult of world-weariness—as the novelist Karl Immermann said in 1836, the curse of the current generation was to "feel unfortunate even without any particular afflictions." Marx did not do so, but he struggled with weak health throughout his entire life; time and again his letters were replete with reports about the condition of his lungs and bronchial tubes, gall bladder, liver, and his furunculosis. For now, though, the fresh country air in the fishing village of Stralau at the gates of the Prussian capital was supposed to reinvigorate the *anaemic weakling.*

Marx had just completed his second semester in Berlin. Initially the *grotesque craggy melody* of Hegelian philosophy remained somewhat foreign to him, but eventually it thoroughly suited his need for rest. *By moonlight* on the shore of Lake Rummelsburger, the patient delved deeply into Hegel *from beginning to end,* ran around *madly in the garden by the dirty water of the Spree,* and in the end fell *into the arms of the enemy* and became a Hegelian. The nineteen-year-old concluded that

> From the idealism which, by the way, I had compared and nourished with the idealism of Kant and Fichte, I arrived at the point of seeking the idea in reality itself. If previously the gods had dwelt above the earth, now they became its centre.

The world was inherently reasonable, even though it was also inherently contradictory. A second conclusion formed during the summer weeks in Stralau:

> In the concrete expression of a living world of ideas, as exemplified by law, the state, nature, and philosophy as a whole, the object itself must be studied in its development; arbitrary divisions must not be introduced, the rational character of the object itself must develop as something imbued with contradictions in itself and find its unity in itself.[11]

Science, Marx learned from Hegel, meant "surrender to the life of the object,"[12] and from this life of the object itself, by means of intellectual abstraction, distilling the concepts and categories that classify and order it. This claim for the potential to obtain absolute knowledge would accompany him throughout his life. Soon Marx would maintain that he himself, not Hegel, had first found the *real*[13]—because it was material—key to this.

For the time being, however, he found in Hegel the key to what his future terminology would call criticism. For Marx and his generation of young Hegelians, viewing the present "critically" meant not accepting it as a given but rather working out from its internal contradictions those principles and tendencies that pointed beyond the present toward the future. A beer garden on the banks of the Spree in Stralau became a laboratory for such thought experiments. In the summer of 1837, this was the meeting place for the Berlin Doctor Club, an eccentric circle of critical students of Hegel that now also included the young student Marx. In this somewhat bohemian atmosphere *many conflicting views were expressed*,[14] presumably quite boisterously and loudly on occasion. The theologian Bruno Bauer, who was to have an especially strong influence on Marx, was initially not among them, being still an orthodox Hegelian at the time. The origins of the Left Hegelians, without whom Marx's further development can scarcely be imagined, lay not in academic seminar rooms or lecture halls but rather in the Stralau tavern and at regular literati meetings in a café in the Französische Straße. They claimed—treating Hegel somewhat one-sidedly—not that reality was necessarily inherently reasonable, but rather that reason was the actual reality. And reason was essentially negating, that is, "critical."

If pursued with reference to the Prussian state, this abstract inquiry could become directly political. Was this state already a reasonable entity for Hegel, or did reason still need to develop into reality within this state? Did not the Hegelian *embodiment of the idea*, the *embodiment of freedom*, Marx asked a little later, also and necessarily require the freedom of unlimited public expression of opinion?[15] Was Prussia thus still inherently a highly unreasonable state?

Hegel would presumably have answered: in principle, no; in its details, yes. In any case, this was how he formulated matters in a letter to State Chancellor Hardenberg when sending him a copy of his *Philosophy of Right*.[16] But Hegel had been dead for six years when Marx delved into his works. Marx essentially became familiar with Hegel's philosophy through his most gifted student, Eduard Gans—which meant Hegel as seen from a liberal perspective. At the time Gans was a celebrated man at the university in Berlin. In the winter semester of 1838/39—Marx's fifth semester in Berlin—Gans resumed his "contemporary historical" lectures about politics and social issues in modern Europe, which he had discontinued five years earlier under pressure from the authorities. A captivating and almost hypnotic speaker whose meetings often attracted hundreds of listeners, he was considered, like his role model Mirabeau, a herald of new liberal confidence during a time of Prussian agony. The students arrived in enthusiastic torchlight processions, and the lecture halls could barely cope with the congestion.

Hegel had taught that the state was the "march of God in the world," the reality of the ethical idea.[17] To be sure, Gans believed this as well, but in contrast to Hegel he held the view that in modern times this "reality" could only be produced through the public and free competition of ideas—through "opposition." "If the state will have nothing to do with opposition," he announced, "then it lapses into laziness." And if in the process an agreement between civil society and the state was not possible—for example, due to the repression of the opposition—then at some point there would inevitably be a revolution,[18] one that by rights would be welcomed by "every better and progressive person."[19] It was the Vormärz: Old Europe found itself at the "beginning of its end," and even Prince Metternich, the architect of the restoration, knew it. There were no prospects for "honorable capitulations."[20]

After 1840, the idea that it might be possible in Prussia to strike a balance between the regime and a rapidly modernizing society slipped ever further away. That year Friedrich Wilhelm IV became king in Prussia. At first it looked as if the new king would, in the words of the Russian envoy Peter von Meyendorff, provide for "une certain couleur libérale,"[21] a certain liberal coloring. He issued an amnesty for political prisoners and courted a number of well-known heroes of the Wars of Liberation and opponents of Metternich's system. The parliaments and press became freer, and a wave of enthusiasm accompanied the change in rulers. However, it very quickly became clear that Friedrich Wilhelm was by no means a liberal.

Marx was among the few who recognized this early on. "Already when the oath of allegiance was taken in Königsberg, he justified my supposition that the question would now become a purely personal one," he noted in retrospect. "He declared that his heart and his turn of mind would be the future fundamental law of the realm of Prussia, of *his* state."[22] The immense and elaborate spectacle Friedrich Wilhelm had staged in Königsberg was born of his desire to invent the sacred tradition of the Prussian monarchy—one that did not exist. He was a Romantic obsessed with the past who wanted to surprise Metternich's cold world of power with something *extravagant*.[23] This extravagance was Friedrich Wilhelm's "Christian state," the fantastical product of a late-Romantic art-religion that raved about Christian regeneration through the spirit of an ancient Christianity, understood more aesthetically than religiously, and the divine origins of royal dignity. He had his "lords" and "cavaliers" and dreamed of a sacred mystical union as hollow as the figure of Christ adorning the courtyard of his Church of Peace in Potsdam, arms outspread to offer protection and blessings. But what he initially promised with respect to a certain liberalization of the press was nothing more than "respectable publicity" inserted into the privilege-based order of his personal rule.[24] He was the living denial of the Fredrickian rational state in which Hegel and, to a lesser extent, his students had placed all their hopes for the potential for reform from within.

In Prussia, Marx noted laconically, in reality *the King is the system*, and it was only a matter of time before the ludicrous historical comedy of this new cavalier would end in tragedy. For while the court *wove fantasies in the old German manner*, elsewhere, people had long ago started to *philosophise in the new German manner*. In other words, Marx and others had possessed the *audacity* of *wanting to turn men into human beings*[25] and had stripped away from them the supposedly divinely willed corset of the Estates and subjects.

It was a radical break in thought, and not only with respect to royal romanticism. The fact that this break had theological origins was very significant for Marx's further development. Around 1840 in the Berlin Doctor Club, a veritable "scientific terrorism"[26] had dawned, led by Bruno Bauer, whom a friend at the time called the "Robespierre of theology."[27] As a consequence, the New Hegelians had announced the "dissolution" of the idea of religion and in the same breath that of the Christian state as well. "Zeitgeist" had been a fashionable word for years, and in 1840 the poet Georg Herwegh noted that the "sword of revolution" is always felt first in literature. In this respect, language too had changed, becoming impetuous "like the pace of the times, cutting like a sword and beautiful like freedom and spring."[28] Among the young Hegelians, the idea spread that they stood on the threshold of a new era of Enlightenment that was unique in history, and they actually began to search within their own ranks for the future German Robespierre and Marat. As Marx confided in his handwritten notes while working on his dissertation, one felt like *Prometheus, who having stolen fire from heaven begins to build houses and to settle upon the earth.*[29] It was quite an intense atmosphere, in which everything flourished.

As Marx began his studies in Berlin, the debate among Hegelian students was completely dominated by the polemic *The Life of Jesus, Critically Examined*, written by the Tübingen theologian David Friedrich Strauß and perceived as a provocation. The Hegelian Strauß, a researcher of myths, assumed that all Christology had been imputed to the historical figure of Jesus of Nazareth. In contrast to the atheists of the French Enlightenment, however, he did not consider this to be a deliberate fraud or a clever invention but rather a myth that expressed a profound truth[30]—namely, the incarnation of God—in the form of an unconscious idea. This truth, however, could not be reduced to whether Jesus was actually born, lived, and was resurrected in the manner described by the Evangelists. The real message was rather that the person "in his immediate consciousness knew himself to be one with God."[31] This view could with some justification call upon Hegel, who likewise polemicized against what he held to be the eighteenth century's abstract theory of priestly fraud and asserted by contrast that even religion possessed truth, albeit "in the form of *picture-thoughts.*"[32] Additionally, writing in the era of the Grimm brothers' research into legends and fairy tales and Niebuhr's source criticism,[33] Strauß could not treat historical sources as naively and unself-consciously as Hegel and Goethe had done— a realization that came to Marx as well. Especially when moving into the individual scientific and scholarly disciplines, speculative philosophy needed to meet the challenge of the factual and empirically demonstrable.

For the time being, however, it confronted the internal contradictions of theory. For several years, the theologian Bruno Bauer was in this respect the dominant figure in the Berlin Doctor Club. He began teaching at the university "Unter den Linden" in 1834 and first drew attention to himself in 1835 when, on the instigation of the orthodox pietist theologian Ernst Wilhelm Hengstenberg, he published a scathing review of Strauß's *Life of Jesus*. In 1840, however, he did a complete about-face, now describing Strauß's text as an event that struck the realm of theological bliss like a contemplative lightning bolt. Shortly thereafter he published his *Critique of the Synoptics,* whose thorough exegesis, as the theologically learned Marx pointed out, proved that the contradictions alone in the reports of the evangelists disqualified them as reliable records of historical fact.[34] It was indeed a solid critical work, and Albert Schweitzer wrote in *The Quest of the Historical Jesus* that Bauer's criticism of the evangelical histories of the synoptists was worth a dozen good Lives of Jesus. To date, Schweitzer insisted, it was the most ingenious and complete index of the problems with the historicity of Jesus's life.[35]

In the 1840s, however, Bauer and his views hit a roadblock, given the radical conclusions he drew from his criticism. He maintained that the Evangelists were the product of a zeitgeist that included not only the stories of the life of Jesus but also set pieces from Jewish, Alexandrian, Greek, and Roman myths and philosophies. In other words, the Evangelists represented nothing more than a late-antique interim stage of human self-consciousness that assumed institutionalized forms in the Christian religion, thereby taking on a life of its own and preserving itself.

Marx, who as a student of Bauer in the late 1830s attended his seminars at the university, was considered a veritable arsenal of ideas among friends in the Doctor Club. Bauer invited him to collaborate on a new edition of the Hegelian lectures on the philosophy of religion, awakening in Marx the desire to write something comparable, although he never realized this goal. The theologian was deeply impressed by the younger man's exuberant intellectual spirit; likewise, Bruno Bauer's influence on Marx can hardly be overestimated.

"The ego was everything and yet it was empty," Bauer wrote about early Christianity in the third volume of his *Critique of the Synoptics*. "It did not dare to conceive of itself as everything and the universal power, that is it remained a religious conception and completed its alienation in that it placed its own universal power over itself and worked in the sight of this power in fear and trembling for its preservation and holiness."[36] Thus in religion the object of the fantasy of human consciousness had assumed independence as its own being. A calcified product of the human spirit began to rule the living. In religion, according to Bauer, the person was bereft of himself, and the being stolen from him was transferred to heaven and thus made into a non-being, a nonhuman.[37]

Marx would never escape from the influence exerted by this intellectual concept of an inverted theology. For him, capital in the modern economic process would remain a general, self-created demiurge that confronts and rules over the person as an alien force. It was a grandiose vision of a world without gods, in which the person was the true source of every society, all politics, the world of ideas, and history; the person was its actual but also dispossessed and alienated "causa sui,"[38] the truth of which, however, could only be recognized once criticism had opened the person's eyes.

When Bauer wrote the work *Christianity Exposed* in 1842, he already saw himself entirely in the role of a radical Enlightenment philosopher, as was supposed to be clear from the allusion to the title of Paul Henri Thiry d'Holbach's atheistic polemic *Le christianisme dévoilé*, written eighty years earlier. Through the critique of religion, Bauer wanted to dispel the "delirium of humanity" and thereby lead humanity to an understanding of itself again.[39] The first political target was Friedrich Wilhelm's Christian state, for a state that according to Bauer would be a creation of self-consciousness could no longer be a Christian state. At the very least, it required the legal acceptance of an enlightened and critical opposition.[40] In political terms, this was a liberal position.

But conditions in Prussia drove Bauer toward increased radicalism. In 1839, following a literary feud with the mighty Hengstenberg, he was transferred as a precaution to Bonn, initially as a *Privatdozent,* albeit with the prospect of soon becoming a professor. He wanted Marx to join him as quickly as possible and pressured him to finally take his "wretched exam," suggesting that the following summer Marx would already be delivering lectures in Bonn.[41] But then Altenstein, the last proponent of liberal academic policy in Prussia, died. His successor, Friedrich von Eichhorn, ensured a fundamental change of course after 1840.

In that year Friedrich Julius Stahl, who considered the state a necessary consequence of humanity's sinful nature, became the successor of the liberal Eduard Gans, who had died young, and in 1841 the elderly Schelling was called from Munich to Berlin to use his authority to smoke out the entire troublesome hive of Hegelianism—the "dragon spawn of Hegelian pantheism, the shallow know-it-allness, and the legal dissolution of domestic discipline," as Friedrich Wilhelm informed him through a confidant.[42] Also in 1841, the police investigated students at Halle University who had petitioned for David Friedrich Strauß's appointment as a professor. Only a theologian, Marx noted shortly thereafter, could believe that this period's confrontations concerned religion as religion.[43] In reality, they were about the ideological pillars of the Christian state. Even for Bruno Bauer, it was not chiefly his critical theology that sealed his doom but rather his invocation of Hegel when, during a visit by the South German liberal Carl Theodor Welcker, he publicly proposed a toast to Hegel and in particular his conception of a constitutional state governed by laws.[44] After this performance, the king himself promptly directed Eichhorn to dismiss Bauer as a *Privatdozent* in Bonn and scuttle his academic career by blocking any further opportunities.

The campaign against Hegel had intensified in the late 1830s. Not only was Hegel's theory of the constitutional state an attack on the personality principle of the pure monarchy, the Silesian monarchist Karl Ernst Schubarth observed in 1839, but it was tantamount to a call for insurrection and rebellion, and the whole speculative dialectic with its so-called specific negations was in reality nothing other than a disguised black mass in which God must humbly request of the Devil "that he help him—as the negation to be sublated—attain his supreme existence."[45] Quite right, replied Bruno Bauer, who had been denied all bourgeois career opportunities. Playing the picaresque role of a strict orthodox pietist, Bauer announced that Hegel was in fact an atheist; he knew how to disguise himself well, but actually, with his message that God as a person was dead, he represented the "root of evil." Strictly speaking, his theory was "Revolution itself."[46] This was to be demonstrated in a public provocation—a satirical "ultimatum" comprised of citations from Hegel's collected works entitled the *Trumpet of the Last Judgment against Hegel the Atheist and Antichrist: an Ultimatum*, published anonymously in October 1841. Marx presumably also participated in this intellectual carnival; at any rate, he was supposed to collaborate on a continuation with a second *Ultimatum*.[47]

At the time, Marx was living in Bonn. Even after Berlin, Bauer joked to Marx that pietists had sensitive noses, a "premonition of a crisis, like animals prior to a change in the life of nature." But the planned response of the left Hegelians would become a catastrophe for the pietists, "terrible and drastic" and "greater and more enormous" than the catastrophe by which Christianity had entered the world.[48] This rhetoric revealed an unintentional theatricality, which the two young "critics," Bauer and Marx, also displayed by riding donkeys through Godesberg on holidays, thereby deeply disturbing Bonn's decent society and greatly amusing themselves by poking fun at the philistines of this officious Prussian administrative town on the Rhine. Were they trying to emulate the eccentric Prince Pückler, whose favorite public appearances included driving a team of deer along Unter den Linden in Berlin? Or did Marx, as a Rhinelander, have in mind the carnivalesque tradition of the *Eselsmesse* (Mass of Asses)? At times they lived (and caroused) in an overstimulated, early-adolescent mood of superiority and boundlessness.

Then the *Trumpet of the Last Judgment* was banned. The *carnival of philosophy* that Marx had discussed in the handwritten notes for his dissertation was no longer a viable option. On 15 April 1841, he received his doctorate with a dissertation on the difference between democritical and epicurean natural philosophy, but the removal of his mentor Bauer from Bonn University suddenly dashed all hopes for a future academic career. Needed now were no longer the intellectual games of *half-hearted minds* in ivory towers, but rather the judgments of *whole-hearted generals*.[49]

Liberalism

One could be forced, like Themistocles when Athens was threatened with destruction, to leave one's home completely and *to found a new Athens at sea, in another different element*, Marx wrote while still working on his doctorate.[50] In other words, he had to dedicate himself to the liberal political opposition that, as the *party of the concept*, was the only party in a position to make *real progress*.[51] Marx was twenty-two years old when he put these words to paper. At twenty-four, well on his way to becoming a familiar personality in Germany, he became a political journalist.

The reason that the Prussian government not only allowed but even encouraged the publication of the *Rheinische Zeitung für Politik, Handel und Gewerbe* (Rhenish newspaper for politics, trade, and industry) on 1 January 1842 was due to confessional disputes in the Rhineland. Since 1837, when a conflict over mixed marriages ended with the imprisonment of the refractory Archbishop Droste zu Vischering of Cologne, Berlin's relationship with its Catholic subjects along the Rhine had been exceptionally tense. Admittedly, Friedrich Wilhelm IV had attempted reconciliation by staging the 1842 festival for the construction of the Cologne cathedral as a kind of ecumenical event in the spirit of pan-German Christianity. Yet the Rhineland's independent will continued to make itself felt. In particular, the Prussians wanted to set up an effective counterpoise to the *Kölnische Zeitung* published by DuMont-Schauberg, which with eight thousand subscribers counted among the leading newspapers in Germany and in Berlin was regarded as a disruptive mouthpiece for Catholic ultramontanism. Thus the concession for the *Rheinische Zeitung* was approved with relative ease.

With steamships and the beginnings of railway construction, Cologne was experiencing a noticeable rejuvenation after a long period of economic agony. Industrialists and bankers like Gustav Mevissen, Ludolf Camphausen, David Hansemann, and Salomon Oppenheim represented a self-confident stratum of the new Rhenish *Großbürgertum* that was striving for political influence. Industry had gained enough strength to become an independent force, noted Mevissen in 1840, and where industry was a strong force, political power and freedom ensued. Even in political terms, a new era was inevitably approaching. Mevissen was among other things a member of the directorate of the Rhenish Railway Society and, in the judgment of

Hans-Ulrich Wehler, an early social liberal.[52] He was undoubtedly the most interesting figure of this affiliated circle of Cologne liberals. Another member, Moses Hess, a scion of a wealthy Jewish family, is credited alongside the conservative Hegelian Lorenz von Stein with introducing France's communist ideas to Germany.

Hess was the first communist Marx personally encountered. Both were from the Rhineland, came from bourgeois families, and were under the influence of Hegel's philosophy. Marx made an "imposing impression" on Hess upon their first acquaintance in September 1841, when Marx was still in Bonn with Bruno Bauer. After their initial encounter Hess had the sense of having met the "greatest, perhaps the only real philosopher now living," one who would soon—Hess was referring here to the lecture halls of Bonn University—"draw upon him the eyes of Germany."[53]

Hess played a leading role in the negotiations over the founding of the *Rheinische Zeitung*. He was actually the spirit of the whole operation, also chairing a socialist club that included Mevissen and the well-to-do solicitor Gustav Jung, a former member of the Berlin Doctor Club.

At this point, the perspectives of socialism and liberalism were still very similar. In contrast to Friedrich Wilhelm's Christian state, liberalism and socialism stood philosophically on the ground of immanentism—happiness on earth. Bound more to Kant's ideas in East Prussia, and in the West more to the traditions of the French Revolution and the Napoleonic period, liberalism was essentially a postrevolutionary movement, just as Hegel's philosophy was a postrevolutionary philosophy of the French Revolution. At first glance, it must come as a surprise that even people from the upper bourgeois circles around the *Rheinische Zeitung* therefore felt close to the radical intellectuals of the Hegelian school. Included among their fundamental demands were the rights to freedom of opinion and the press, whereas conservatives advocated the view that there could only be freedom for the truth as they themselves defined it. The liberals also demanded actual representative bodies, understanding them in the decidedly Hegelian sense as institutions of realized reason. Overall, as Thomas Nipperdey has noted, a kind of crypto-politics in vogue at the time was turning into actual politics. Standing behind all of the parties was basically a metapolitical philosophy, a secularized theology.[54]

The coalition of the *Rheinische Zeitung* was also metapolitical when the newspaper was summoned to life with share capital amounting to 20,000 Taler. One of its most important members was Dagobert Oppenheim, who had fallen in with the young Hegelians in Berlin and now lived in Cologne as a co-owner of the banking house Salomon Oppenheim Jr. & Cie. He had arranged the financing in 1841 with a prospectus for a limited partnership in the founding of a new newspaper.

Marx's first article in the *Rheinische Zeitung*, on the Rhineland Landtag's debate over freedom of the press, appeared on 5 May 1842. Remarkable in a time of argumentative feuilletons, it reported well-researched, concrete details. One could say that it clearly indicated that its author was moving from philosophical speculation toward solid ground. Citing individual speakers and imparting a view of the narrow interests of the different estates, it concluded by persuading readers that a censorship law was not a law but rather a police measure, and that in contrast, only a law granting freedom of the press could be a *real law because it is the positive existence of freedom.*[55] Thus was Hegelian legal philosophy applied to concrete daily events, and on this issue the Rhenish liberals around Mevissen and Camphausen were largely of one mind. They could feel themselves understood even in Marx's sharp polemic against the historical school of law, for in reality its target was the king himself, whom Marx was accusing of representing the *right of arbitrary power.*[56] If there had ever been a Christian state, Marx insisted, it would have been Byzantium, for only in this caesaropapist entity were the dogmas of religion simultaneously matters of state.[57] All of this thought still followed Hegelian paths.

Yet the historical experience of Marx's generation was already completely different from that of Hegel's. When the latter published his *Philosophy of Right,* the Prussian provincial Landtäge did not yet exist. But increasingly parties began to form out of the Estates, something Freiherr von Stein noted as a positive development shortly before his death in 1831.[58] And although Hegel had imagined otherwise, the Estates themselves were less and less capable of representing bourgeois society. Basically, the Estates were "natural"—or, as Marx would say, zoology—whereas parties represented the principle—appropriately suited for modernity—of the reasonable, or at least informed, spirit. "Without parties there is no development," wrote Marx in the *Rheinische Zeitung* on 14 July 1842, the anniversary of the French Revolution, adding, "without demarcation there is no progress."[59] In this too he could rest assured that he was in agreement with Rhenish liberals, so much so that, even after the March Revolution in 1848, Prussian Minister of Finance David Hansemann toyed with the idea of bringing the talented young man to Berlin for the business of politics.

Marx was twenty-eight years old when, on 15 October 1842, he was appointed editor in chief of the *Rheinische Zeitung*. Since summer he had found himself increasingly involved in editorial work, especially since Adolf Rutenberg, the chief editor at the time and Marx's best friend from the days of the Doctor Club in Stralau, was increasingly discrediting himself with alcoholic excesses. In practical terms, Marx had already replaced Rutenberg in July. Rutenberg was *absolutely incapable*, he wrote at the time to Arnold Ruge, publisher of the young Hegelian *Deutsche Jahrbücher* (German yearbooks) in Dresden, and *sooner or later he will be shown the door*.[60] These words clearly anticipated the parlance of the "Dictatorship of Marx," as the Prussian censorship authorities called the period when he was editor in chief. Mevissen described him as "domineering, impetuous, passionate" and "full of boundless self-confidence," but also "deeply earnest and learned."[61] But above all Marx was often internally restless and occasionally somewhat driven, as his contemporary, the journalist Karl Heinzen, described him, and at the same time he enjoyed exercising his power over others. "I will destroy you," he once hissed at Heinzen on the occasion of a controversy about the Prussian bureaucracy.[62] But the dispute with Rutenberg also involved objective reasons.

Rutenberg had given his Berlin friends—"The Free" from the former Doctor Club, whose behaviors were increasingly bohemian—too much free rein. In June in the *Rheinische Zeitung*, Edgar Bauer, for example, railed against the "juste milieu" of the upper bourgeoisie, the exact opposite of those who, like him, wanted radically and critically to push "principles to their extremes."[63] The rhetoric was not very effective, but articles like this very much displeased the publishers, leading Marx to announce a corrective realignment of editorial policy in a letter to Dagobert Oppenheim. Under no circumstances did he want to challenge the censors with senseless provocations. Above all, though, he was fundamentally opposed to this kind of light, provocative feuilleton.

"The concrete theory," he informed Oppenheim, "must be made clear and developed within the concrete conditions and on the basis of the existing state of things."[64] He demanded the demonstration of *more expert knowledge* and not, for example, en passant and *inappropriately* smuggling communist and socialist *doctrine* into theater reviews and similar edifying articles.[65] Briefly put, he wanted journalism that was well grounded and empirically detailed, in contrast to the style of his old friends, whom he soon mocked as the inspired congregation of a new holy family. "As you already know, every day the censorship mutilates us mercilessly, so that frequently the newspaper is hardly able to appear," he reported at the end of November to Ruge:

> Because of this, a mass of articles by "The Free" have perished. But I have allowed myself to throw out as many articles as the censor, for Meyen and Co. sent us heaps of scribbling, pregnant with revolutionizing the world and empty of ideas, written in a slovenly style and seasoned with a little atheism and communism (which these gentlemen have never studied). Because of Rutenberg's complete lack of critical sense, independence and ability, Meyen and Co. had become accustomed to regard the *Rheinische Zeitung* as *their own*, docile organ, but I believed I could not any longer permit this watery torrent of words in the old manner. This loss of a few worthless creations of "freedom," a freedom which strives primarily "to be free from all thought," was therefore the first reason for a darkening of the Berlin sky.[66]

Ruge replied: such "absurdities of student shallowness," carelessly bandied about with buzzwords like "atheism, communism, decapitation, and guillotining," must at all costs be kept at arm's length.[67] The last report in the *Rheinische Zeitung* from the pen of one of Berlin's "The Free" ran on 8 December 1842.[68] It was Marx's first great political divorce for reasons of principle, though many more would follow.

Once the Rheinische Zeitung had departed from the form of the zeitgeist's argumentative Berlin feuilleton and increasingly turned to *questions of the real state, practical questions*,[69] and the specific problems of the Rhineland, the newspaper's circulation noticeably increased—from under a thousand copies in October to over three and half thousand prior to Christmas in 1842. From its very inception, interference and prohibitions would threaten the newspaper time and again, but for the moment its basic pro-Prussian, *North-German*–oriented spirit,[70] directed against the ultramontanism of the *Kölnische Zeitung*, gave it special status, even for Eichhorn.

While working there, Marx grew familiar with concrete politics: the Landtag with its Estates—distinguished by virtue of status and property—and its narrow-minded interests, whose reality completely contradicted the ideal condition of Hegelian political philosophy. One subject he chose to address, as the Landtag debated laws regarding the theft of wood, was a preindustrial problem that incidentally also preoccupied Mevissen: the hardship of pauperism, which, alongside child labor and poorly paid women's labor, was widespread. Indeed, since 1830 poverty had become a massive problem in Germany, and by the mid 1840s the Cologne Poor Roll listed around 25,000 persons—out of a city population of 95,000.[71] But Marx chiefly provoked irritation by justifying a Mosel correspondent's report on the misery of the peasants in the Mosel region, caused by the open borders of the German Customs Union. He began by stating that given a *lively press movement*, the entire truth would become apparent bit by bit.[72] The details, facts, and statistics he provided penetrated all the way to Berlin and even embarrassed the king's uninformed advisors, who rambled on somewhat helplessly about unavoidable transitional phenomena. The fact that these matters were even made public was in itself scandalous, for Friedrich Wilhelm IV had made it known that Prussia was to be regarded as a blessed and fortunate country. As a rule, the censors energetically suppressed reports of social distress, including the famine in Upper Silesia.

Thus the modest freedoms of the liberal Cologne press came to an end in the wake of the investigative reports from the Mosel, which stultified censors and the state's highest officials; the sharp criticism of censorship itself; and not least the pressure the czar brought to bear personally. Dr. Marx, with his "extraordinary talents" and "admirable dialectic," noted the *Mannheimer Abendzeitung*, had undoubtedly been the guiding spirit of the *Rheinische Zeitung* and endowed it with its first historical significance.[73] But the banning of the "Hurenschwester" (sister-of-a-whore),[74] as Friedrich Wilhelm put it, meant the end of Marx's exclusive weapons of criticism for the time being.

The Riddle of Modernity

The *Rheinische Zeitung*, Marx observed after the crackdown, had only ever asserted claims that according to its conviction were reasonable, whether they proceeded from one side or the other. In contrast, he saw the monarchy's reaction as resembling a reprise performance by those obscurantists who at one time, in defiance of all reason, had put the Copernican world system on the Index, declaring it invalid.[75] The banning of the *Rheinische Zeitung* had clearly shown that the use of force would assure that the ideas prevailing in Prussia would be those of the current ruling class, regardless of how unreasonable and outdated they were. Marx's first idea—that of reasonable freedom—had failed because of the Prussian circumstances of his time. It was this failure that led him toward the path of revolution.

As Jenny von Westphalen, his wife of many years, wrote to him when he became an editor for the *Rheinische Zeitung*, he had gotten mixed up in the most dangerous (*Halsbrechendste mengelirt*) thing imaginable, namely, politics. His hopes of finally attaining the respectable position of a good match as a husband had suddenly vanished. He rejected an offer, presumably made through Jenny's half brother, Ferdinand (later the Prussian interior minister), to enter the state service in Berlin, refusing to allow himself to be bought by Prussia.[76] As the Cologne censor Saint-Paul wrote with covert admiration in his final evaluation to Berlin, Marx was someone who might be accused of "anything, but not a lack of principles."[77] Meanwhile, Arnold Ruge had a plan: now that his *Deutsche Jahrbücher* was also suppressed, he would continue his project abroad "as long as this police fury lasts"[78] in order to thereby escape the "self-castration of the German spirit." "Could you get by with a fixed income of 550 or 600 Taler?" he inquired of the still editor in chief of the *Rheinische Zeitung*.[79] Including the honorariums he could expect to receive as a writer, Marx could count on an annual income of 850 Taler as copublisher of Ruge's new project. Once the contract was finalized, this would provide an acceptable basis for his long-desired marriage. "I have been engaged for more than seven years," he informed Ruge in mid March, "and for my sake my fiancée has fought the most violent battles, which almost undermined her health, partly against her pietistic aristocratic relatives, for whom 'the Lord in heaven' and the 'lord in Berlin' are equally objects of religious cult, and partly against my own family, in which some priests and other enemies of mine have ensconced themselves."[80]

To escape the pressure against this liaison from Jenny's half brother Ferdinand, Jenny's sympathetic mother, Caroline von Westphalen, promptly brought her daughter along for a long stay at the spa in Kreuznach, whose fashionable new bathhouse had just been completed that year. Without family—and without the Civil Code ceremony that was common on the left side of the Rhine—the marriage took place on 19 June 1843 in Kreuznach's St. Paul's Church on the bank of the Nahe. After a honeymoon of several weeks in Switzerland and Baden, the couple returned to Kreuznach and remained there for another quarter of a year in the house of Jenny's mother.

Now that the *Rheinische Zeitung* was no more, Marx seized this opportunity *to withdraw from the public stage to my study*, which meant flooding his mother-in-law's salon with books, excerpts, and manuscripts so that, in the wake of his recent Prussian experiences, he could grapple more intensely with Hegelian legal philosophy. Summarizing the laboratory of his thoughts at the time, he later wrote:

> My inquiry led me to the conclusion that neither legal relations nor political forms could be comprehended whether by themselves or on the basis of a so-called general development of the human mind, but that on the contrary they originate in the material conditions of life, the totality of which Hegel, following the example of English and French thinkers of the eighteenth century, embraces within the term "civil society"; that the anatomy of this civil society, however, has to be sought in political economy.[81]

In other words, he found himself on the way to his second idea—historical materialism.

But the steps taken in his studies in Kreuznach initially led him from liberalism toward a systematic theory of democracy. For a certain period, this position brought him into proximity with Arnold Ruge. The latter's demand to elevate "in all spheres the free person to a principle and the people to a purpose"—in short, a "dissolution of liberalism into democratism"[82]—had led to the prohibition of his *Deutsche Jahrbücher* in early 1843. The fronts of the Vormärz began increasingly to radicalize. Even Marx concluded from his Kreuznach engagement with Hegel's constitutional law that only in a democracy could a constitution be what it essentially needed to be, namely, a *free product of man*. "Hegel proceeds from the state," he noted in the first of what would later become his famous philosophical inversions, "and makes man into the subjectified state; democracy starts with man and makes the state objectified man; just as it is not religion that creates man but man who creates religion, so it is not the constitution that creates the people but the people which creates the constitution."[83] But the issue here was something other than pure philosophy: it was about establishing parties. Until 1848, Prussia did not have a constitution at all, not even a Hegelian one. At this particular time it was thus crucial to know what the world should look like after the foreseeable fall of the Ancien Régime. Liberalism wanted constitutional limitations, the containment of state power by means of constitutional law, and, in the best-case scenario, selective suffrage for the representative organs. By contrast, the movement for radical democracy taking shape in Germany wanted unlimited sovereignty of the people and majority rule.

Marx, newly married to his secretary in the Kreuznach salon, saw the outcome of his critique of Hegel as the conception of a political system without mediation. The entire construction of Hegelian constitutional law was obsolete—but not because it rested on the antiquated construction of the representation of Estates and the presumption of a leading role for the state bureaucracy. Rather, its obsolescence lay much more in the claim that the modest pluralism in these institutions was able to produce a balance between the interests of the state and civil society, a task that today falls to the system of parties and associations. Basically, Marx wanted a political system without any differentiation because he had come to see that mediating entities were unable to reconcile the interests of the state and civil society. This is one of the earliest examples of his mode of thought, which Georges Gurvitch once called an "inflation of antinomies."[84] "Real extremes," Marx wrote, "cannot be mediated precisely because they are real extremes. Nor do they require mediation, for they are opposed in essence." He wanted to resolve this ostensibly irreconcilable opposition between state and society into a democracy, or in any event into what he considered as such, for in a *true democracy* the political state was in actuality nothing more than *a particular form of existence of the people.*

Hegel admittedly demonstrated a certain depth by perceiving the division between civil and political society as a *contradiction*, but by recommending a mediating entity he had wrongly declared the appearance of a resolution to be the resolution itself. With the mediating entities of the three-step dialectical approach of the universal, particular, and individual, Marx declared in the spirit of a modern proponent of Enlightenment, speculative philosophy admittedly gave *political body to his logic*, but it did not develop—as would be appropriate—*the logic of the body politic.*[85] But what was the logic specific to a body politic supposed to be? An emanation, or the *particular form of being of a people*? Presumably Marx had something similar in mind with these dark words. But then his criticism did not strike at Hegelian constitutional law alone; more forcefully, it called into question any structured constitutional law whatsoever.

Above all, however, the Hegelian demand for differentiation cannot, as Marx suggests, simply be dismissed as the voluntarism of forcing logical categories onto empirical circumstances. This demand was largely the result of experiences during the French Revolution and the dead end of the Jacobin phase of *absolute freedom*, whose unstructured nature Hegel regarded as having led inevitably to the Terror. Indeed, in his *Phenomenology of Spirit*, Hegel devoted a chapter to the dialectic of the Enlightenment. Here he described Jacobin rule as one where "all social groups or classes which are the spiritual spheres into which the whole is articulated are abolished," as the "corpse of the vanished independence of real being or the being of faith," and as a mere "fury of destruction."[86] But Marx's generation had evidently already forgotten this chapter. The call for differentiation and mediating entities between state and society had much more to do with this historical experience than with the arbitrary application of philosophical ontology to political circumstances. Even if the details of Hegel's institutional doctrine were open to critique, it nonetheless clearly represented an attempt to conceptualize anew, in a modern and more complex world, what he saw as the world-historical impulse of the French Revolution so that this impulse could be preserved.

But for Marx's generation, the French Revolution was considered an unfinished event for other reasons. It appeared not to have solved the modern riddle of the world's duplication into state and society. In Kreuznach, Marx held that an unlimited direct democracy along Rousseauian lines—where *all wish individually to share in the legislature*—could overcome this problem and sublate the division of state and society through the movement of a dialectical treatment. Namely, once *everyone* operated without difference as parts of the same political body, then its abstraction would be carried so far to the extreme that it would directly bring about the *transcendence* [Aufhebung] *of the abstraction*.[87] Was this dynamic perhaps supposed to comprise the "real" *logic of the body politic* Hegel had called for? For a young man who had just set out to devastate philosophical speculation, these were highly speculative thoughts. Shortly thereafter

Marx would radicalize his conception so that the riddle would only be solved when the *real, individual man* reabsorbed in himself *the abstract citizen* and *as an individual human being* became the *species-being* in his empirical life, individual work, and individual condition.[88] When dealing with the future, Marx's conceptions always remained vague and philosophically undefined. They sustained themselves, in Jürgen Habermas's formulation, on the illusion that in principle all objectified, systematically autonomized social relationships could be led back to the horizon of the world of lived experience.[89] Basically, these were surprisingly simple answers to extremely complicated questions.

But the questions had been raised, and they had something to do with the new problems and contradictions of a rising industrial society. As early as 1831, the French socialist Pierre Leroux wrote in the *Revue encyclopédique:* "For forty years, one state form follows the next and one after the other collapses similarly into an abyss. All the while the Sphinx of the Revolution still wears its mysterious headband upon which is written the formulation of the task assigned to us by our fathers: liberty, equality, fraternity."[90] Basically, Eugène Delacroix's "Freedom at the Barricades" was the first icon of this sphinx, a "strange blending of Phryne, poissarde, and goddess of liberty," as Heinrich Heine described it.[91] During the 1830s and 1840s, French socialists and communists labored on this sphinx with a variety of plans for the future; now, from the same angle, Marx approached the question about the riddle of modernity. He became a communist shortly thereafter, moving with Jenny from Kreuznach to Parisian exile.

There were real communists in the French capital, and although they initially formed, in Heine's words, a small "ecclesia pressa" (suppressed church), they played a significant role in the city. They were the only party in France, Heine noted in mid 1843, that deserved resolute attention[92] in the early capitalist society of "Enrichissez-vous," which otherwise was mainly characterized by the eternal conflict of a present addicted to enrichment and lacking any moral footing in its heroic revolutionary past—by the "anger of a madman at a ghost."[93] On this ship of fools, Heine added, the communists were the only force driven by "dæmonic necessity." They were the "predestined servants by whom the supreme will sets forth its vast intentions," and Pierre Leroux, the publisher of the *Revue independence*, had already taken on a role as one of their "Church

Fathers."[94] Incidentally, Marx, who came to know Heine personally in December 1843 in Paris, would soon make his—Hegelian—idea of the predestined servants his own, albeit without sharing the cultural pessimism that Heine associated with such prognoses.

Pierre Leroux was among the French whom Marx and Ruge wanted to win over to their yearbook project in Paris, especially since Ruge, looking at the range of authors of Leroux's *Revue,* saw the *Revue* as a model for the new project. Heine described Leroux, who was around fifty years old at the time, as a typical "child of the people" whose external appearance itself already revealed "the indignations of the *proletary.*"[95] A close friend of the author George Sands, Leroux was in fact a proletarian only in the sense of romantically aspiring to be one. Disgusted with Mammon, he had quit his job as a stockbroker and become a typographer, a typesetter, and above all an influential journalist.[96] He represented the typical French *engagé* of his time, for whom philosophy, as Heine put it, consisted primarily of engaging in "general researches on social questions"—which greatly appealed to Marx. Leroux was certainly one of the most interesting of the socialist theorists of his time, notwithstanding Heine's mockery of his utopian plans as pathways into a "visioned moonshine of the future" or a "yet undiscovered star in the Milky Way."[97] As a social theorist who, even prior to Marx, had traced the class differences of the new industrial society back to economic conditions, Leroux could be taken very seriously.[98]

However, because Leroux had a deeply religious—though pantheistic—streak, he was highly suspicious of the offers made by the radically democratic atheists who had arrived from Germany. For the same reason, Marx and Ruge fared no better with the likes of Alphonse de Lamartine, Felicité de Lamennais, Louis Blanc, or Pierre-Joseph Proudhon. Ultimately, the challenging project heralded as the *Deutsch-Französische Jahrbücher* (German-French yearbooks) did not include a single French contributor, even though in his introduction Ruge attested that the French represented a "cosmopolitan mission" in its true sense. Any national hatred toward France was nothing but a "blind aversion to political freedom."[99] In this period of renewed rampant German hatred of the French after the 1840 Rhine crisis, this was a respectable European program for democracy.

The Bureau des Annales—the editorial office of the *Deutsch-Französische Jahrbücher*—resided in the ground floor of Rue Vaneau

22 in the seventh arrondissement, in a house with a small front garden. The printing was done at Worms & Cie on the Boulevard Pigalle, an enterprise that was part of the Paris community of German guest workers and emigrants, which then numbered at least eighty thousand people. Through painstaking archival research, Jacques Grandjonc has remarkably identified by name seventy-four emigrant periodicals for the period between 1830 and 1848 that had to be published abroad because of censorship in Germany.[100] Yet the *Jahrbücher* attained an extraordinary status among the many emigrant organs and in fact managed to announce an acquisition in Paris—namely, Heinrich Heine. As early as fall 1842, Heine identified a need to harmonize with Ruge's *Hallische Jahrbücher* and Marx's *Rheinische Zeitung* and "call the bad by its proper name and defend the good without regard for the world."[101] In the first and only edition of the *Deutsch-Französische Jahrbücher*, he contributed a satirical hymn in praise of King Ludwig of Bavaria.

A different kind of German contribution would have been almost completely in vain, even though in the end it characterized the entire spirit of the *Jahrbücher*. The independent scholar and philosopher Ludwig Feuerbach was represented with what amounted to a single page. Basically, this was not even an article but rather only the printing of a letter Feuerbach had written to Ruge in June 1843, in which he opined that the prohibition of Ruge's *Deutsche Jahrbücher* was as disastrous for Germany's freedom as the demise of Poland.[102] At the moment, however, Feuerbach himself—sitting at his desk in his castle in Bruckberg—would rather leave matters to "quiet workings."[103] It was Marx, with his sharp pen, who saw to it that there would be more to the *Jahrbücher* than simply these "quiet workings." In the course of Marx's studies during his months in Kreuznach, Feuerbach had been a veritable revelation. As Engels wrote in retrospect, Marx absorbed Feuerbach's criticism of Hegel quite "enthusiastically."[104] As Engels noted, Feuerbach taught Marx to upend Hegel, that is, to turn philosophical speculation on its head,[105] which he had attempted for the first time in his Kreuznach critique of Hegelian constitutional law.

1842 witnessed the publication of Feuerbach's *Vorläufigen Thesen zur Reform der Philosophie* (*Preliminary Theses on the Reform of Philosophy*) and summer 1843 the publication of Ruge's *Anekdota zur neuesten deutschen Philosophie und Publizistik* (Anecdotes on the most recent German philosophy and journalism) in Zurich and

Winterthur. The *Preliminary Theses* argued that one need only "invert" speculative philosophy to grasp the unveiled truth. "Thought arises from being," wrote Feuerbach, "but being does not arise from thought."[106] Marx would later say that being determines consciousness. As novel as this might have appeared to a generation under the spell of Hegelian speculation, the situation was otherwise for those who had at one point glanced at, for instance, John Locke's *Essay Concerning Human Understanding* or the writings of Locke's students. Locke's act of liberation in 1690 was a rebellion against Aristotelian speculation, which at the time in Oxford was treated as a codified holy ritual. After Locke, philosophy was to be based on facts.

John Locke was the actual founder of modern thought, although his claim resounded far more modestly than the euphoria celebrating Feuerbach that took hold in Kreuznach and Paris. Locke taught that thought and all social life arise from sensation—from being. This simple idea opened all doors to unbiased science in a single blow. All historical knowledge, which in his tradition was understood as empirical thought, was thus always a kind of historical materialism as well. However, Locke was aware that precisely this turn toward researching facts established certain limits with respect to knowledge. "Our business here," he wrote, "is not to know all things."[107]

Feuerbach's break with Hegelian speculation, by contrast, was not principally directed toward the world of facts. He wanted to reveal a secret. "The secret of theology is anthropology," he announced in the *Preliminary Theses*, "but the secret of speculative philosophy is theology."[108] Feuerbach's critique of religion not only called into question God as an absolute subject but also, along with God, the absolute Idea of speculative philosophy. He saw these as illusory duplications of the human person who had been robbed of his natural foundations and whose consciousness of species had therefore developed within these ideological alienations instead of his natural reality. God and the Idea were nothing more than false mirrored reflections of a complete "real" human person. Feuerbach's effect was like an inspiration. *The real* henceforth became an almost magical phrase for Marx.

"Dear Sir," Marx wrote on 11 September 1844 from the Rue Vaneau to Feuerbach in Bruckberg, "I am glad to have the opportunity of assuring you of the great respect and—if I may use the word—love, which I feel for you." Despite their limited scope, Marx continued, Feuerbach's more thesis-like articles of recent times were nonetheless more important than all of contemporary German literature put together. With his writings, Feuerbach had namely finally provided a *philosophical basis for socialism*. And further: "The unity of man with man, which is based on the real differences between men, the concept of the human species brought down from the heaven of abstraction to the real earth, what is this but the concept of *society*?"[109] Hiding behind these sentences was an entire program holding far more than the announcement of a future sociology. Marx meant that the *concept of society* held the key to understanding the entire riddle of history.

In a certain way, Hegel had already argued in sociological terms. Well aware of the significance of John Locke's act of liberation, he had also always been in favor of empirical research. But he felt that the facts needed to be ordered systematically and situated in their appropriate place in the Spirit's history of the world and being. Yet the further intrusion of empirical research into his system led to an erosion of Hegelian metaphysics. This was exemplified in the reasoning of Eduard Gans, who, on the basis of his intensive work in legal history, came to believe that from the outset, the idea of law was just as nonexistent as its realization in history; instead, the idea and its realization exhibited a "course that ran parallel with history."[110] This was not so much Hegelian metaphysics but rather more a secular intellectual history. Another example of secular intellectual history was David Friedrich Strauß. And the importance of Lorenz von Stein, whom Moses Hess characterized as a "Hegelian of the center," also deserves mention.[111] With *Socialismus und Communismus des heutigen Frankreich* (Socialism and communism in today's France), published in 1842, Stein was the first to draw the German public's attention to the new political trends in the neighboring country and also to make compelling reference to the serious social problems and irreconcilable class differences of the new capitalistic industrial society developing in Europe, problems that largely still lay ahead for Germany. Stein held that "the order of society dominates the constitution of the state," and that at the core this order was a "system of production."[112] According to Herbert Marcuse, Stein's work constituted the first German sociology.[113] But Hess reproached Stein for believing in the possibility of a "mediation of the contradictions in the situation of strife." In other words, with his drastic depiction of exploitation, immiseration, and the proletarian countermovement that could be observed in France, Stein argued for decidedly preventive state social policies instead of socialism. According to Hess, Stein was nothing more than a cold "political rationalist."[114]

But Marx was not. For him, history had a definite goal and thus an inherent truth, namely, the practical sublation of the alienation of the person, something he regarded as the necessary result of the premises of Feuerbach's dialectical critique of ideology. The radical change, for Marx, came from philosophical—not empirical—research, and when he spoke of *reality*, he primarily meant the earthly rather than the illusory world of human beings; seldom was this the world of facts. The fact that this moved him beyond Feuerbach toward empirical research of the earthly world had its own logic, and his extensive work is evidence of the dedication with which he undertook this task. But the question is whether empiricism ever played a substantially different role for Marx than it did for Hegel, or whether he instead founded a kind of new materialistic pantheism of history.

That is to say, he developed a materialistic teleology, in the light of which he now also arranged his French experiences. "You would have to attend one of the meetings of the French workers," he informed Feuerbach at his country estate, "to appreciate the pure freshness, the nobility which burst forth from these toil-worn men. The English proletarian is also advancing with giant strides but he lacks the cultural background of the French. But I must not forget to emphasise the theoretical merits of the German artisans in Switzerland, London and Paris." It was in any case obvious, he informed his intellectual inspirator of ideas, that what was being readied among these *barbarians of our civilized society* was *the practical element for the emancipation of mankind*,[115] which Feuerbach called the heart of philosophy: "the source of sorrow, finitude, need, sensualism."[116] Feuerbach would presumably have understood the allusion to the late-antique *translatio imperii*, but he hardly saw matters as Marx did. As Boëthius had done at the court of Theodoric, king of the Goths, Feuerbach preferred to take precautionary refuge in the comfort of philosophy. New lineages, new spirits would arise, Feuerbach wrote to his young admirer a month later, "as once before from the coarse Germanic tribes," but the dismal, even if unintentional, result of communism would merely consist of turning "the top to the bottom, and the bottom to the top."[117]

Marx's essays in the *Deutsch-Französische Jahrbücher* were wholly permeated with the enthusiastic spirit of his new idea, inspired by Feuerbach. They announced a downright Copernican turning point in the historical and political view of the world. "Religion is only the illusory sun which revolves around man as long as he does not revolve round himself," he wrote: "The *task of history*, therefore, once the *world beyond the truth* has disappeared, is to establish the *truth of this world*. The immediate *task of philosophy*, which is at the service of history, once the *holy form* of human self-estrangement has been unmasked, is to unmask self-estrangement in its *unholy forms*. Thus, the criticism of heaven turns into the criticism of the earth, the *criticism of religion* into the *criticism of law*, and the *criticism of theology* into the *criticism of politics*."[118] In the year 1844, this was the ambitious program of his own, individual version of historical materialism. Through the method of the immanent critique of *the world*, Marx wanted to develop *new principles for the world out of the world's own principles*[119] and to force *these petrified relations ... to dance by singing their own tune to them*.[120]

A year later the new doctrine was complete. Let us allow Marx himself to speak in a few longer passages. "The premises from which we begin are not arbitrary ones, not dogmas, but real premises from which abstraction can only be made in the imagination," states a manuscript on German ideology written with Friedrich Engels in 1845/46: "They are the real individuals, their activity and the material conditions of their life, both those which they find already existing and those produced by their activity. These premises can thus be verified in a purely empirical way." And again:

> The fact is, therefore, that definite individuals who are productively active in a definite way enter into these definite social and political relations. Empirical observation must in each separate instance bring out empirically, and without any mystification and speculation, the connection of the social and political structure with production. The social structure and the State are continually evolving out of the life-process of definite individuals, however, of these individuals, not as they may appear in their own or other people's imagination, but as they *actually* are; i.e. as they act, produce materially, and hence as they work under definite material limits, presuppositions and conditions independent of their will.

Continuing on:

Men are the producers of their conceptions, ideas, etc., that is, real active men, as they are conditioned by a definite development of their productive forces and of the intercourse corresponding to these, up to its furthest forms. Consciousness [*das Bewusstsein*] can never be anything else than conscious being [*das bewusste Sein*], and the being of men is their actual life-process.

So far, so matter-of-fact. So British, one could almost say, if one takes Marx's language about the new empirical science seriously.

But as already mentioned, his problem was something different. He wanted to demonstrate that the previous history was *upside-down*, that people were dominated by the products of their own activities, and that this contradiction was driving toward resolution *in the present era*. A few pages later, he continues:

This fixation of social activity, this consolidation of what we ourselves produce into a material power above us, growing out of our control, thwarting our expectations, bringing to naught our calculations, is one of the chief factors in historical development up till now and out of this very contradiction between the interest of the individual and that of the community the latter takes an independent form as the *State*, divorced from the real interests of individual and community, and at the same time as an illusory communal life, always based, however, on the real ties existing in every family and tribal conglomeration—such as flesh and blood, language, division of labour on a larger scale, and other interests—and especially, as we shall enlarge upon later, on the classes, already determined by the division of labour, which in every such mass of men separate out, and of which one dominates all the others. It follows from this that all struggles within the State, the struggle between democracy, aristocracy, and monarchy, the struggle for the franchise, etc., etc., are merely the illusory forms in which the real struggles of the different classes are fought out among one another.[121]

There was a significant addendum in 1859. "Mankind thus inevitably sets itself only such tasks as it is able to solve," Marx wrote in the preface to his *Critique of Political Economy*,

since closer examination will always show that the problem itself arises only when the material conditions for its solution are already present or at least in the course of formation. In broad outline, the Asiatic, ancient, feudal and modern bourgeois modes of production may be designated as epochs marking progress in the economic development of society. The bourgeois relations of production are the last antagonistic form of the social process of production.

With that, Marx continued, *the prehistory of human society* would reach its conclusion[122] and *social evolutions* cease to be *political revolutions*.[123] Thus history not only assigned people tasks, but in a mysterious way it also provided them with solutions—namely, *replacing the domination of circumstances and of chance over individuals by the domination of individuals over chance and circumstances*.[124] Then all the reversals and alienations would be resolved, and along with them the doubling of the world into state and society. As a radical democracy led back to the species-life of the social human individual, communism would produce an *association* in which there could be *no more political power properly so-called*.[125] By this Marx meant the complete recovery and appropriation by human individuals of what had now become a transparent world, which would render the state superfluous as an illusory and domineering doubling of society.

These were the most important hypotheses in Marx's historical materialism, which at its core was purely a philosophy of history and a secular narrative of an impending redemption. Incidentally, that narrative, with its so-called *progressive epochs*, leaned heavily on Hegel's developmental stages of reason on its way from Asia to Central Europe, only Hegel's "progress in the consciousness of freedom" was now regarded materialistically as the purposeful extrication of the human individual from nature. The fact that this developmental path of humanity was paved with torpidity and alienation could already be read in Hegel. The theory of alienation was in itself definitely an important discovery, insofar as it aided understanding of the structures of power and rule inherent in all systematic autonomizations. To be sure, these did not necessarily need to end in eschatology. Yet Marx believed that with his conceptualization he had simultaneously both understood and intellectually overcome the fascinating and frightening riddle of industrial modernity, into which the Europe of these years had tumbled headlong, as if into a magical time machine.

Predestination

The modern *system of industry and trade*, Marx wrote to Ruge in May 1843, *of ownership and exploitation of people*, leads inevitably to a rupture within society *because it does not heal and create at all, but only exists and consumes.* In case of the *impending Revolution*[126]—which he also expected soon in Germany—Marx was now in search of that universal class of which Abbé Sieyès had once said at the beginning of the heroic October Days in 1789: it is nothing and must be everything. This was Marx's third idea. "Only in the name of the general rights of society can a particular class lay claim to general domination," he wrote in early 1844, alluding to the French Revolution. "For one estate to be *par excellence* the estate of liberation, another estate must conversely be the obvious estate of oppression." But a dramatic intensification like the one the opposition between the nobility and bourgeoisie had sparked in 1789 could no longer be expected in the epic chaos of the postrevolutionary world, especially given the *philistine mediocrity* of the German bourgeoisie. Now, in contrast to 1789, a revolutionary situation required a class with *radical chains*, one that possessed a *universal character by its universal suffering*, that was the *complete loss of man*, that could emancipate itself only through the *complete rewinning of man*—that thus was nothing and needed to be everything. The dissolution of society as a particular Estate, according to Marx, was the modern proletariat, which could no longer invoke a historical title but now *only a human title*.[127]

His prognosis referred to an impending revolution in Germany, which admittedly largely lacked a real modern proletariat at the time, despite suffering massive poverty. Within the territory of the German Customs Union in the mid 1840s—not including mining operations and work in the textile industry (most of which was carried out in homes)—barely 170,000 workers were employed in 13,600 factories.[128] Industrialists like Friedrich Harkort in 1844 saw the wide-ranging problem of pauperism as evidence that the "proper path had been missed"; for Gustav Mevissen it was the "harbinger of a social crisis" that without timely reforms would inevitably lead to a revolution.[129] But Marx thought principally in terms of antinomies, perhaps because his generation in particular experienced the upheavals of the 1840s, oscillating between progress and destitution, as especially traumatic.

Apart from that, Marx's presentation of his construction of the proletariat as a universal class was not much more convincing than, for example, Hegel's derivation of the monarchic principle from Nature. Hegel thought that something "against which caprice is powerless" could be found only in Nature, and not in civil society's conflict-ridden world of interests; therefore it was imperative that the ultimate self of the state's will be determined "in an immediate, natural, fashion" through the monarch's "birth in the course of nature."[130] Marx held that the *social existence* of the proletariat escapes, so to speak, just as naturally from civil society's world of interests, a point classically summed up a little later in his reckoning with his former young Hegelian friends entitled *Die heilige Familie* (*The Holy Family*). "It is not a question of what this or that proletarian, or even the whole proletariat, at the moment *regards* as its aim," Marx and Engels stated in *The Holy Family*: "It is a question of *what the proletariat is*, and what, in accordance with this *being*, it will historically be compelled to do. Its aim and historical action is visibly and irrevocably foreshadowed in its own life situation as well as in the whole organization of bourgeois society today."[131] This antithesis, which pressed for a new synthesis, occupied him throughout his life and, as a philosophically founded objective, would prefigure all of his scientific curiosity as well as its results.

Arnold Ruge, who was ten years Marx's senior, found all this to be pretentious and overly epigrammatic, too much of an artificial "formlessness and super-form." Despite Marx's indisputable critical talent, Ruge saw his theses as flights of fancy, "occasionally degenerating into arrogance."[132] Unsurprisingly, their partnership met with dissonance before long. The project of the *Jahrbücher* did not go as expected. At the end of February 1844, the first double issue was published, but the Prussian police confiscated a few hundred copies during an effort to smuggle them across the border. The French showed little interest in the journal, which declared itself to be binational but was effectively exclusively German. In Berlin, meanwhile, arrest warrants were issued for Marx, Heine, and Ruge.

Ruge was also increasingly disturbed by Marx's sudden communistic euphoria and his proximity to groups that "wish to liberate people by turning them into artisans."[133] Marx personally knew members of these groups. —The teacher German Mäurer, for example, who lived at Rue Vaneau 43 and was a leading member in the communist League of the Just, and the doctor Hermann Ewerbeck, a supporter of the communist utopias of Etienne Cabet. Ruge criticized Marx for his too-vivacious carryings-on with these "one-and-a-half artisanal blokes" and at the same time for his "sybaritism," his bohemian life of dissolution, and his penchant for the elegant salons of the liberal Russian aristocracy. Ruge also found fault with Marx's friendship with Georg Herwegh, who had just married the wealthy daughter of a banker and, it was said, taken up shortly thereafter with the Countess d'Agoult, the former lover of Franz Liszt. Ruge felt that when a man got married, he needed to know what he was doing, and that Marx, somewhat arrogantly and indignantly, had wrongly judged Herwegh to be a genius and Ruge's views of marriage to be quite philistine. "After that," Ruge wrote in late May 1844, "we did not see each other again." According to Ruge, Marx had gone mad with arrogance and bile.[134] For Marx, on the other hand, Ruge was just *a Prussian*, which became clear above all in light of Ruge's restrained evaluation of the Silesian weavers' uprising in 1844. Cheap competition from the mechanized textile industry in England had precipitated such a rapid drop in piecework rates for Silesian weavers in Peterswaldau and Bielau, who still worked in cottage industry, that soon many could no longer feed their families. On 4 June, three thousand of them formed a protest procession in Peterswaldau, and when their demands for higher wages were mockingly rejected by the local employer they stormed his house, tore up the account books and papers, and smashed the machines. In Ruge's eyes the significance of this uprising was exclusively local, and it had no political consequences worth mentioning.

In Berlin, however, the riot was perceived as an assault on the foundations of the state, and on 6 June it was quashed by the military. Four cannons and cavalry were deployed in the process, and among the weavers eleven died, including women and children. Almost a hundred weavers were arrested and turned over to the Breslau higher regional court. "No mercy, no reflection anymore," noted Karl August Varnhagen von Ense on 16 June in his diary: "But there will be the Court of Lord. Just wait, the outcome will be quite different!"[135] The state's overreaction, mixed with its moral cynicism and indifference to misery, allowed the rebellion to attain national significance. Whereas previously the opposition to be feared had most likely been the liberals from the bourgeois classes, now the order of the Christian state faced a new and potentially far more dangerous opponent: the pauperized classes arising in insurrections due to the misery of their condition. "We're weaving busily night and day; / Thy shroud, Old Germany, now weave we," wrote Heinrich Heine: "A threefold curse we're weaving for thee, — / We're weaving, we're weaving!"[136]

Presumably it was Marx who led Heine to this view of the matter. "The Silesian uprising," Marx wrote in *Vorwärts* on 10 August in Paris, "*begins* precisely with what the French and English workers' uprisings *end*, with consciousness of the nature of the proletariat. The action itself bears the stamp of this *superior* character. Not only machines, these rivals of the workers, are destroyed, but also *ledgers*, the titles to property. And while all other movements were aimed primarily only against the *owner of the industrial enterprise*, the visible enemy, this movement is at the same time directed against the banker, the hidden enemy." What he drew here was a colossal portrait, quite in contrast to Ruge's miniature. Nor was there a lack of eschatological imagery. The German proletariat's *gigantic infant shoes*, which he wanted to attribute to the Silesian weavers, held something of the mythical archetype of the "puer senex"—the grown boy—with which Vergil once proclaimed the Golden Age, and which also appeared in the manger in Bethlehem. An industrial uprising, thought Marx, could be ever so partial, but it fundamentally had *within itself a universal soul*. Only a social revolution possessed therefore the *point of view of the whole*—and by this he meant, still completely in Feuerbach's sense, the point of view of the human being in contrast to the mere state citizen. Precisely this was what he would have liked to see, from the distance of Paris, in the events in Peterswaldau and Bielau.

In reality, the rebellion was a preindustrial form of social protest with decidedly archaic characteristics. It was directed not against the system of exploitation itself but rather against individual agents whose especially cynical behavior had provoked the weavers' anger. Others were spared. At the house of the agent Fellmann, the rebels even allowed themselves to be placated with a one-time payment of five silver groschen each and then moved on. Ruge had seen things far more realistically than Marx. Yet Marx found himself surprisingly in agreement (though from the opposite viewpoint) with the hysteria that had broken out among the ruling circles in Berlin and elsewhere. The same forces that unleashed panicky fears in Berlin led Marx to the euphoria of an anticipated historical synthesis. Just as the French Revolution was the *classic period of political intellect*, he maintained, the Silesian uprising was the first visible sign of the age of revolutionary reason. *Not one of the French and English workers' uprisings*, he insisted in all seriousness, possessed *such a theoretical and conscious character* as the Silesian weavers' rebellion.[137] Setting aside the completely overblown view of the events, these passages reveal a strange, unconscious pantheistic aspect in his way of thinking. Marx did not want to say that the weavers were theoreticians. Rather, he meant that in their actions themselves—in the *real movement*, the way he interpreted it—a hidden revolutionary reason was at work. As he formulated matters a little later in a polemical dispute with the French socialist Pierre-Joseph Proudhon, as a theoretician Marx only had to give an account of the reality playing out before his eyes and to *become its mouthpiece*.[138]

Phenomenology of Communism

Compared to his view on the Silesian uprising, Marx regarded the communism he encountered in Paris as nothing more than incomplete *dogmatic abstraction*. "This communism," he wrote in the *Deutsch-Französische Jahrbücher*, is itself only "a special expression of the humanistic principle, an expression which is still infected by its antithesis—the private system." It was no coincidence, then, that other socialist doctrines arose alongside communism, "because it is itself only a special, one-sided realisation of the socialist principle." By this Marx meant above all the conceptions of Charles Fourier and Claude-Henri de Saint-Simon, who as philosophers of history and sociologists had turned to the problems of the present from different perspectives and with different imaginative approaches. In Paris he dealt very intensely with both these schools and the communist groups, predicting the sublation of their one-sidedness—according to the model of Hegel's phenomenological stages of a *consciousness that is unintelligible to itself*.[139]

"The transcendence of self-estrangement follows the same course as self-estrangement," he wrote in a quite Hegelian fashion in his posthumously published *Paris Manuscripts*, mentioning Proudhon, who denounced property as theft; Fourier, who regarded standardized and divided—and thus unfree—labor as the source of an alienated existence; and Saint-Simon, who was the first to look at *industrial labor* as such and from that drew formulations for improving conditions for workers. The communist schools had finally reached the stage of the positive transcendence of private property, even if still only imperfectly, Marx wrote. The first positive annulment of private property—crude communism, he stated further in his Hegelian manner—is thus merely one form of the vileness of private property, a *culmination of this envy* and an *abstract negation of the entire world of culture and civilization*. Some of the forms of this communism were still of a political nature, democratic or despotic, and others wanted to abolish the state without dealing further with the nature of private property and thus the alienation of man. In any form, according to Marx, communism demanded the reintegration or return of man unto himself. But because it had not dealt with the nature of private property, with its ideas of egalitarian distribution it was still entirely captive to and infected by it. It had admittedly grasped its concept, but *not its essence*.[140]

Parisian communism of the 1840s was a child of the French Revolution. For a long time it was intellectually dominated by its overlord, Filippo Buonarroti, who died in 1837. Buonarroti was a descendant of the Italian artist Michelangelo and a former member of the Parisian Jacobin Club, and for a while he moved within Robespierre's intimate circle. In 1795 he got to know "Gracchus" Babeuf, who after the attempt to lead the poor from the suburbs in an uprising under the slogan "bread and the constitution of 1793!" served time in the Collège du Plessis prison until, as a republican, he was again released after a royalist revolt. Driven underground for good by Napoleon in 1796, Babeuf had formed the Conspiracy of Equals, a secret communist organization with a strongly centralized leadership. With his book, *Conspiration pour l'Egalité dite de Babeuf*, published in 1828, Buonarroti made the history of the organization popular again in the 1830s. Babeuf and Buonarroti represented what Marx called "crude" communism in its despotic form.

Buonarroti in particular, a Rousseauist of the purist order, was of the view that in a morally corrupt society, the journey to societal happiness inevitably had to be enforced by an uncompromising educational dictatorship. This was, according to Marx, the first *idea of the new world order*[141] to emerge from the French Revolution. Maximilien de Robespierre was Buonarroti's great hero, and Buonarroti introduced to the world the myth, popular since the 1830s, that the measures of the Jacobin Committee of Public Safety—the first people's republic in history and the model for all future insurgencies—would ultimately have led to an egalitarian society, had they not been violently interrupted by Robespierre's arrest and execution. His program was followed by a significant neo-Babouvist movement, whose most important leading figures included Robespierre's admirer

Albert Laponneraye; Theodore Dézamy, who in Marx's eyes was the most scientific of all of the French communists; and the conspirator Louis-Auguste Blanqui, who in a certain sense would become the legitimate heir to Gracchus Babeuf and whom Marx always regarded with a very ambivalent love-hatred. The neo-Babouvists supported class struggle and had as their objective, as Laponneraye put it, "the abolition of the exploitation of man by man."[142]

The more democratic form of communism mentioned by Marx was represented by Etienne Cabet. With around two hundred thousand supporters, he was by far the most influential communist of his time, among other reasons because of the widely distributed periodical *Populaire* and the five editions of his *Travel and Adventures of Lord William Carisdall in Icaria*, a description of a communist society in the form of a literary travelogue. In Icaria, common property prevailed and a central planning commission looked after production and distribution as justified by need. The political organization of his utopian future state followed the model of direct democracy. For the real future of France, Cabet envisioned a democratic republic that, without an overthrow or violent expropriations, would introduce communism in a democratic manner within a transition period of fifty years.[143] However, in the mid 1840s, while Marx was living in Paris, Cabet became increasingly radical, ever more convinced that communism would only be possible as the result of an organized workers' movement.[144] Later, Marx still considered him respectable for this reason, that is, *for his practical attitude towards the French proletariat*. Marx viewed the socialist Louis Blanc similarly—at least, until 1848; at one point Blanc was supposed to be recruited to collaborate on the *Jahrbücher*, and his call for the "organization du travail"—for the elimination of competition through the organization of labor—was very popular and helped inspire Marx's ideas about planned economies.

Marx considered Proudhon's first work, *What is Property?*, to be by far his best. In this text, according to Marx, Proudhon acted with respect to Saint-Simon and Fourier much as Feuerbach had done with respect to Hegel: he drew attention to the right problems and, by questioning the legal basis of property, managed an act of liberation without even being a serious theoretician. But such sensationalistic writings could play their catalytic role in the sciences just as well as they did in fiction. And in fact, in terms of theory Marx owed a far greater debt to Saint-Simon and Fourier than to the communist schools of his period, or even to Proudhon, who at the time was at height of his fame and with whom, during the summer of 1844, Marx sat and debated throughout the night.[145] Communism offered projects, but it did not offer a real philosophy of history.

Even later, Friedrich Engels saw Saint-Simon and Fourier as the first Enlightenment thinkers who were enlightened about the Enlightenment and, next to Hegel, the most important representatives of the dialectic of Enlightenment of their time. During the course of the French Revolution the state of reason had gone to pieces; Rousseau's social contract found its reality during the Jacobin Terror. The promise of eternal peace turned into Napoleon's endless wars of conquest, and the society of reason had shown itself to be unsupportable without the poverty and misery of the working masses.[146] According to Engels, these were the problems that Saint-Simon and Fourier saw themselves confronted with.

Marx and Engels got to know each other better during that summer of 1844. The first long conversation between just the two of them took place on 28 August as they sat at a marble table in the Café de la Régence, a hub for chess players that was rich in tradition, having been frequented by Voltaire and Rousseau and described by Diderot in *Rameau's Nephew*. Marx and Engels had already met in Cologne during the period of the *Rheinische Zeitung*, but at the time Marx, seeing Engels as an excited envoy of the "Free Ones" in Berlin, had shown little interest in a closer relationship. In the meantime, however, he had changed his mind, above all because of the two articles Engels submitted to the *Deutsch-Französische Jahrbücher*. In particular, Engels's "Outlines of a Critique of Political Economy" (long afterward, Marx still called it a *brilliant essay*[147]) had an inspirational effect on Marx, who was always open to impulses.

Engels had just returned from Manchester, where his father had sent him as an agent for the Elberfeld textile company Ermen & Engels. There he was confronted with the harsh world of labor in modern industrialized society. Soon he saw England as nothing but a vile class state ruling over a class society. Even in the words of philanthropic Tories like Lord Ashley and Benjamin Disraeli, England was really composed of "two nations" that found themselves in a state of war. From the outset, the young man from Elberfeld, strongly influenced by the enthusiastic communist ideas of his Rhenish friend Moses Hess, viewed the irritating modern world on the other side of the Channel through the eyes of a man awash in chiliastic expectations of crises. His later book on the condition of the working classes in England—in large part an impressive achievement of early empirical sociological research—revealed these chiliastic traits in its discussion of the consequences of industrialization for the immediate future. During this first visit to England, Engels began to write for Robert Owen's communist *New Moral Order* and the *Northern Star* of the radical Chartist George Julian Harney. Initially he was completely under the influence of Proudhon, whom Engels called the "most important writer"[148] among the French socialists because he considered property the crux of the explanation of the modern world's contradictions.

Apart from dealing with the classics of English economics, however, the "Outlines of a Critique of Political Economy" revealed clear signs that Engels had closely studied Charles Fourier, particularly regarding the destructive effects of trade crises. Civilization, by which Fourier meant developing industrial society, was moving in a faulty cycle. Industry was developed in order to create workplaces, but in reality it only increased the army of the unemployed; by increasing production, one caused crises of overproduction; by increasing abundance, one exacerbated poverty. Civilization, "the most recent of our scientific illusions,"[149] according to Fourier, in reality meant nothing more than industrial anarchy. It was a topsy-turvy world. The twenty-three-year-old Engels saw things the same way. "What are we to think of a law," he asked with an eye to the repeatedly recurring trade crises of the preceding years, "which can only assert itself through periodic upheavals? It is certainly a natural law based on the unconsciousness of the participants." The system of free trade that had been erected on Adam Smith's *Wealth of Nations,* thought Engels, had in reality brought the world nothing but "hypocrisy, inconsistency and immorality."[150] It was irrational, self-destructive, and as a consequence, transitory. This made a strong impression on Marx, and over the next one and a half weeks they elaborated these ideas during daily meetings in the Rue Vaneau. "When I visited Marx in Paris in the summer of 1844," Engels remembered, "our complete agreement in all theoretical fields became evident and our joint work dates from that time."[151] It was the beginning of a lifelong friendship between two thoroughly kindred spirits.

By the time Marx and Engels resided in Paris, the Saint-Simon school had long been defunct. Its adherents, among them Pierre Leroux, had long ago moved elsewhere, yet its core ideas lived on. In its heyday in the late 1820s and early 1830s, Leroux had published the Saint-Simonian periodical *Globe*[152] and Saint-Amand Bazard conducted an exposition of the systematized doctrines of Saint-Simon in weekly Wednesday lectures on the Rue Taranne 12, the former house of the philosophe Baron Paul Thiry d'Holbach.[153] Soon the "belle formule" of the Saint-Simonists, as Heinrich Heine called it in the early 1830s—the catchphrase about the "exploitation de l'homme par l'homme,"[154] the exploitation of man by man—was on everyone's lips.[155]

In the ongoing social crisis since the French Revolution, the Saint-Simonists saw the creation of a cycle. The Revolution could not be understood because it was still ongoing, but it was still ongoing because it could not be understood. And the reason it was not understood, Bazard thought, was that so few understood exploitation. In reality the modern world was not characterized by reason but rather by the "final transformation" of slavery, the "relation of the master to the wage worker." But property formed the "basis of the political order," and like everything else in the world it was subject to the law of progress. The exploitation of man by man must end, Bazard announced before a well-read public of intellectuals and artists, and consequently the constitution of property in which the exploitation persisted also had to disappear. The industrial crises caused by the constitution of property were due solely to the absence of a general plan.

Yet the future, Bazard taught with explicit reference to Leibniz's concept of tendency, had already begun in the "germs" of the present. A "Plan of Providence"[156] was in force, and its agenda was the continuation of the divine work of creation on earth, that is, the replacement of the antagonisms of exploitation and competition with a rationally controlled social administration aided by the sciences, unified under a general metaphysical principle, and the systematic organization of industry.[157] The nuclei of almost all of the noneconomic ideas of later socialism, thought Engels with a certain amount of justification, were already present in Saint-Simon.[158]

Despite the reference to providence, however, evidence of teleological necessity from the so-called *real* course of history was still missing. For this reason Marx, shortly after his brief Feuerbach euphoria, found himself in Paris, compelled to return to Hegel. All the elements of criticism were hidden in the latter's *Phenomenology of Spirit*, he wrote in his *Parisian Manuscripts*; they were *already prepared and elaborated in a manner often rising far above the Hegelian standpoint.* The greatness of the *Phenomenology* lay in the fact that Hegel grasped the self-education of man as a process, and objectification as loss of the object, as alienation, and as transcendence of this alienation; that he thus grasped the *essence of labor* and understood objective man—true man, because he was real—as the result of man's own labor.

Here, for Marx, also lay hidden the unresolved question Proudhon had raised about the essence of property. "We have already gone a long way to the solution of this problem," Marx noted,

> by *transforming* the question of the *origin of private property* into the question of the relation of *alienated labor* to the course of humanity's development. For when one speaks of *private property*, one thinks of dealing with something external to man. When one speaks of labor, one is directly dealing with man himself. This new formulation of the question already contains its solution.

The subjective essence of private property was nothing other than labor, just as, for Hegel, the essence of the master was the servant. The whole of human servitude, Marx continued, was involved in the relation of the worker to production, and "all relations of servitude are but modifications and consequences of this relation."[159] With his "Outlines," Engels had drawn Marx's attention to the fact that, according to economists, capital was "stored-up labour." The division between capital and labor that followed from private property, Engels thought, is thus nothing other than an "inner dichotomy of labour."[160] From this Marx concluded that here lay a *developed state of contradiction—hence a dynamic relationship driving towards resolution.*

This required yet another reversal of Hegel, leading Marx beyond Feuerbach and then away from him again. Marx maintained that when Hegel grasped wealth, state power, and so on as concepts estranged from the human being, he grasped them only in their form as thoughts. "The whole process therefore ends with absolute knowledge,"[161] according to Marx—that is, with a mere interpretation of the course of the world as a trail of human self-alienation. Hegel's path to consciousness had thereby completed a negation of the negation, but this only led to the intellectual transparency of a self-made history without abolishing the real alienations and the objectified power structures of an inverted world determined by these alienations. Only at the Copernican turning point of communism as the *truth of this world*, in which man, instead of moving around an illusory sun, moves around himself in real life,[162] thought Marx, did a *true*—material—abolishment of alienation become possible. Only communism is thus the actual negation of the negation, and finally the *riddle of history solved*[163] as the movement of material history itself. Private property, Marx and Engels argued with an eye to their immediate present, *drives itself in its economic movement toward its own dissolution*, and the proletariat only executes the sentence that private property pronounces on itself by producing the proletariat.[164] This was nothing less than the prognosis of an imminent final judgment, in which the real people—the proletariat, as Marx prophesized—might appear as *puer robustus, sed malitiosus, as a robust and angry boy*.[165] Fantasies? Yes, and big ones!

Marx's oft-misunderstood and frequently cited eleventh thesis about Feuerbach, written in 1845, states: "Philosophers have only *interpreted* the world in various ways; the point is to change it."[166] The entire thesis makes sense only in relation to Hegel's construction of absolute knowledge. But if it is put this way, the materialist philosopher who is unwilling to abandon the aim of abolishing self-alienation is then forced to become a revolutionary politician. Hegel ultimately reconciled himself to the world the way it was, but he interpreted this world as a product of people and wanted to make it transparent as such. As a consequence, naturally this could result in a demand for change, but never a demand for the abolishment of a complex differentiation that was almost foreordained by the development of history. Was Marx aware that this was precisely what the result of his conceptualization had to be? Or did he merely automatically follow an idea once it had taken hold? Compared to Marx, Karl Löwith once said, Hegel was in any case far more of a realist.[167]

The Discovery of Simplicity

Marx's fourth idea also concerned a leveling of complexities. It involved his thoughts about politics and the state as a repressive institution of the ruling class. Neither Hegel nor the French Revolution was the ground from which these thoughts were mined. Family and civil society were the *actual components* of the state;[168] quite distinct and opposite from Hegel's construction, they were the *genuinely active elements*, as Marx had previously stated in his Kreuznach critique of Hegelian constitutional law. A little later, his criticism of German ideology would maintain that the state *issues* from the real material life-process and thus does not have its own history. Material life—the mode of production—was *the real basis of the state* and remained so at every stage, which incidentally is something Thomas Hobbes had already recognized in a certain way in *Leviathan*, where power represents the basis for all law. The state did not arise through a dominant will, Marx maintained, but vice versa, the state that emerged from the material mode of human life also took on the form of a dominant will.[169]

His actual problem, however, remained the modern state and how it had classically come into being through the French Revolution and contemporary civil society. During this time Marx delved intensively into the history of the French Revolution, in particular more recent works by a number of liberal historians who had been influenced by Saint-Simon—among them François Auguste Mignet, who described the drama of the French Revolution as a struggle between all the classes involved that had arrived at a certain peace only under the bourgeois government of the Directory after the fall of Robespierre. Just as the English Revolution had ushered in an era of new forms of government, so did the age of a new society in Europe begin with the French Revolution. Mignet also put forth the thesis that in the founding acts of history there had as yet been "no sovereign but force,"[170] ushering in a concept that would be central for Marx: that of *class struggle*. "Modern Europe was born in the struggle of the different social classes," François Pierre Guillaume Guizot announced in 1828 before the tiered lecture hall of the Parisian Faculté des lettres: "The struggle between them did not become the starting point of stagnation but rather the cause of progress." Guizot had already described property relations as the basis of every class struggle[171] in his 1826 history of the English Revolution and thereby also revised his earlier thesis that ultimately referred back to Henri de Boulainvilliers's *Recherches sur l'ancien gouvernement de la France*, namely that the development of classes in France was based solely on the conquest of Gaul by a caste of Frankish warriors. Guizot, however, considered the class oppositions to be a given fact and therefore sought, like Hegel, the mediation of those oppositions by the state as a universal third party.[172] Apart from that, he also felt that in modern Europe "national unity" would allow the class struggle to find peace.[173] This was before the July Revolution.

But to every attentive observer, French society after 1830 made Guizot's prognosis look like a fleeting chimera. The July Revolution, noted the conservative Hegelian Lorenz von Stein in 1850, was nothing other than the signal for a series of fierce new battles, and "the condition that followed it was a permanent state of war."[174] At the time of Marx's residence in Paris, Guizot was the exterior minister, but in reality he was the actual strongman in the cabinet of Louis Philippe, the "citizen king." The catchphrase issued by this French Calvinist, "Enrichissez-vous par le travail et par l'éspargne"—enrich yourselves through work and frugality—significantly aggravated the social climate during the July Monarchy.

In 1830 the bourgeoisie finally managed to fulfill its wishes from the year 1789, Marx noted at the time.

> with the only difference that its *political enlightenment* was now *completed*, that it no longer considered the constitutional representative state as a means for achieving the ideal of the state, the welfare of the world and universal human aims but, on the contrary, had acknowledged it as the *official* expression of its own *exclusive* power and the *political* recognition of its own *special* interests.[175]

And in fact, with the possible exception of England, nowhere had there ever been such unrestrained bourgeois rule as in France during the period of the July Monarchy, which made its debut with the words of the finance magnate Lafitte at the Paris Hôtel de Ville: *From now on the bankers will rule*.[176]

Marx made a theory out of this. Soon thereafter he wrote:

> By the mere fact that it is a class and no longer an estate, the bourgeoisie is forced to organise itself no longer locally, but nationally, and to give a general form to its mean average interests. Through the emancipation of private property from the community, the State has become a separate entity, beside and outside civil society; but it is nothing more than the form of organisation which the bourgeois necessarily adopt both for internal and external purposes, for the mutual guarantee of their property and interests.

And further:

> Since the State is the form in which the individuals of a ruling class assert their common interests, and in which the whole civil society of an epoch is epitomised, it follows that the State mediates in the for-

mation of all common institutions and that the institutions receive
a political form. Hence the illusion that law is based on the will, and
indeed on the will divorced from its real basis—on free will.[177]

Naturally, it was not merely experience that spoke in these sentences but primarily the view of the state and politics that necessarily followed from his new base/superstructure paradigm of historical
materialism.

In any case, the state by no means represented for him a neutral
and positively configured legal order—or even parts of it. Marx saw
even the doctrine of the division of powers as merely a dominant
idea—elevated to the status of an eternal law—of a transition period during which the monarchy, aristocracy, and bourgeoisie *are
contending for domination.*[178] With respect to Montesquieu this idea
was perhaps somewhat correct, but as a general thesis it suffered from
sociological reductionism and a complete lack of understanding of
the complex political institutions and rules that generally remained
characteristic of Marx's historical materialism. All political struggles
were for him nothing more mere *manifestations* of social collisions,[179]
and the democratic representative state with its *emancipated slavery* was only a *spiritualistic-democratic* illusion. "What a terrible illusion,"[180] he railed indignantly in a style that was almost reminiscent
of Fourier's satirical polemics.

Marx had difficulty giving this theory a consistent form. Particularly when it came to supporting his philosophical-systematic explanation with empirical details, he occasionally lapsed into platitudes
that elsewhere he would certainly have mocked as the shallowness
of British utilitarian thought. The modern state, he wrote for instance in *The German Ideology*, had gradually been purchased by the
taxes of private property holders. Through the national debt, the
state had fallen entirely into their hands, and through the rise and
fall of state funds on the stock exchange it had become wholly de-
pendent on commercial credit.[181] Even if that was somewhat true for
the July Monarchy—in 1832 Heine called the Parisian market price
for state funds the "thermometer of popular prosperity" and the
halls of the stock market the place "where the interests are at home
which in this our time decide peace and war"[182]—it was neither a
systematic nor profound theoretical explanation. It also did not develop any further. Engels would repeat it almost verbatim in 1884
in *The Origin of the Family, Private Property, and the State,* even the

thesis about the spiritualistic-democratic illusion. In a democratic republic, Engels maintained, wealth exercises its power "indirectly, but all the more surely," especially with universal suffrage. As long as the oppressed class is "not yet ripe" for its self-liberation, argued Engels, "it will in its majority regard the existing order of society as the only one possible and, politically, will form the tail of the capitalist class, its extreme Left wing."[183] In short, the democratic state would remain a class state until the majority of the workers had become Marxists and abolished it. One can hardly call this a modern theory of the state.

New Species

Marx's fifth idea was the dictatorship of the proletariat as the *necessary* result of the modern class struggle. He never systematically explained this thesis, yet from early on he considered it the most important result of his actual discoveries. Writing to a friend in New York in 1852, Marx noted:

> Now as for myself, I do not claim to have discovered either the existence of classes in modern society or the struggle between them. Long before me, bourgeois historians had described the historical development of this struggle between the classes, as had bourgeois economists their economic anatomy. My own contribution was 1. to show that the *existence of classes* is merely bound up with *certain historical phases in the development of production*; 2. that the class struggle necessarily leads to the *dictatorship of the proletariat*; 3. that this dictatorship itself constitutes no more than a transition to the *abolition of all classes* and to a *classless society*.[184]

The concept of the dictatorship of the proletariat appeared for the first time in the 1850 statutes of the Universal Society of Revolutionary Communists.[185] It pertained to an agreement—co-signed by Marx—between German communists, Blanquists, and revolutionary Chartists who had been influenced by an English translation of Buonarroti's book about Babeuf. The society did not exist for very long. Nonetheless, the statutes are of historical interest because they show that Marx appropriated the designation "dictatorship of the proletariat" from the Blanquists. Actually, it was the concept of a purely educational dictatorship. Faced with the question from the

democratic socialist Théophile Thoré: "Why do you need a dictatorship if you have the people behind you?" the *Égalitaire* responded
in 1840: because of the hundreds of years of being accustomed to de-
moralizing tyranny.[186] The neo-Babouvists and Blanquists evidently
did not see a contradiction between sovereignty of the people and
an educational dictatorship. They simply resolved it in a political
"contrat pédagogique," an educational contract analogous to that
in the fourth book of Rousseau's *Émile*. "Make me free," Émile says
to his educator, "by guarding me against the passions which do me
violence; do not let me become their slave; compel me to be my
own master and to obey, not my senses, but my reason."[187] The people were thus sovereign only insofar as they voluntarily subjugated
themselves for their own good.

In his third thesis about Feuerbach, Marx had already objected
to such ideas, maintaining that they divided *society into two parts,
one of which is superior to society,* and that it had been forgotten that
the educator himself had to be educated.[188] In detail, the statutes of the
universal association were a political compromise. But it is revealing that Marx felt closer to the Blanquists than to any other stream
of French socialism and communism—not because he considered
them great theorists, but because they were resolute proponents of
class struggle and unconditionally affirmed the creative role of violence in history. Beyond that, they were proponents of a concept
of permanent revolution. In his eyes, all of this gave them an unconscious depth, for they bluntly—if also somewhat crudely—proclaimed *what the proletariat is, and what, in accordance with this being,
it will historically be compelled to do.*[189]

Thus he spoke with admiration about that revolutionary socialism *for which the bourgeoisie has itself invented the name of Blanqui.*
This Blanquist socialism was the declaration of the permanence of
the revolution. The class dictatorship of the proletariat was a necessary way station along the road to the abolition of class distinctions
in general, the abolition of all the relations of production on which
they rest, the abolition of all the social relations that correspond
to these relations of production, and the overthrow of all the ideas
that result from these social relations[190]—precisely points two and
three of Marx's supposed actual discoveries. Basically, he had simply
thrown the philosophical mantle of his historical materialism over
the legacy of the Conspiracy of Equals and inserted the dictatorship
of the proletariat into an eschatological figure of the negation of the

negation. Only because of this did the Blanquist *project* become a historical *necessity*, the painfully riven but unavoidable transition period at the end of the prehistory of humanity. "O sacred head, now wounded"—the death of an inverted and resurrection of a redeemed modernity. What distinguished Marx from Blanqui, however, was his idea that a determined minority could introduce communism at any time with a deftly engineered coup d'état. "The longer the time that events allow to thinking humanity for taking stock of its position, and to suffering mankind for mobilising its forces," he thought, "the more perfect on entering the world will be the product that the present time bears in its womb."[191] Marx always held the view that the emancipation of the working class had to be achieved *by the working class itself*[192] and not by a small avant-garde. But this supposedly most important point of his political theory also remained the cloudiest, and it became the critical Achilles' heel in the history of communism. Regarding the task of the worker, he asked in his text about the 1850 class struggles in France, *who accomplishes that?* The Revolution was by no means a short-lived affair. And he followed with a puzzling sentence: *The present generation is like the Jews whom Moses led through the wilderness:* "It has not only a new world to conquer, it must go under in order to make room for the men who are able to cope with a new world."[193] Thus spoke Zarathustra as well, when he proclaimed the *Übermensch* to be the meaning of the earth.[194] Paradoxically, the museum curators who kept the eschatological flame in the secular nineteenth century were not so much the great theologians but the worldly-pious atheists like Marx—and Nietzsche.[195]

Notes

1. Karl Marx, "Introduction," *Contribution to the Critique of Hegel's Philosophy of Law*, in Karl Marx and Frederick Engels, *The Collected Works of Marx and Engels* (henceforth MECW), electronic edition (InteLex Corporation: 2003), vol. 3, 182.
2. Marx, Announcement, 17 March 1843, in *MECW*, vol. 1, 376.
3. Marx, "The Ban on the *Leipziger Allgemeine Zeitung* within the Prussian State," in *MECW*, vol. 1, 311.
4. Marx to Ruge, 25 January 1843, in *MECW*, vol. 1, 397f.

5. Heinrich Heine, *Ludwig Börne*, in *Werke und Briefe in zehn Bänden*, ed. Klaus Briegleb, 10 vols. (Munich, 1976), vol. 7, 50.

6. Benedetto Croce, *History of Europe in the Nineteenth Century*, trans. Henry Furst (New York, 1933), 102.

7. Georg Wilhelm Friedrich Hegel, *The Philosophy of History*, trans. J. Sibree (Kitchener, Ontario, 2001), 471.

8. Hanns-Günter Reissner, *Eduard Gans: Ein Leben im Vormärz* (Tübingen, 1965), 131.

9. Günter Busch, *Eugène Delacroix – Die Freiheit auf den Barrikaden* (Stuttgart, 1960), 16.

10. Karl Gutzkow, *Wally the Sceptic* (Frankfurt am Main, 1974), 39.

11. Marx to his Father, 10 November 1837, in *MECW*, vol. 1, 10, 18, 12. Translator note: some of the words here are translated directly from the German version: Karl Marx and Friedrich Engels, *Werke* (hereafter *MEW*), 39 vols., 2 suppl. vols. (Berlin, 1956–1990), suppl. vol. 1, 9.

12. Georg Wilhelm Friedrich Hegel, preface to *Phenomenology of Spirit*, in *G.W.F. Hegel: The Oxford University Press Translations*, electronic edition (Oxford, 2000), 32.

13. Karl Marx and Friedrich Engels, *The German Ideology*, in *MECW*, vol. 5, 37.

14. Marx to his Father, 10 November 1837, in *MECW*, vol. 1, 19.

15. Marx, "Debates on Freedom of the Press and Publication of the Proceedings of the Assembly of the Estates," in *MECW*, vol. 1, 154.

16. Hegel to Hardenberg, mid October 1820, in *Briefe von und an Hegel*, ed. Johannes Hoffmeister, 4 vols. (Hamburg, 1954), vol. 2, 249.

17. Georg Wilhelm Friedrich Hegel, *Philosophy of Right*, Additions, §258, in *G.W.F. Hegel: The Oxford University Press Translations*, 279.

18. Eduard Gans, *Naturrecht*, in *Philosophische Schriften*, ed. Horst Schröder (Berlin, 1971), 136, 124f.

19. Eduard Gans, *Rückblicke auf Personen und Zustände*, in *Philosophische Schriften*, 87.

20. Golo Mann, *Friedrich von Gentz: Geschichte eines europäischen Staatsmannes* (Frankfurt am Main, 1972), 304; quotations translated by Bernard Heise.

21. Barclay, David. *Frederick William IV and the Prussian Monarchy 1840–1861* (Oxford, 1995), 91.

22. Marx to Ruge, May 1843, "Letters from the Deutsch-Französische Jahrbücher," in *MECW*, vol. 3, 139.

23. Ibid., 139.

24. Reinhart Kosellek, *Preußen zwischen Reform und Revolution* (Stuttgart, 1987), 423.

25. Marx to Ruge 1843, Letters from the Deutsch-Französische Jahrbücher, in *MECW*, vol. 3, 139f.

26. August von Cieszkowski as quoted in David McLellan, *The Young Hegelians and Karl Marx* (London, 1969), 52.

27. Arnold Ruge as quoted in McLellan, *Young Hegelians*, 52.

28. Georg Herwegh, "Die Literatur im Jahre 1840," in *Werke in einem Band* (East Berlin, 1975), 320.

29. Marx, *Notebooks on Epicurean Philosophy*, Sixth Notebook, from the Preparatory Materials, in *MECW*, vol. 1, 491.

30. David Friedrich Strauß, *Das Leben Jesu*, in *Die Junghegelianer: Ausgewählte Texte*, ed. Hans Steussloff (Berlin, 1963), 30.

31. David Friedrich Strauß, *Allgemeines Verhältnis der Hegelschen Philosophie zur theologischen Kritik*, in *Die Hegelsche Linke*, ed. Ingrid Pepperle (Berlin, 1978), 65, 61, 66; quotation translated by Bernard Heise.

32. Hegel, *Phenomenology of Spirit*, 321.

33. Strauß, *Allgemeines Verhältnis*, 55.

34. Marx, "Yet Another Word on *Bruno Bauer und die Akademische Lehrfreiheit*," in *MECW*, vol. 1, 211–214.

35. Schweitzer, Albert, *Geschichte der Leben-Jesu-Forschung* (Tübingen, 1933).

36. Bruno Bauer, *Critique of the Synoptics*, vol. 3, quoted in McLellan, *Young Hegelians*, 57.

37. Bruno Bauer, "Die gute Sache der Freiheit und meine eigene Angelegenheit," in Bruno Bauer, *Feldzüge der reinen Kritik* (Frankfurt am Main, 1968), 122.

38. Bruno Bauer, *Das entdeckte Christentum*, quoted in David McLellan, *Die Junghegelianer und Karl Marx* (Munich, 1974), 70.

39. Bauer, "Die gute Sache der Freiheit," 122; quotation translated by Bernard Heise.

40. Bruno Bauer, "Der christliche Staat und unsere Zeit," in *Feldzüge der reinen Kritik*, 29, 32.

41. Bauer to Marx, 11 December 1839, quoted in McLellan, *Young Hegelians*, 70.

42. Xavier Tiliette, *Schelling: Biographie* (Stuttgart, 2004), 392.

43. Marx and Engels, *The Holy Family*, in *MECW*, vol. 4, 108f.

44. Bruno Bauer to Edgar Bauer, 9 December 1841, in Bruno Bauer, *Feldzüge der reinen Kritik*, 237.

45. Karl Ernst Schubarth, "Über die Unvereinbarkeit der Hegelschen Staatslehre mit dem obersten Lebens- und Entwicklungsprinzip des Preußischen Staats (1839)," in *Materialien zu Hegels Rechtsphilosophie*, ed. Manfred Riedel, 2 vols. (Frankfurt am Main, 1970), vol. 1, 256, 250.

46. Bruno Bauer, *Die Posaune des jüngsten Gerichts über Hegel, den Atheisten und Antichristen: Ein Ultimatum*, in Pepperle, *Die Hegelsche Linke*, 297, 236, 300; quotation translated by Bernard Heise.

47. Marx to Ruge, 5 May 1842, in *MEW*, vol. 27, 397.

48. Bauer to Marx, 5 April 1840, in Pepperle, *Die Hegelsche Linke*, 297, 236, 300; quotations translated by Bernard Heise.

49. Marx, *Notebooks on the Epicurean Philosophy*, sixth notebook, in *MECW*, vol. 1, 491, 492.

50. Ibid., 492.

51. Marx, *Difference between the Democritean and Epicurean Philosophy of Nature*, in *MECW*, vol. 1, 86.

52. Hans-Ulrich Wehler, *Deutsche Gesellschaftsgeschichte*, vol. 2, (Munich, 1996) 199, 426.

53. Moses Hess to Berthold Auerbach, 2 September 1841, in *Erinnerungen an Karl Marx* (Berlin, 1953), 111.

54. Thomas Nipperdey, *Deutsche Geschichte 1800–1866: Arbeitswelt und Bürgergeist* (Munich, 1994), 287, 377f.

55. Marx, "Debates on Freedom of the Press," in *MECW*, vol. 1, 162.

56. Marx, *The Philosophical Manifesto of the Historical School of Law*, in MECW, vol. 1, 209.
57. Marx, "The Leading Article in No. 179 of the *Kölnische Zeitung*," in MECW, vol. 1, 199f.
58. Nipperdey, *Deutsche Geschichte 1800–1866*, 378.
59. Marx, "The Leading Article in No. 179 of the *Kölnische Zeitung*," 202.
60. Marx to Ruge, 9 July 1842, in MECW, vol. 1, 391.
61. Quoted in David McLellan, *Karl Marx: His Life and Thought* (Bristol, 1973), 53.
62. Karl Heinzen, "Erlebtes," in *Der negative Marx: Marx im Urteil seiner Zeitgenossen*, ed. Siegfried Weigel (Stuttgart, 1976), 57.
63. Bruno Bauer, "Das Juste-Milieu," *Rheinische Zeitung*, 5 June 1842, in McLellan, *Young Hegelians*, 82.
64. Marx to Dagobert Oppenheim, 25 August 1842, in MECW, vol. 1, 392.
65. Marx to Ruge, 30 November 1842, in MECW, vol. 1, 394.
66. Ibid., 393.
67. Ruge to Marx, 4 December 1842, in Pepperle, *Die Hegelsche Linke*, 856f.
68. Ruge to Moritz Fleischer, 12 December 1842, in Pepperle, *Die Hegelsche Linke*, 859.
69. Marx to Oppenheim, 25 August 1842, in MECW, vol. 1, 392.
70. Renard's Letter to Oberpräsident von Schaper, in MECW, vol. 1, 283.
71. Heinrich Lutz, *Zwischen Habsburg und Preußen: Deutschland 1815–1866* (Berlin, 1985), 114ff.
72. Marx, "Justification of the Correspondent from the Mosel," in MECW, vol. 1, 333.
73. Richard Friedenthal, *Karl Marx: Sein Leben und seine Zeit* (Munich, 1983), 173, 151.
74. Lutz, *Zwischen Habsburg und Preußen*, 222.
75. Marx, Randglossen zu den Anklagen des Ministerialreskripts, MEW, suppl. vol. 1, 425, 420.
76. Heinz Frederick Peters, *Die rote Jenny: Ein Leben mit Karl Marx* (Munich, 1984), 42, 48.
77. Friedenthal, *Karl Marx*, 174.
78. Ruge to Prutz, 25 January 1843, in Pepperle, *Die Hegelsche Linke*, 863.
79. Ruge to Marx, 1 February 1842, in Pepperle, *Die Hegelsche Linke*, 866.
80. Marx to Ruge, 13 March 1843, in MECW, vol. 1, 399.
81. Marx, preface to *A Contribution to the Critique of Political Economy*, in MECW, vol. 29, 262.
82. Arnold Ruge, foreword to Arnold Ruge, *Eine Selbstkritik des Liberalismus*, in Pepperle, *Die Hegelsche Linke*, 573.
83. Marx, *Contribution to the Critique of Hegel's Philosophy of Law*, in MECW, vol. 3, 29.
84. Georges Gurvitch, *Dialektik und Soziologie* (Berlin, 1965), 145.
85. Marx, *Contribution to the Critique of Hegel's Philosophy of Law*, in MECW, vol. 3, 88, 30, 75, 48.
86. Hegel, *Phenomenology of Spirit*, 357f.
87. Marx, *Contribution to the Critique of Hegel's Philosophy of Law*, in MECW, vol. 3, 118, 121.

88. Marx, "On *the Jewish Question*," in *MECW*, vol. 3, 168.
89. Jürgen Habermas, *Der philosophische Diskurs der Moderne* (Frankfurt am Main, 1988), 83.
90. Pierre Leroux, *Die Gesellschaft liegt im Staube*, in *Die frühen Sozialisten*, ed. Frits Kool and Werner Krause, 2 vols. (Munich, 1972), vol. 1, 277; quotation translated by Bernard Heise.
91. Heinrich Heine, *The Works of Heinrich Heine*, trans. Charles Godfrey Leland, 20 vols. (London, 1893), vol. 4, 25.
92. Ibid., vol. 8, 449.
93. Ibid., vol. 4, 153.
94. Ibid., vol. 8, 450.
95. Ibid., vol. 8, 458.
96. Kool and Krause, *Die frühen Sozialisten*, vol. 1, 258ff.
97. Heine, *Works*, vol. 8, 457.
98. Kool and Krause, *Die frühen Sozialisten*, vol. 1, 261.
99. Arnold Ruge, "Plan der Deutsch-Französischen Jahrbücher," in *Deutsch-Französische Jahrbücher* [1844], ed. Arnold Ruge and Karl Marx (Frankfurt am Main, 1973), 90.
100. Jacques Grandjonc, "Deutsche Emigrationspresse in Europa während des Vormärz 1830–1848," in Akademie der Wissenschaften der DDR, Zentralinstitut für Literaturgeschichte and Centre d'Histoire et d'Analyse des Manuscrits Modernes am Centre National de la Recherche Scientifique, eds., *Heinrich Heine und die Zeitgenossen: Geschichtliche und literarische Befunde* (East Berlin, 1979), 229–297.
101. Heine to Laube, 7 November 1842, in *Werke und Briefe*, vol. 9, 99; quotation translated by Bernard Heise.
102. Feuerbach to Ruge, June 1843, in Ruge and Marx, *Deutsch-Französische Jahrbücher*, 122.
103. Feuerbach to Ruge, 20 June 1843, in Pepperle, *Die Hegelsche Linke*, 877.
104. Engels, *Ludwig Feuerbach and the End of Classical German Philosophy*, in *MECW*, vol. 26, 364.
105. Marx, *Capital*, vol. 1, Afterword to the Second German Edition, in *MECW*, vol. 35, 19.
106. Ludwig Feuerbach, *Vorläufige Thesen zur Reformation der Philosophie*, in Ludwig Feuerbach, *Philosophische Kritiken und Grundsätze* (Leipzig, 1969), 170, 186.
107. John Locke, quoted in Paul Hazard, *Die Krise des europäischen Geistes 1680–1715* (Hamburg, 1939), 284, 281, 287.
108. Feuerbach, *Vorläufige Thesen*, 169; quotation translated by Bernard Heise.
109. Marx to Feuerbach, 11 August 1844, in *MECW*, vol. 3, 354.
110. Eduard Gans, "Über Lerminier introduction à l'histoire du droit," in Gans, *Philosophische Schriften*, 241; quotation translated by Bernard Heise.
111. Moses Hess, "Socialismus und Communismus: Vom Verfasser der europäischen Triarchie," in *Einundzwanzig Bogen aus der Schweiz* [1843], ed. Georg Herwegh (Lepizig, 1989), 175.
112. Lorenz von Stein, *Die industrielle Gesellschaft: Der Sozialismus und Kommunismus Frankreichs von 1830 bis 1848* (Munich, 1921), 1, 34.
113. Herbert Marcuse, *Vernunft und Revolution: Hegel und die Entstehung der Gesellschaftstheorie* (Berlin, 1962), 327.

114. Moses Hess, "Socialism and Communism," in Moses Hess, *The Holy History of Mankind and Other Writings*, translated and edited with an introduction by Shlomo Avineri (Cambridge, 2004), 110 and 112.
115. Marx to Feuerbach, 11 August 1844, in *MECW*, vol. 3, 355.
116. Feuerbach, *Vorläufige Thesen*, 181.
117. Feuerbach to Friedrich Kapp, 15 October 1844, in Werner Schuffenhauer, *Feuerbach und der junge Marx* (East Berlin, 1972), 125; quotation translated by Bernard Heise.
118. Marx, introduction to *Contribution to the Critique of Hegel's Philosphy of Law*, in *MECW*, vol. 3, 176.
119. Marx, *Letters from the Deutsch-Französische Jahrbücher*, in *MECW*, vol. 3, 144.
120. Marx, introduction to *Critique of Hegel's Philosphy of Law*, in *MECW*, vol. 3, 178.
121. Marx and Engels, *The German Ideology*, in *MECW*, vol. 5, 31, 35f., 47f.
122. Marx, *A Contribution to the Critique of Political Economy*, in *MECW*, vol. 29, 263f.
123. Marx, *The Poverty of Philosophy*, in *MECW*, vol. 6, 212.
124. Marx and Engels, *The German Ideology*, in *MECW*, vol. 5, 438.
125. Marx, *The Poverty of Philosophy*, in *MECW*, vol. 6, 212.
126. Marx to Ruge, "Letters from the Deutsch-Französische Jahrbücher," in *MECW*, vol. 3, 141.
127. Marx, introduction to *Critique of Hegel's Philosophy of Right*, in *MECW*, vol. 3, 184, 185, 186.
128. Nipperdey, *Deutsche Geschichte 1800–1866*, 195.
129. Kosellek, *Preußen zwischen Reform und Revolution*, 620.
130. Hegel, *Philosophy of Right*, § 281, § 280, in G.W.F. Hegel: *The Oxford University Press Translations*.
131. Marx and Engels, *The Holy Family*, in *MECW*, vol. 4, 37.
132. Franz Mehring, *Karl Marx: The Story of His Life* (London, 2003), 68.
133. Ruge to his mother, 28 March 1844, quoted in McLellan, *Karl Marx*, 99.
134. Ibid., 99; Fritz J. Raddatz, *Karl Marx: Eine politische Biographie* (Hamburg, 1975), 78; quotation translated by Bernard Heise.
135. Karl August Varnhagen von Ense, Diary entry for 16 June 1844, in *Kommentare zum Zeitgeschehen* (Leipzig, 1984), 132.
136. Heinrich Heine, "The Silesian Weavers," in *The Poems of Heine*, trans. Edgar Alfred Bowring (London, 1866), 395.
137. Marx, "Critical Marginal Notes on the Article 'The King of Prussia and Social Reform: by a Prussian,'" in *MECW*, vol. 3, 201, 201, 205, 199, 201.
138. Marx, *The Poverty of Philosophy*, in *MECW*, vol. 6, 177.
139. Marx, "Letters from the Deutsch-Französische Jahrbücher," in *MECW*, vol. 3, 136, 143, 144.
140. Marx, Economic and Philosophic Manuscripts of 1844, in *MECW*, vol. 3, 237, 295, 296.
141. Marx and Engels, *The Holy Family*, in *MECW*, vol. 4, 119.
142. Jean Bruhat, "Französischer Sozialismus von 1815 bis 1848," in *Geschichte des Sozialismus*, ed. Jacques Droz, 4 vols. (Frankfurt am Main, 1974), 192.

143. Joachim Höppner and Waltraud Seidel-Höppner, *Von Babeuf bis Blanqui: Französischer Sozialismus vor Marx*. 2 vols. (Leipzig, 1976), vol. 1, 318–327; Bruhat, "Französischer Sozialismus von 1815 bis 1848," 189–191.

144. Christopher H. Johnson, "Etienne Cabet und das Problem des Klassenantagonismus," in *Vormarxistischer Sozialismus*, ed. Manfred Hahn (Frankfurt am Main, 1974), 212.

145. Marx, "On Proudhon," in MECW, vol. 20, 31, 26, 28.

146. Engels, *Socialism: Utopian and Scientific*, in MECW, vol. 24, 289.

147. Marx, *Contribution to the Critique of Political Economy*, in MECW, vol. 29, 264.

148. Engels, "Progress of Social Reform on the Continent," in MECW, vol. 3, 399.

149. Charles Fourier, *Ökonomisch-philosophische Schriften* (Berlin, 1980), 57; quotation translated by Bernard Heise.

150. Engels, "Outlines of a Critique of Political Economy," in MECW, vol. 3, 433f, 420

151. Engels, "On the History of the Communist League," in MECW, vol. 26, 318.

152. Kool and Krause, *Die frühen Sozialisten*, vol. 1, 259.

153. Gottfried Salomon-Delatour, introduction to *Die Lehre Saint-Simons*, ed. Gottfried Salomon-Delatour (Neuwied, 1962), 19ff.

154. Heinrich Heine, French introduction to the French edition of *Reisebilder*, in Heinrich Heine, *Sämtliche Schriften in zwölf Bänden*, ed. Klaus Briegleb, 20 vols. (Munich, 1976), vol. 3, 677.

155. Eliza Marian Butler, *The Saint-Simonian Religion in Germany* (New York, 1960), 60: "The newspaper-reading German public could no more be in ignorance of Saint-Simonism than of the cholera."

156. Salomon-Delatour, *Lehre Saint-Simons*, 117, 105, 108f., 117, 209, 225.

157. Otto Warschauer, *Saint-Simon und der Saint-Simonismus* (Leipzig, 1892), 62.

158. Engels, "Socialism: Utopian and Scientific," in MECW, vol. 24, 293.

159. Marx, *Economic and Philosophical Manuscripts of 1844*, in MECW, vol. 3, 332, 333, 281, 280.

160. Engels, "Outlines of a Critique of Political Economy," in MECW, vol. 3, 430.

161. Marx, *Economic and Philosophical Manuscripts of 1844*, in MECW, vol. 3, 294, 331.

162. Marx, introduction to *Contribution to the Critique of Hegel's Philosophy of Law*, in MECW, vol. 3, 176.

163. Marx, *Economic and Philosophical Manuscripts of 1844*, in MECW, vol. 3, 297.

164. Marx and Engels, *The Holy Family*, in MECW, vol. 4, 36.

165. Marx, "The Communism of the Rheinischer Beobachter," in MECW, vol. 6, 233.

166. Marx, "Theses on Feuerbach," in MECW, vol. 5, 5.

167. Karl Löwith, *Weltgeschichte und Heilsgeschehen: Die theologischen Voraussetzungen der Geschichtsphilosophie* (Stuttgart, 2004), 61.

168. Marx, *Contribution to the Critique of Hegel's Philosophy of Law*, in MECW, vol. 3, 8.

169. Marx and Engels, *The German Ideology*, in MECW, vol. 5, 329.
170. François Auguste Mignet, *Geschichte der Französischen Revolution von 1789 bis 1814* (Leipzig, 1975), 409ff., 13, 15.
171. François Guizot, *Cours d'histoire, histoire générale de la civilisation en Europe*, Lecture 7, quoted in Rudolf Herrnstadt, *Die Entdeckung der Klassen* (East Berlin, 1965). Quotation translated by Bernard Heise.
172. François Pierre Guillaume Guizot, *Die Demokratie in Frankreich* (Grimma, 1849) 49, 67, 71.
173. Francois Guizot, *Cours d'histoire*, Lecture 7, quoted in Herrnstadt. Quotation translated by Bernard Heise.
174. Stein, *Die industrielle Gesellschaft*, 5.
175. Marx and Engels, *The Holy Family*, in MECW, vol. 4, 124.
176. Marx, *The Class Struggles in France 1848–1850*, in MECW, vol. 10, 48.
177. Marx and Engels, *The German Ideology*, in MECW, vol. 5, 90.
178. Ibid., 59.
179. Marx, "Public Prosecutor Hecker and the Neue Rheinische Zeitung," in MECW, vol. 7, 488.
180. Marx and Engels, *The Holy Family*, in MECW, vol. 4, 122.
181. Marx and Engels, *The German Ideology*, in MECW, vol. 5, 90.
182. Heine, *Works*, vol. 7, 126.
183. Engels, *Origins of the Family, Private Property and the State*, in MECW, vol. 26, 271f.
184. Marx to Weydemeyer, 5 March 1852, in MECW, vol. 39, 62ff.
185. Universal Society of Revolutionary Communists, in MECW, vol. 10, 614f.
186. Höppner and Seidel-Höppner, *Von Babeuf bis Blanqui*, vol. 1, 373.
187. Jean-Jacques Rousseau, *Emile* (Teddington, 2007), 274.
188. Marx, "Theses on Feuerbach," in MECW, vol. 5, 7.
189. Marx and Engels, *The Holy Family*, in MECW, vol. 4, 37.
190. Marx, *Class Struggles in France*, in MECW, vol. 10, 127.
191. Marx to Ruge, May 1843, in MECW, vol. 3, 141.
192. Marx, Provisional Rules of the Association, in MECW, vol. 20, 14.
193. Marx, *Class Struggles in France*, in MECW, vol. 10, 117.
194. Friedrich Nietzsche, *Thus Spoke Zarathustra: A Book for All and None*, trans. Adrian Del Caro (Cambridge, 2006), 5f.
195. Löwith, *Weltgeschichte und Heilsgeschehen*, 76.

Deeds

Futurism

The railway's conquest of the earth was one of the earliest dreams motivating Count Henri de Saint-Simon. At the end of the 1840s, only its modest beginnings were visible outside of England and America. Yet ever since the Congress of Vienna, the increasing speed of travel had begun to open up the landscape with a vengeance. Express postal routes along new highways soon reduced the travel time from Berlin to Munich by way of Cologne from 130 to 78 hours. In 1825, horse-drawn omnibuses were introduced to inner-city traffic in Berlin. By 1847, Prussia boasted 3,200 kilometers of railway lines. Tunnels penetrated mountains, bridges spanned valleys and rivers, and railway embankments were soon an intrinsic part of landscape imagery, classically captured by Adolph Menzel's 1847 oil painting *Die Berlin-Potsdamer Eisenbahn*. Whereas Menzel's steaming colossus still came across as an irritating disruption in a mortally wounded landscape, William Turner's *Rain, Steam and Speed, the Great Western Railway* of 1844 represented the full-blown apotheosis of the new era in which everything was bathed in the glowing reddish light of the new fires of industry. "The shining steel glides to and fro / And, driving other parts, all show / A striving to one goal," wrote the harp maker J. A. Stumpf, living in London: "The great machine / Obeys the master's mind, it may be seen."[1] The atmosphere of the time was futuristic.

Even the *Communist Manifesto*, which Marx and Engels wrote in Brussels in 1847, breathed this futuristic spirit. "The bourgeoisie," it states, "has disclosed what man's activity can bring about. It has accomplished wonders far surpassing Egyptian pyramids, Roman aqueducts, and Gothic cathedrals; it has conducted expeditions that put in the shade all former exoduses of nations and crusades." This revolution, the likes of which the world had never seen, was occurring before the very eyes of contemporaries who had just recently learned to cultivate the niches and favorite everyday things of the domesticated Biedermeier period. "The bourgeoisie, during its rule of scarce one hundred years, has created more massive and more colossal productive forces than have all preceding generations together," the *Manifesto* continues:

> Subjection of Nature's forces to man, machinery, application of chemistry to industry and agriculture, steam-navigation, railways, electric telegraphs, clearing of whole continents for cultivation, canalisation of rivers, whole populations conjured out of the ground— what earlier century had even a presentiment that such productive forces slumbered in the lap of social labour?[2]

As Marx had already written in his doctoral dissertation, it was in fact a time that recalled Prometheus's theft of fire from the gods in heaven.[3] There was something almost frightening about the speed and extent of the human world's accumulation of powers that seemed to transport the entire earthly sphere into a state of permanent industrial, economic, and communicative revolution.

Marx believed this sudden and ultra-pharaonic violence and strength of capitalism was too fragile to last very long. "Modern bourgeois society," the *Communist Manifesto* states, "with its relations of production, of exchange and of property, a society that has conjured up such gigantic means of production and of exchange, is like the sorcerer who is no longer able to control the powers of the nether world whom he has called up by his spells." For decades already, the history of industry and trade had been a history of the revolt of modern productive forces against modern conditions of production, which came to light especially in the periodic commercial crises that *put the existence of the entire bourgeois society on its trial,* each time more threateningly. The entire paradox of capitalistic modernity revealed itself in these societal epidemics, which the old world, always suffering from scarcity, had not known. They were indeed *epidemics of over-production* that were leading to a *universal war of devastation*, for unregulated overabundance due to the sudden stagnation of the markets created dramatic shortages of goods, whereupon humanity unexpectedly found itself thrown back into a *state of momentary barbarism* during the economic crisis.[4] Only the regulated, rational world of communism was in a position to lead humanity out of this chaos and really consummate the work of Prometheus.

Marx had meanwhile become a member of the Communist League. A failed attempt to assassinate Friedrich Wilhelm IV had abruptly ended his first stay in Paris. On the morning of 26 July 1844, as the Prussian king and queen set out from the busy Berlin Schlosshof for their usual summer vacation in Silesia, the former Storkow Bürgermeister Heinrich Ludwig Tschech approached them with a double-barreled pistol; Tschech got off two shots, but they narrowly missed their target. The Parisian *Vorwärts* reported on the event—not particularly reverentially—and thereafter the government of His Majesty in Berlin had, with increasing anger, demanded that measures be taken against the radical German emigrants in Paris, among them Marx. In mid August, Marx again disrespectfully issued solemn remarks about Friedrich Wilhelm in *Vorwärts*, saying that *the hand of God* had providentially deflected the bullets, and now, *while looking upward to the divine Savior* and with the *certainty of victory*, he was applying a firm hand to the work *of combating evil*.[5] French scruples kept Guizot from expelling Heinrich Heine, whose mocking political poetry made him hated in Berlin above all others. Guizot paid respect to Heine's international renown as a European author—and, as was common knowledge at the time in France, "one does not arrest Voltaire." But Marx had to go.

He received his deportation order on 1 January 1845. On 3 February he left with the mail coach for Brussels, where he would remain until the outbreak of the European Revolution in February 1848. Jenny followed him ten days later. For a month they lived in the Hotel Bois Sauvage, and in May 1845 they moved into a row house on the eastern edge of the town on Verbondsstraat, which at the time was still called Rue de l'Alliance in French. Shortly thereafter Caroline von Westphalen, Jenny's mother, sent them Helene Demuth, the daughter of a Trier baker, as a housemaid. "Lenchen" would henceforth manage the household until Marx's death.

"In those days Brussels teemed with all sorts of refugees and emigrants," wrote the author Alfred Meißner in his memoirs: "There was no shortage of troubled creatures who had avoided the police of Louis Philippe."[6] Marx was now among those who, expelled by the police of Louis Philippe, had gathered in the capital city of this the most liberal constitutional monarchy on the continent. In early 1847 he became a member of the Communist League. The league had originally been founded in Paris in 1836 under a different name. "During my first stay in Paris," Marx recalled later, "I established personal contact with the leaders of the League living there as well as with the leaders of the majority of the secret French workers' associations, without however becoming a member of any of them." But in Brussels, *where Guizot's expulsion order had sent me*, he joined the league after receiving the offer, together with Engels, to formulate anew the league's program on the basis of his own views. Marx had, in the time since his arrival, become an authority among German communists abroad.

This fact was due substantially to the many different activities that he undertook in Brussels, usually with Engels. He later recalled:

> We published a series of pamphlets, partly printed, partly lithographed, in which we mercilessly criticized the hotchpotch of Franco-English socialism or communism and German philosophy, which formed the secret doctrine of the League at that time. In its place we proposed the scientific study of the economic structure of bourgeois society as the only tenable theoretical foundation. Furthermore, we argued in popular form that it was not a matter of putting some utopian system into effect, but of *conscious participation in the historical process revolutionizing society before our very eyes.*[7]

Thus, as Engels wrote in retrospect, Marx was convinced that the materialistic conception of history he had formed through the reversal of Hegel was "of immediate importance for the contemporary workers' movement."[8] This, his first and most important political paradigm, was basically the paradigm of a new kind of absolute knowledge. Underlying it was nothing less than the claim of being the only self-conscious and authentic mouthpiece of the historical will of the ostensibly real historical objective of Marx's own present.

Increasingly, his sense of superiority also set the tone of his debates. The first to experience this was the theorizing communist tailor Wilhelm Weitling, whose *brilliant writings*, Marx had attested in 1844, marked the *vehement and brilliant literary debut of the German workers.*[9] Since 1836, Weitling had played an important role in the precursor organizations of the Communist League, and for a long time his writings—among them *Humanity as It Is and Ought to Be, The Poor Sinner's Gospel,* and *Guarantees of Harmony and Freedom*—were considered authoritative catechisms for the conspiratorial secret organization. He moved to Brussels in February 1846 upon his release from a year in prison.[10] "But," as Engels described him after his arrival,

> he was no longer the naive young journeyman-tailor who, astonished at his own talents, was trying to clarify in his own mind just what a communist society would look like. He was now the great man, persecuted by the environs on account of his superiority, who scented rivals, secret enemies and traps everywhere—the prophet, driven from country to country, who carried a recipe for the realisation of heaven on earth ready-made in his pocket, and who was possessed with the idea that everybody intended to steal it from him.[11]

In late March 1846, during a longer debate about communist future perspectives in which the liberal Russian landowner Pavel Annenkov—a friend of Marx—also participated, things came to a head with Marx. Assigning himself the role of mouthpiece of historical truth, Marx could react quite sharply and arrogantly in such debates. Weitling was circuitously presenting his future projects when Marx impatiently interrupted him by saying that it was simply a fraud against the people to incite them without providing a solid, well thought-out basis for their activities, as fantastic hopes never lead to the salvation of the sufferers but rather to their demise. As Annenkov reports, Marx concluded with a quotation from Spinoza: "Ignorance is not an argument,"[12] (*ignorantia non est argumentum*). As Weitling noted afterward, Marx was evidently insisting on a critical examination of the Communist Party.[13] And in fact this got to the heart of the matter, for the priority now, according to Engels, was "to win over the European, and in the first place the German proletariat to our conviction."[14]

The second rebuff—Annenkov was the first to hear of this case as well—concerned Pierre Joseph Proudhon. Marx and Engels planned to set up an international Communist Correspondence Committee in Brussels, an archetype for every subsequent International. It was supposed to help prepare for the coming European revolution. Of every conceivable contact person, Proudhon was originally one of the most important to Marx, for whom only the crowing of the Gallic rooster could assure the beginning of a new revolutionary Spring of Nations in Europe. Connections must be established between German, French, and English socialists, he wrote to Proudhon in May 1846, to settle existing differences of opinion through impartial criticism, and he could not imagine a better correspondent in France.[15] This attempt was Marx's first foray into practical politics. What he meant by impartial criticism would soon become apparent.

Proudhon cautiously declined the request for collaboration with the Communist Correspondence Committee. "Let us seek together, if you wish, the laws of society," wrote Proudhon, "but, for God's sake, after having demolished all the a priori dogmatisms, do not let us in our turn dream of indoctrinating the people."[16] France was difficult terrain, as the vain search for French collaborators for the *Deutsch-Französische Jahrbücher* had already demonstrated.

Marx did not respond. "Mr. Proudhon confuses ideas and things," he wrote to Annenkov that December after reading from Proudhon's new book *The System of Economic Contradictions or the Philosophy of Misery*, using the occasion to once again lay out the central basic theses of his own historical materialism.[17] As a response to the failure to set up a collaborative correspondence, he produced *Misère de la Philosophie—The Poverty of Philosophy*. Written in French, it was an intellectual execution of Proudhon, with the final chapter spelling out their core political differences. The book got out of hand, like *The Holy Family*, which had been published a year earlier as a polemic against his former young Hegelian friends; both volumes betrayed a personal overexcitement that could by no means be blamed solely on the subject at hand.

Revealing his seemingly near-manic compulsion to repeat himself, Marx's anti-Proudhon text awkwardly zeroed in on an invisible enemy: Hegel, whom Proudhon, incidentally, had not even invoked and knew only rudimentarily at best from lectures the German emigrant Heinrich Ahrens had given at the Collège de France.[18] Page after page, Marx depicted Proudhon as philosophically foolish instead of coming to the point. Much of it reads like a theological dispute akin to those at the Berlin Doctor Club, including the constantly repeated allegation that Hegel—and with him, Proudhon—was reducing everything to logical categories instead of proceeding from real conditions. After the book appeared, Proudhon called Marx the "tapeworm of socialism," thereby quite accurately striking a nerve, and referred to his opponent ironically as "my dear philosopher."[19]

The leaders of the Communist League had already written Weitling off when Marx suggested in mid May that they collaborate with his international Correspondence Committee. Many of them had fled to London after the suppression of the 1839 uprising organized by Auguste Blanqui, in which they had participated. Among them in particular was Karl Schapper, who after the Parisian uprisings had been imprisoned for a considerable period and then expelled from France by Louis Philippe's police. Schapper, a former member of Georg Büchner's conspiratorial Society for Human Rights in Hesse, had been among the armed assailants who stormed the constabulary watch in Frankfurt in early April 1833; in 1834 he joined Giuseppe Mazzini's Young Europe movement. Now home to Schapper, the cobbler Heinrich Bauer, and the watchmaker Joseph Moll, London in the early 1840s had become a new center for the league.[20]

After the unsuccessful Blanquist uprising, Schapper came to understand that it was just "as easy to compel a tree to grow as to inculcate new ideas into mankind by force."[21] This change increasingly distanced him from Weitling's revolutionary voluntarism and drew his curiosity to the work of Marx and Engels in Brussels, where they were running a workers' association through which Marx, for example, held lectures about the irreconcilable opposition between wage labor and capitalism. There, to an audience of around a hundred, he explained among other things that capital's modern relations of production were at heart characterized by the exploitative *dominion of accumulated, past, materialised labour over direct, living labour that turns accumulated labour into capital.*[22] Marx and Engels also presided over the *Deutsche Brüsseler Zeitung*, a forum for their opinions. Their writings were well known—at least to the initiated—especially Engels's text about the "the condition of the working class in England," which appeared in 1845 and opened with the statement that the world-historical significance of the industrial revolution was only now gaining recognition. It ended with the words "I think the people will not endure more than one more crisis."[23]

In spring 1847, Joseph Moll showed up at Marx's in Brussels and shortly thereafter at Engels's in Paris, requesting on behalf of his London comrades that they join the Communist League. Moll and his comrades had dissociated themselves from the old conspiratorial tradition and now wanted to give Marx and Engels the opportunity to present their critical communism as a new league doctrine at a league congress. But to do so they had to become members.[24] In the rooms of the communist Workers' Educational Society in London's Drury Lane 191, after weeks of debate in which communists from a variety of nations participated, the *Communist Manifesto* was finally unanimously accepted as the official program of the Communist League at the beginning of December 1847.[25] The program had an international orientation from the outset and was supposed to be translated into Europe's most important languages[26]—and it was the first sign of the deep suggestion that proceeded from Marx and his view of history to the damned of the earth.

In his text about Proudhon, Marx had written: "For the oppressed class to be able to emancipate itself it is necessary that the productive powers already acquired and the existing social relations should no longer be capable of existing side by side. *Of all the instruments of production, the greatest productive power is the revolutionary class itself.*"[27] Transformed according to the spirit of Marx's definition, the Communist League members were now supposed to elevate the self-consciousness of this revolutionary productive power—the working class—so that it became aware of its own mission. The *Communist Manifesto* formulated it this way: "The Communists ... theoretically ... have over the great mass of the proletariat the advantage of clearly understanding the line of march, the conditions, and the ultimate general results of the proletarian movement." On the one hand, they were not a particular party vis-à-vis other workers' parties; but on the other hand they always kept the *interests of the movement as a whole* in sight and thus considered themselves practically as the *most advanced and resolute section* of the working-class parties of every country. *In the movement of the present,* according to Marx and Engels, the communists also *represent and take care of the future of that movement,*[28] and this maxim would also determine their options for forming coalitions in a future revolution. For only *if all the conditions are at hand,* according to the assumptions of Hegelian logic shared by the authors of the manifesto, could something actually come into being.[29] Basically, Marx and Engels were developing the dynamic concept of permanent revolution. Especially with respect to Germany, which would play a major role in the coming European Revolution, they predicted that the imminent bourgeois revolution would *be but the prelude to an immediately following proletarian revolution.*

Marx and Engels anticipated a revolution in Germany along the lines of what had occurred in France between 1789 and 1794, among other reasons because, according to their conceptions, bourgeois society as a system lacked a stabilizing dynamic; therefore, once a revolution was underway it would inevitably become more radical. Theoretically, this conception relied on the prognosis of the inevitable immiseration of the worker in the modern world of capital. "The modern labourer," states the *Communist Manifesto*, "instead of rising with the progress of industry, sinks deeper and deeper below the conditions of existence of his own class. He becomes a pauper, and pauperism develops more rapidly than population and wealth. And here it becomes evident, that the bourgeoisie is unfit any longer to be the ruling class in society, and to impose its conditions of existence upon society as an over-riding law."[30] It was an end-times prognosis. Unlike the situation after the fall of Robespierre, at this point no new bourgeois Directory could halt the dynamic of a revolution against the system of the Holy Alliance.

The social-democratic theoretician Franz Mehring, Marx's first biographer, thought that the *Manifesto* was still informed by the law of wages as it had been developed by the British economist David Ricardo with the help of Malthusian population theory. Therefore, according to Mehring, it too one-sidedly envisioned the possible reaction to the trend of immiseration in terms of a political revolution. For precisely this reason, Marx and Engels saw the near future taking shape according to the model of the French Revolution. Only during Marx's work on *Capital* was this model called into question, upon the discovery of the "elasticity" of the law of wages, which acknowledged that wage levels were influenced by factors that were culturally acquired or gained through the struggles of unions. This opened up perspectives with political consequences that Marx, however, never really managed to clarify. In any case, in 1848 Jacobinism was for him still materially anchored in the theory of immiseration. Incidentally, the *Communist Manifesto*, written during a period marked by constitutional struggles, contained not a single word about the future constitution. Dolf Sternberger once quite rightly observed: "But how the class will begin to govern, administer, and dispense justice is not considered, or in any event explained."[31] The *real movement* would come up with something and create the corresponding institutions.

World War

At the time, Marx and Engels were deeply convinced that after the outbreak of the revolution, the German bourgeoisie's transitory rule would last a few years at most. "So just fight bravely on," wrote Engels at the end of January, 1848, "[i]n recompense whereof you shall be allowed to rule for a short time. You shall be allowed to dictate your laws, to bask in the rays of the majesty you have created, to spread your banquets in the halls of kings, and to take the beautiful princess to wife—but do not forget that the hangman stands at the door!"[32] Shortly thereafter Engels himself sat at a dining table in the royal chambers of the Tuileries in Paris with a friend who was a former French refugee from Brussels. On 24 February the people of Paris had risen up, declaring the Republic. Those wounded in the street fighting were now recovering and smoking their pipes in the apartments of the overthrown Citizen King Louis Philippe, who had fled to England. Outside, to the sound of the Marseillaise, the National Guard and armed people were saluting the funeral procession of a revolutionary worker who had died of his wounds.[33] At the same time, the author Fanny Lewald observed huge piles of torn-up cobblestones in the Parisian streets, as well as broken bread wagons and overturned omnibuses that had been used to build barricades in February. At the Palais Royal, now called the Palais National, she saw that all the windows and many of the window frames and scaffolds were broken, and the royal guardhouse lay in ruins, blackened by smoke. The trees along the boulevards had been felled, well pipes and pillars had been torn down, and the tricolor flew everywhere—on the theaters, over the church entries, and on all public buildings.[34]

The year had begun with an uprising in Palermo, after which King Ferdinand of the two Sicilies had had to agree to a constitution on 29 January. The storm unleashed in the French capital in late February had completely different dimensions, however. With lightning speed it engulfed all Europe, for the first time demonstrating to the world the great drama of the historical unity of European life. As Benedetto Croce once wrote, it was as if all the great impediments against which one had vainly struggled for half a century had suddenly, with the sound of trumpets, lost all of their frightening magic, almost like the walls of Jericho.[35] The revolt against the coercive system of Europe's Holy Alliance and the police state it entailed had already been heralded in the *Communist Manifesto*. Marx had predicted as early as 1844 that the revolution would begin with the crowing of the Gallic rooster. Since July 1847 the republican opposition in France had been campaigning for the introduction of universal suffrage, a goal the Guizot regime strictly opposed. Then, with the prohibition of a voting-rights assembly on 22 February 1848, the situation escalated. The first street battles erupted on 23 February. In Paris, barricades were erected and the military's advance on the Boulevard des Capucines resulted in over fifty fatalities and many wounded. An angry crowd laid the dead on wagons and paraded them through the city by torchlight, and the next day the uprising spread to all of Paris. On the evening of 24 February the Republic was proclaimed.

The news reached Brussels on 26 February. Thereupon King Leopold allowed the spread of a rumor that he was prepared to abdicate, should the people wish it. In reality, thought Marx, this was just a feint to get the Belgian democrats to refrain from any undertakings against such a benevolent monarch. And in fact, the Belgian authorities began compiling lists of persons who were to be arrested as potential disturbers of the public order. The first arrests took place in a hail of beating fists, kicks, and slashing sabers. The foreigners among those arrested were squeezed into prison wagons and brought to the French border.[36] The Belgian government, Marx noted, suddenly positioned itself entirely on the side of the Holy Alliance. On 3 March, at five o'clock in the evening, Marx received the order to leave the kingdom within twenty-four hours. That night, after a meeting of the central authority of the Communist League, ten policemen arrested him at the Hotel Bois Sauvage, and the next morning he and his wife Jenny found themselves in a dark cell of the city prison in the Rue de l'Amigo, not far from the Grand Place.[37] Escorted to the border by the police, they arrived in Paris a short time later. Ferdinand Flocon, a democratic socialist and now a member of the provisional regime, had already sent news to the "brave and loyal Marx" on 3 March: "Tyranny has banished you, free France opens her doors to you."[38] Marx felt that the martial reaction of the Belgian government would spark enthusiasm on Metternich's part.[39] But his days, too, were numbered.

On 9 March, Engels's report of tremendous news from Germany reached Marx in Paris—full-blown revolution in Nassau, an uprising in Munich because of the king's mistress Lola Montez, freedom of the press and a National Guard in western Germany. The People's Assembly of Mannheim had given the signal on 27 February, issuing demands for the arming of the people and the free election of officers, freedom of the press, jury courts based on the English model, and the immediate convocation of a German parliament. These then circulated throughout Germany as the so-called March Demands, to be once again presented in Karlsruhe to thousands of people who had come by train from Mannheim and Heidelberg, and likewise, on 4 March, in Wiesbaden. Again it was the railway—which the *Communist Manifesto* had already predicted would play the role of a future revolutionary locomotive[40]—that allowed ten thousand people to gather in front of the ducal palace. Liberal so-called March regimes, mostly led by bourgeois persons, sprang up overnight throughout Germany. "If only Frederick William IV digs his heels in!" Engels wrote to Marx, referencing the all-important Prussian king. "Then all will be won and in a few months' time we'll have the German Revolution. If he only sticks to his feudal forms! But the devil only knows what this capricious and crazy individual will do."[41]

First, however, the spark ignited a fire at the center of the Habsburg monarchy—shown over the last decade to be hardly capable of reform—where the Metternich system had been exercised most rigorously. On 13 March, the Parisian virus gripped its first German metropolis, Vienna, initiating a whole year of democratic revolutions in every state of the German Confederation and the bordering European countries. "The Paris Revolution struck the darkness of our situation like a lightning bolt," Saxony's legation councilor in Vienna, Carl Friedrich Graf Vitzthum von Eckstädt, wrote to his mother as early as 5 March: "The malaise is universal, und I only fear that it will not be perceived as such from above, as is necessary."[42] Eight days later, open insurrection prevailed in Vienna. "The gates are closed," wrote Vitzthum von Eckstädt on 13 March: "Cannons are positioned at the court, in front of the castle, in front of the state chancellery. Heavy patrols are moving through the streets. In some alleyways barricades are being erected. One hears shouted: Hurray! The constitution!"[43] At around four in the afternoon, a few thousand demonstrators gathered under the windows of the state chancellery and demanded the resignation of Klemens von Metternich, whom they loudly called Austria's fox. That morning in the Ministerial Council, the chancellor had still opposed all concessions to the rebels and categorically denied the possibility of a revolution in Austria, even as shots were fired outside his window. All that, he insisted, was "only Jews, Poles, Italians, and the Swiss who are stirring up the people."[44] But by evening, the once supremely powerful police dictator of the European Restoration had to surrender all of his offices and leave in disguise through the back door of the Hofburg, fleeing to London by way of Prague. On this same evening of 13 March, initial disturbances were also reported from Berlin. Under tents in the Tiergarten, a people's assembly demanded that the king establish a Ministry of Labor, for the people were being "oppressed by capitalists and usurers."[45] The crown, however, summoned the military to the city, prompting initial skirmishes and a few isolated fatalities. On 15 March the news of Metternich's fall reached Berlin, sending the court into a panic, according to the young doctor Rudolf Virchow in the Berlin Charité. Friedrich Wilhelm reacted as Engels had feared: he made concessions, agreeing to the abolition of censorship and the convocation of a unified Landtag on 2 April. "A proclamation was made in a grandiloquent style," Virchow commented on this half-hearted royal act.[46] But as news of the proclamation spread, thousands of Berliners streamed enthusiastically to the city palace. Actually they were celebrating the onset of a new era in Prussia and wanted to thank the king for conceding; a loud hurrah initially greeted the king as he appeared on the palace balcony. But the mood among the demonstrators changed suddenly when they noticed the concentrated power of the dragoons assembled in the palace square to protect the king. Demands were made for the military to withdraw, and the atmosphere increasingly became so hostile that the uncertain king, suddenly feeling threatened by the change in the mood of the crowd, gave General von Moellendorff an ill-considered order to clear the square. The people who had in fact gathered to pay tribute to the king were violently driven from the square by saber-swinging dragoons. But this was not a crowd that could be dissolved in the usual manner. It was—as Friedrich Wilhelm should have known, in light of the disturbances in recent days and the events in Paris and Vienna—the beginning of a state crisis.

"From this moment the revolution began," according to Rudolf Virchow, who actively participated: "Everything screamed betrayal and revenge. In a matter of hours all of Berlin was barricaded, and anyone who could get weapons armed himself."[47] The big battles that would change Prussia for the foreseeable future broke out just before noon on 18 March 1848. Late in the evening at Alexanderplatz, after a heated battle that lasted many hours, the royal troops were forced to flee. It was a bright moonlit night, as the painter Adolph

Menzel reported, on which the lathe-turned rifles of the citizens' marksman guilds often proved to be much more accurate than the simple commissioned rifles of the royal infantry.[48] A citizens' brigade led by the veterinarian Urban captured General von Moellendorff and brought him to the marksman guild's house, where he was compelled to sign an order to the Kaiser Franz and Alexander regiments to cease fire immediately and retreat to the barracks. A message sent to the king stated that if another shot was fired, the general would be shot dead immediately. Friedrich Wilhelm signed an appeal to his "dear Berliners" and promised to withdraw all troops. From this moment forward, all shooting ceased.

On 22 March, the coffins of the fallen insurrectionists were laid out on a large scaffold in the Neue Kirche at the Gendarmenmarkt. Male choirs sang funeral marches and spiritual songs. Around ten o'clock a funeral procession moved toward the palace. On the balcony stood an adjutant with a black funeral flag, and across from him an officer of the citizens' militia held the black-red-gold flag high. Each time a new procession of coffins passed, the king appeared, bareheaded, and remained standing until the procession had gone by. "His head shone from afar like a white spot," noted Adolph Menzel, observing the almost surreal staffage with a painter's keen eye for unreal aesthetic effects.[49] According to Menzel, it could well have been the most dreadful day of the king's life. On the streets people filed by with black ribbons and black-red-gold cockades. The flag waved black-red-gold from the homes of citizens. A black-red-gold flag had even been affixed at the palace of the prince of Prussia, with an inscription reading "Property of the Entire Nation."

The day before, the king had undertaken his first ride through Berlin since the revolution, accompanied by the prince, a few generals, and the ministers of his short-lived transitional government. Everyone, including the king himself, wore black-red-gold armbands. A royal proclamation of the day announced that he had adopted "the old German colors," establishing the legend that black, red, and gold were actually the colors of the Holy Roman Empire and its now-mythical Emperor Friedrich Barbarossa. In other words, during this period of critical emergency, the political romantic on the royal throne deftly tried to associate his backward-looking imperial idea, bound to the divine right of kings, with the symbols of the revolution and thereby tacitly appropriate them for himself. As Engels had shrewdly guessed, it was almost impossible to anticipate the chess moves the founder of the Christian state and the sacred Hohen-zollern tradition—"this capricious and crazy individual"—could still manage to make.

At this point Marx, who was living in a side street to the Bou-levard Beaumarchais in the vicinity of the Bastille, was initially completely occupied with keeping the German communists in Paris together. On 16 March, he wrote to Engels, the bourgeoisie there were *again becoming atrociously uppish and reactionary, mais elle vera.*[50] In his view a second armed conflict was imminent, this time be-tween the bourgeoisie and the proletariat, and would decide the fate of the revolutionary movement across Europe; thus he called on the communists to remain in Paris and prepare for the coming battle. The central authority of the Communist League was reorganized, and on 10 March Marx became its formal president. Then came the news on 19 March from Vienna and on 20 March from Berlin. The first thousand printed copies of the *Communist Manifesto* had just been sent from London to Paris, and now four hundred Ger-man communists set off toward their old homeland, carrying these copies as well as the demands of the Communist Party in Germany. Marx himself left Paris at the beginning of April; traveling by way of Mainz, he arrived in Cologne on 10 March. Jenny followed with their two children, going first to Trier and three months later to the Rhine.

The demands of the Communist Party exceeded the March De-mands—discussed widely at the time throughout the land—in only a few points. Feudal estates, mines, and all means of transportation were to be nationalized; inheritance rights restricted; high progres-sive taxes introduced; nationalized work sites established; and the existence of all workers secured.[51] Entirely in keeping with the ideas of Marx and Engels, the events in Germany, of course, did not pertain to an imminent socialist revolution but rather a bourgeois revolution in which it was nonetheless desirable from the outset to embed certain demands that would necessarily develop a dynamic extending beyond the demands themselves. This was the only way, in their view, to foster the desired radicalization and ultimately the shift into a proletarian revolution. Thus they decisively rejected independent political actions by German workers for the time be-ing. But such actions did exist. "The workers are beginning to bestir themselves a little, still in a very crude way, but as a mass. They at once formed coalitions," Engels informed Marx from Wuppertal in mid April, "But to *us* that can only be a hindrance."[52] Such actions took place in Cologne as well.

On 3 March, long before the street battles in Berlin, a few thousand people had gathered at Cologne's Rathausplatz and a delegation forced its way into the town hall meeting room to present the March Demands. Its leaders were communists named Andreas Gottschalk (a doctor for the poor), August von Willich, and Friedrich Anneke (both former Prussian lieutenants). The main points were the right to work and free child education, demands that were decidedly popular among the masses of paupers in the city. A battalion of the 16th Cologne Regiment dispersed the crowd around nine o'clock that evening, killing a few people and wounding others with bayonets. Gottschalk, Willich, and Anneke wound up in prison,[53] although two weeks later they would again be free because of the Berlin revolution. After these events, a certain balance of power prevailed in Cologne between the city militia—subject to the local democrats—and the Prussian garrison. Gottschalk founded a workers' association that soon included eight thousand members, and in mid May he left the Communist League, having fallen out with Marx over the question, in particular, of the elections to the Prussian parliament and the Frankfurt National Assembly. He was also disturbed by Marx's short-lived efforts—entirely in keeping with his concept of a dynamic revolution—to get involved in the founding of a democratic association.

At first Marx even entertained certain hopes that left-leaning circles of the wealthy bourgeoisie would support his new newspaper project, which would be called the *Neue Rheinische Zeitung.* He even had Engels approach his *old man* in Barmen, but Engels responded that there was "damned little prospect" for the newspaper's shares in those circles. Basically, he informed Marx, "even these radical bourgeois here see us as their future main enemies and have no intention of putting into our hands weapons which we would very shortly turn against themselves"[54]—which was indeed the case. Otto Camphausen, the brother of one of Marx's former supporters from the days of the *Rheinische Zeitung,* had warned early on of the "danger of complete mob rule";[55] Gustav Mevissen thought that one must "seize the moment" and agree to a "constitution with the crown."[56] In March 1848 they felt that they had achieved the aim that, five years earlier, had spurred them to create the *Rheinische Zeitung* as a liberal oppositional newspaper with Marx as the chief editor. On

29 March, Ludolf Camphausen became the minister president and David Hansemann the finance minister in Prussia. No contribution to the project could be expected from them now—or from anyone else. Marx had reckoned on amassing thirty thousand Taler in share capital but barely managed to raise thirteen thousand. He had to finance his new paper largely through an advance on his inheritance.

The *Neue Rheinische Zeitung* conceived of itself as an "organ of democracy." But at no time did it see itself as a newspaper for Frankfurt's parliamentary Left; rather, it considered its primary task to be to journalistically monitor these democrats from its own political viewpoint. In certain respects, this viewpoint was a provisional Girondism from a self-enlightened Montagne perspective that had learned above all that striking *too soon* could be a ruinous mistake—as could retreating too soon. Entirely in accordance with the dynamic principles of the *Communist Manifesto*, it attempted *in the movement of the present* to *represent and take care of the future*.[57] As understood by the *Neue Rheinische Zeitung*, for reasons of the historical sequence of events the current movement happened to be a bourgeois-democratic revolution in the countries of the German Confederation. This was also why the newspaper ran so little reportage on the concurrent developments of the workers' movement in Germany, which in 1848 were in fact quite significant.[58]

Schapper and Moll stretched a web of communist workers' associations across the Rhineland and Westphalia. Stefan Born, a former typesetter for the *Deutsche Brüsseler Zeitung* and an old member of the Communist League, found himself in Berlin shortly after the outbreak of the revolution. There he founded the Workers' Brotherhood, which soon boasted a substantial membership of twelve thousand workers in the large cities of Prussia and Saxony as well as in Franken and Wurttemberg; it was thus the most important workers' association on the continent.[59] The Berlin proletariat was revolutionary through and through, Born reported to Marx in early May, and he was doing his best to keep it from engaging in "useless riots." Marx would have agreed, but he was bothered by Born's penchant for strike movements, state-assisted reforms, and projects involving unions and production cooperatives when what really mattered was using political victories to further the breakthrough of the dynamic revolutionary process in Germany and Europe. In Marx's conception, the downfall of the monarchies and a bourgeois transition period would by necessity end with the rule of the proletariat.[60] At that point, the minor everyday problems the Workers' Brotherhood bandied about would no longer play a role anyway. With respect to the Communist League as such, wrote Born in the same letter, he had nothing to report: it seemed to have dissolved.[61] Indeed, as Marx later wrote, the league's activities had almost ceased completely because, as he saw it, there were more effective ways available to pursue his goals[62]—above all, editing the *Neue Rheinische Zeitung*, as he wanted to drive the European revolution forward through its journalistic stance.

But Cologne was not Paris. From there it was hardly possible to have a national effect. Although the paper was later celebrated as by far the best political newspaper of the 1840s, it was only regionally significant. What had worked to the advantage of its predecessor—namely, its concentration on the Rhineland—very much limited the newspaper's effective radius in real revolutionary times. In all likelihood Marx was orienting himself along the lines of large Parisian publications like *Réforme* and others, which were backed by actual groups that played real roles in the National Assembly and government. Marx, however, did not have any connections with the radical Left in the Palatinate and Baden, or even with the left-wing representative Ludwig Simon in his hometown of Trier, and he viewed Stefan Born's activities, as already mentioned, with considerable suspicion.

To be sure, he had correspondents and emissaries from the Communist League milieu, such as the loyal Wilhelm Wolff in Breslau.[63] But in principle, during the revolution the *Neue Rheinische Zeitung* remained an agent of political philosophy that provided critical commentary on contemporary events along the lines of the principles of the *Communist Manifesto*. It appeared fourteen days after the first meeting of the parliaments convened for constitutional deliberations in Frankfurt and Berlin, and they were the subject of its first critique. For example: "The Assembly at Frankfurt is engaged in parliamentary school exercises and leaves it to the governments to act." But a constituent National Assembly, according to the *Neue Rheinische Zeitung*, must above all be "an active, revolutionarily active assembly."[64] A left-wing minority led by the South Germans Hecker and Struve had already made such demands in the Frankfurt preliminary parliament; when they failed, Hecker—in a decidedly putsch-like fashion—proclaimed the German Republic in

Constance in mid April. The whole thing ended in a debacle. The *Neue Rheinische Zeitung* criticized the democratic party for abandoning itself to the intoxicating delirium of its first victory, noting that a *proclamation* was not a *realization*. What really mattered now was that it *should understand its position*.[65] Germany was difficult. After a revolution, the *Neue Rheinische Zeitung* announced, every provisional state would require a dictatorship, *and an energetic dictatorship at that*.[66] With this kind of reminder of the *comité du salut public*, however, Marx remained a lonely voice in the German territories. Therefore he initially placed all his hopes on a revival of the revolution in France.

By 22 June, this point had been reached. In a matter of hours, workers in the east of Paris erected over fifteen hundred barricades, generally along the axis stretching from Rue Saint-Denis to Rue Saint-Jacques. This was a response to the brutal dissolution of the National Workshops, through which February's provisional regime had attempted to solve the problem of unemployment. After the bourgeois republicans prevailed in the late-April elections to the National Assembly, this coalition ceased to exist. On 22 June, the National Guard in the east joined the insurgents, while the National Guard in the west, together with the army, opposed them. The second armed conflict, which Marx had expected in March, was imminent. Reporting "the latest news received from Paris," on 27 June the *Neue Rheinische Zeitung* wrote:

> Paris bathed in blood; the insurrection growing into the greatest revolution that has ever taken place, into a revolution of the proletariat against the bourgeoisie. Three days which sufficed for the July revolution and the February revolution are insufficient for the colossal contours of this June revolution, but the victory of the people is more certain than ever. The French bourgeoisie has dared to do what the French kings never dared—it has itself cast the die. This second act of the French revolution is only the beginning of the European tragedy.[67]

Never again in his entire life would Marx find himself in such a state of revolutionary euphoria as on this day.

Marx saw the June revolution as the first that actually "divided all society into two large hostile armed camps"[68]—exactly as the *Communist Manifesto* had predicted. Yet, contrary to Marx's hopes that day, the uprising failed to bring about the defeat of the bourgeoisie.

The republican general and appointed military dictator Cavaignac declared a state of emergency and had artillery brought to Notre Dame; he even entertained the idea of setting the entire quarter ablaze. Five thousand insurgents were killed during the battles; fifteen hundred were summarily executed; twenty-two thousand were arrested and in large part deported to Algeria. With extreme severity, the "fraternité" of the February Days was drowned in blood. Looking back, Marx came to understand that these days had decided the fate of the European Revolution of 1848. "If the June insurrection raised the self-assurance of the bourgeoisie all over the Continent, and caused it to league itself openly with the feudal monarchy against the people," he wrote in 1850, "who was the first victim of this alliances? [sic] The continental bourgeoisie itself."[69] This diagnosis rings true, if one takes into account that in the German states and Habsburg monarchy almost all of the structures of monarchic-military domination survived the commotion of the revolution intact. Later, in 1852, Marx maintained that the June uprising had revealed to everyone that the bourgeois republic in reality only meant *the unlimited despotism of one class over other classes;* in any case, he continued, the republic was only the *political form of the revolutionising of bourgeois society* and by no means *its conservative form of life.*[70]

During the June Days of 1848, Cavaignac moved against the Parisian workers with greater brutality that even Windisch-Graetz would dare use against the insurgents in Prague or Radetsky against the rebels in northern Italy. Marx believed only two alternatives remained: radical revolution or complete counterrevolution. Prior to 1848, he noted, revolution had meant the *overthrow of the form of government;* now, after the events of June, it could only mean the *overthrow of bourgeois society.*[71] After a battle like that of June 1848, wrote the *Neue Rheinische Zeitung*, "only terrorism is still possible," conducted by one side or the other.[72] Marx now came under pressure to radicalize, something that Saint-Just had referred to during the French Revolutionary Wars as the consequence of the "*force des choses,*" a force arising from the circumstances themselves in the struggle of life and death.

Marx developed an affinity for actionism. This included the *Neue Rheinische Zeitung*'s constant propagandistic call for a world war against Russia, the bulwark of the European reaction, modeled on the French "levée en masse" of 1792. Eric Hobsbawm once described this revolutionary war as the first total war in history, for even then it had been a question of either the revolution's total victory, or its utter defeat and the victory of the counterrevolution.[73] Revolutionary Germany's war could only be a war against Russia, the *Neue Rheinische Zeitung* declared on 12 July 1848—a war in which Germany could "cleanse herself of her past sins" and muster the courage to also defeat her own autocrats.[74] By "past sins," Marx meant the combined effort with Russia and Britain to eliminate Napoleon, for had French legislation and administration been employed back then to provide the Germans with a solid basis for their national unification, they would have been spared thirty-three years of humiliation and tyranny.[75]

On New Year's Eve 1848 in Cologne, Marx and the author Ferdinand Freiligrath were invited to have dinner with Mr. Keene from Britain's *Daily News*. They discussed the past year's events and raised their glasses to the revolution in Vienna; to the October uprising, with its marked proletarian characteristics and its suppression by Prince Windisch-Graetz and the Croatian General von Jellachich; and to the Hungarian insurrection led by Lajos Kossuth. After the events in Vienna, Marx had remarked on the *cannibalism of the counterrevolution* in the *Neue Rheinische Zeitung*, expressing the conviction that the only way to shorten, simplify, and concentrate the murderous death throes of the old society was *revolutionary terror*.[76] On this New Year's Eve they still felt that the bloody suppression of the Viennese was only a partial defeat within the grand European drama.[77]

On the next day, 1 January 1849, the *Neue Rheinische Zeitung* articulated for its readers the scenario of an entire world of enemies:

> The defeat of the working class in France and the victory of the French bourgeoisie was at the same time a victory of East over West, the defeat of civilisation by barbarism. The suppression of the Rumanians by the Russians and their tools, the Turks, began in Wallachia; Croats, Pandours, Czechs, Serezhans and similar rabble throttled German liberty in Vienna, and the Tsar is now omnipresent in Europe. The overthrow of the bourgeoisie in France, the triumph of the French working class, and the liberation of the working class in general is therefore the rallying-cry of European liberation. But *England*, the country that turns whole nations into her proletarians, that takes the whole world within its immense embrace, that has already once defrayed the cost of a European Restoration, the country in which

class contradictions have reached their most acute and shameless form—England seems to be the rock against which the revolutionary waves break, the country where the new society is stifled even in the womb.[78]

Precisely in England, where more than anywhere else all the necessary conditions obtained, realizing the revolutionary cause was the most difficult. Therefore the revolution had to be induced through violence from the outside. Old England could be overthrown only through world war, the sole path to creating the conditions in which the Chartists—the party of the organized English workers—could effectively rise up against their powerful oppressors. According to Marx, this war would be waged in Canada and Italy, in India and Prussia, in Africa and along the Danube. *Revolutionary rising of the French working class, world war*—thus read the table of contents for the year 1849.[79]

World war against Russia and England was indeed much more than an unrestrained "puer robustus, sed malitiosus." This was not to involve hanging aristocrats from streetlights or decapitating kings. Rather, the revolutionary terrorism of the old revolutionary wars was to be reintroduced on a more modern, globally expanded level. What kind of Super-Napoleon would bring this about?

From the perspective of the *Neue Rheinische Zeitung*, the war against Denmark in the fall of 1848 over Schleswig and Holstein was "the first *revolutionary war* waged by Germany," and it had the newspaper's explicit support. Marx and Engels thought anyway that Scandinavianism was a "brutal, sordid, piratical" business, so they also perceived this war as an armed conflict waged with the "right of civilisation as against barbarism, of progress as against stability," and to that extent legitimated by the final judgment of history.[80] As part of the German Confederation subject to the Danish monarchy, Schleswig-Holstein was governed by a revolutionary provisional territorial regime when on 21 March 1848, after an annexation resolution in Copenhagen, Danish troops marched into the region. On 12 April, the German states declared a confederate war led by Prussia against Denmark, which turned out, however, to be incredibly complicated and ended on 26 August with a cease-fire in Malmö, negotiated unilaterally by Prussia. The Frankfurt National Assembly rejected the cease-fire on 5 September, and only after protracted negotiations and two votes was the assembly narrowly convinced to accept the agreement. Had it not, the war Marx and Engels so fervently desired with Russia and England (without any realistic appreciation of the comparative strengths) might presumably have come to pass. Imperialistic undertones colored the debates over Schleswig-Holstein in the National Assembly; especially the speakers on the Left were explicitly nationalistic. Jakob Venedey from Cologne spoke of the "humiliation" that would be imposed upon Germany, as had occurred with the Peace of Westphalia; it could be avoided only if one did not fear "going to war with the entire world to become a unified Germany." Carl Vogt, later a close friend of Marx, reminded the delegates of the French Revolution and the national war declared by the Convention.[81]

Meanwhile, the *Neue Rheinische Zeitung* struck a completely new chord in the debate by addressing the topic of peoples with and without history. Marx and Engels appropriated this distinction from Hegel, who had claimed, with respect to so-called peoples without history, that they had "no movement or development to exhibit."[82] The real capital of Denmark, Engels insisted for example, was not Copenhagen but rather Hamburg, for within the realm of the Danish crown the German cultural element that would otherwise be missing from the "primitive" Scandinavian nation could only be found in Altona.[83] Later, when "Croatian freedom and order" under the command of General Jellachich raged in Vienna with "arson, rape, [and] looting,"[84] judgment was pronounced collectively against Croatia and Slovenia, nations that had "long ago degenerated and were devoid of all historical power of action," unable to accomplish anything apart from supporting the Austrian reaction.[85] In the next world war, according to the *Neue Rheinische Zeitung*, not only reactionary classes and dynasties would vanish from the earth but also "entire reactionary peoples. And that, too, is a step forward."[86]

Engels especially held the view that the Slavs—and here he always explicitly excluded the Poles, even wanting to grant their republic the Baltic coastline all the way to Riga—were everywhere the major tools of the counterrevolution, born "oppressors of all revolutionary nations."[87] Ultimately, he called for an "inexorable life-and-death struggle" against the "Slavs who betray the revolution; an annihilating fight and ruthless terror—not in the interests of Germany, but in the interests of the revolution!"[88] These were more than simply alarming words, even if they are not over-interpreted in light of the experiences of the twentieth century. By annihilation Engels largely meant cultural assimilation, though certainly he could well imagine deploying drastic, violent measures to execute this cultural enterprise. Incidentally, power-political considerations doubtless also played an important role. Croatia and Slovenia, thought the Pan-German Engels and Marx along with him, must by all means be kept from cutting off German and Hungarian access to the Adriatic.[89] Such was the minimum tribute that "people without history" had to pay to the historical revolutionary nations.

This was the almost inevitable verdict of what Hegel in a Christian tradition called the World Court, one that could also be rendered elsewhere. "Or is it perhaps unfortunate," asked Friedrich Engels, "that splendid California has been taken away from the lazy Mexicans who could not do anything with it?"[90] Later the theme of peoples without history even helped Marx justify colonialism. The question, he wrote in 1853 in the *New York Tribune*, is "not whether the English had a right to conquer India, but whether we are to prefer India conquered by the Turk, by the Persian, by the Russian, to India conquered by the Briton. England has to fulfill a double mission in India: one destructive, the other regenerating—the annihilation of old Asiatic society, and the laying of the material foundations of Western society in Asia."[91] This strange revolutionary variant of the dogma of "the white man's burden" was understandable only from the perspective of the conception of history in Marx's historical materialism, in which only the titanic efforts of the British bourgeoisie could one day include a country like India in the process of the proletarian world revolution.

In any case, the conflict between "advanced" and "reactionary" nations contributed in no small way to the failure of the European revolution. The "defection from God," as Friedrich Wilhelm IV described the events beginning in March 1848 in a letter to a confidant, was almost over by the spring of 1849. That same letter featured what would soon become a common phrase: "The only thing that helps against democrats are soldiers."[92] The German Revolution ended with the capitulation of the Rastatt fortress on 23 July 1849. So began the long years of systematic reactionary politics and repressive police measures that—classically represented by the main character Diederich Hessling in Heinrich Mann's *Der Untertan*—left deep traces in the German mentality. And in France, Louis Napoléon's coup ended the brief years of the Republic in 1851.

This provided Marx with occasion to draw a preliminary conclusion about the revolutionary years. Bourgeois revolutions like those of the eighteenth century, he maintained, moved dramatically—*set in sparking diamonds*—but were short-lived and inevitably ended with a hangover of prosaic circumstances. In contrast, the proletarian revolutions of the nineteenth century, which created their poetry out of the future, *constantly criticized themselves* until they attained their objectives. By this Marx meant the *real* crises of the revolutionary courses of action, not just theoretical criticism. Against the backdrop of recent events, this also applied to the bloody criticism wrought by weapons—and the defeats that followed, like the rout Cavaignac's troops delivered to the insurgent Parisian proletariat in June 1848. Proletarian revolutions derided with *cruel thoroughness* all the half-measures of their first attempts, until at some point there arose a situation that made *all turning back impossible, and the conditions themselves cry out: Hic Rhodus, hic salta!*[93] It was an epic scenario of a devouring and purifying purgatory, almost Shakespearian, with the masses as heroes and villains. The French Revolution of 1789 seemed in contrast like a sober tragedy by Racine.

The Trauma of Exile

The Revolution was a feverish dream; the subsequent renewed exile, a trauma. "A more signal defeat," noted Engels in retrospect, "than that undergone by the continental revolutionary party—or rather parties—upon all points of the line of battle, cannot be imagined."[94] Engels had participated in the fighting almost to the very end in the South German uprising. The remains of the revolutionary army from Baden and the Palatinate fled over the border into Switzerland on 12 July 1849. Engels remained in Switzerland until September, met Stefan Born in Bern, and in Geneva got to know the former revolutionary fighter Wilhelm Liebknecht, who would later play a leading role in the history of social democracy in Germany. At the end of August, Marx informed Engels that he intended to go to London and found a new journal—a political-economic review in the spirit of the *Neue Rheinische Zeitung*. He had already secured part of the funding. "So you must leave for London at once," Marx wrote. "In any case your safety demands it. The Prussians would shoot you twice over."[95]

Marx had left Cologne on 19 May, expelled from the country as a non-Prussian. In Frankfurt, he and Engels unsuccessfully urged the

left-wing representatives of the National Assembly to put themselves at the fore of the South German uprising, which did not stand
a chance from the outset; in Baden, likewise unsuccessfully, they
tried to convince the South German rebels to march against Frankfurt. Engels, who as a young man in Berlin had completed military
training, joined the revolutionary army of Baden; and on 2 June
Marx moved on to Paris. The stay was brief: only six weeks later a
deportation order he received from the French government offered
him the seclusion of a lonely spot in Brittany. He would not consent
to such a *veiled attempt on his life*, he wrote Engels, "So I am leav-
ing France."[96] He headed for the docks of Dover aboard the *City of
Boulogne*, and subsequently the railway brought him to London. On
17 September, Jenny arrived there as well with what were now three
small children. On 5 October, Engels reported to his old Chartist
friend George Julian Harney from Genoa that, wind and weather
permitting, he would board the schooner *Cornish Diamond* and arrive in London in mid November.[97]

Marx had come to know Harney during a trip to England with
Engels in summer 1845. Harney edited the *Northern Star*, at the time
a mass-circulation socialist newspaper with a press run of fifty thousand, to which Engels regularly contributed. The years of continental
revolution had radicalized Harney as had the experience of the large
Chartist rally in April 1848. Ten thousand people had marched on
Westminster to present more than five million signatures to Parliament in support of universal suffrage. But the strong hand of the elderly Wellington arranged for hundreds of mounted police, cavalry,
and artillery to take up positions on the Thames Bridge and in the
side streets. The Chartist leader Feargus O'Connor called off the un-
dertaking for fear of a bloodbath. The disappointment was great, but
the decision left Chartism with its spine intact, and it became more
radical. Throughout the spring of 1848 in the industrial regions of
north England, assemblies and demonstrations trumpeted revolutionary slogans. In 1850 Harney's new journal, the *Red Republican*,
announced that the working classes had taken leave of the hope for
political reform and now advocated the idea of social revolution. It
also published an English translation of the *Communist Manifesto*.[98]
At this time Marx was residing with his family on Dean Street in
Soho. A Prussian spy reported to Berlin that they occupied two
rooms in what was virtually the worst, tawdriest quarter of London.

At first Marx believed that his exile would be brief and it was only a matter of time before another revolutionary wave would break out in Europe, especially in France. To the degree that the reaction had advanced, he noted at the beginning of the year, the power of the revolutionary party was naturally also growing as well.[99] And in March he prophesized an imminent commercial crisis with consequences far more significant than those of all earlier crises. Above all, it would inevitably expand from England to the continent, where it would unleash revolutionary crises of an *incomparably more pronounced socialist character*—especially in Germany.[100]

Therefore in April, with Harney and a few Blanquists, Marx founded the previously mentioned Universal Society of Revolutionary Communists, which expressly committed itself to the overthrow of all privileged classes, the dictatorship of the proletariat, and the permanent revolution.[101] As Marx informed the members of the now reorganized Communist League in June 1850, the actual proletarian party of France, whose leader Louis-Auguste Blanqui was imprisoned on Belle-Île, had joined them to prepare for *the next French revolution*, as had revolutionary leaders of the Chartist party,[102] including Julian Harney. The Chartists, Marx maintained, had resumed their own party activity against the bourgeoisie *with increased vigour* and therefore could be an important *ally of the revolutionary Continent* during a future revolution.[103] During his first months of exile, Marx simply did not want to recognize the realities of the era of the European Reaction, which was accompanied by a phase of economic growth. His opinions were rarely as radical and fanciful as during this short period of his stubborn denial of defeat.

For the impending revolution, a "secret and indissoluble" cadre organization was to arise from the Communist League until the proletarian revolution had attained its final objective. All members had to "abide unconditionally" by the resolutions and subordinate themselves to the Central Committee as the executive organ. Anyone expelled for violating the rules was to be brought under surveillance "just like any suspect individual."[104] As the leading organization, the reorganized league was supposed to guarantee the political "independence of the workers" that Marx and Engels had valued so little in the years 1848/49. Now they expected that the democratic petty bourgeoisie would have to be drawn against its will into the ongoing dynamic process of permanent revolution, as had happened two years earlier with respect to the liberal bourgeoisie. "Above all things" decreed the Central Committee (i.e., Marx and Engels),

> the workers must counteract, as much as is at all possible, during the conflict and immediately after the struggle, the bourgeois endeavours to allay the storm, and must compel the democrats to carry out their present terrorist phrases. They must work to prevent the direct revolutionary excitement from being suppressed again immediately after the victory. On the contrary, they must keep it alive as long as possible. Far from opposing so-called excesses, instances of popular revenge against hated individuals or public buildings that are associated only with hateful recollections, such instances must not only be tolerated but the lead in them must be taken.[105]

It was an almost desperate revival of revolutionary fire—perhaps also a result of the trauma of exile—lacking traction and flaunting a final unhesitating recollection of the purifying apocalyptic terror modeled by the French Revolution and the unleashed "puer robustus, sed malitiosus." The Universal Society of Revolutionary Communists would not have a very long life. In part because of the continuing phase of prosperity in England, Julian Harney increasingly lost his faith in revolutionary solutions,[106] and the alliance with the Blanquists eventually became a casualty of the division of the Communist League.

In June 1850, Marx resumed his intensive study of economics and to that end was known to frequent the reading room of the British Museum. In that same summer of 1850, when he was closest to Blanquism, his prognoses of an imminent revolution became increasingly cautious. Marx was not a political romantic but rather chose to focus on the causes of the 1848/49 revolution. His studies showed that the world economic crisis of 1847 had been the real mother of the February and March revolution, and the subsequent prosperity—which entirely failed to lead to the crisis-laden panic Marx and Engels had predicted for July or August—was the real vitalizing force of the European Restoration.[107] The revolutionary party, Marx and Engels declared in the fall of 1850, had everywhere been forced from the stage. "With this general prosperity, in which the productive forces of bourgeois society develop as luxuriantly as is at all possible within bourgeois relationships, there can be no talk of a real revolution." A new revolution was only possible as the result of a new crisis. But the former would come just as surely as the latter.[108]

One of the reasons for the shift in opinion and mood was the California gold rush. It signaled not only a tremendous influx of money into international capital markets but also the prospect of an intensified globalization that the *Communist Manifesto* had only dreamed about in broad strokes. As the *Neue Rheinische Zeitung Revue* noted:

> In a few years we shall have a regular steam-packet service from England to Chagres and from Chagres and San Francisco to Sydney, Canton and Singapore. Thanks to Californian gold and the tireless energy of the Yankees, both coasts of the Pacific Ocean will soon be as populous, as open to trade and as industrialised as the coast from Boston to New Orleans is now. And then the Pacific Ocean will have the same role as the Atlantic has now and the Mediterranean had in antiquity and in the Middle Ages—that of the great water highway of world commerce; and the Atlantic will decline to the status of an inland sea, like the Mediterranean.[109]

Thus the bourgeoisie's titanic predestination was still very much slated for a great future in the screenplay of history. Marx and Engels sometimes spoke about this class, which they simultaneously deeply admired and despised, with a surprising degree of pathos. Contrary to the prophecies of the *Communist Manifesto*, the bourgeoisie was evidently far from being finished.

According to a certain logic, however, the analysis above led Marx and Engels to adopt a wait-and-see attitude for the time being to avoid falling back into the futuristic tinkering and voluntarism of the movements they had energetically criticized prior to 1848 as incomplete or misguided stages of history's self-consciousness. On 15 September 1850, this issue resulted in a split in the Communist League. A number of members, Willich and Schapper among them, accused Marx and Engels of being well on their way to betraying the revolution. Thereupon the Central Committee they controlled, responding in the same tone used in the earlier disagreement with Weitling, stated that it could no longer work with people who held the view that one need have "only the right intentions" to obtain "power immediately during the next revolution." Such people also revealed a tendency to return to the "universal asceticism and social leveling in its crudest form" that had long been overcome.[110] The accusation also pertained to the Blanquists, who had joined them in founding a revolutionary Universal Society that April but now were taking sides with Willich and Schapper. Instead of babbling about coups in the manner of those "London hotspurs,"[111] in the coming period of economic prosperity Marx and Engels would focus primarily on the education of the workers closest to them and the scientific development of their theory.

Marx's correspondence with Engels during this period was full of questions about the economic problems that occupied him during his studies in the British Museum. The lengthy article in the *Revue Neue Rheinische Zeitung's* 1 November 1850 "Revue" presented itself as an analysis replete with comprehensive statistical material of the most recent economic developments; much of it could just as easily have appeared in *The Economist*. The article maintained that a crisis generally erupts first in the area of speculation, leading then to a collapse of the banking system and a breakdown of the credits system before taking hold of production itself. *The Economist* was in fact quoted approvingly with words to the effect that the current prosperity distinguished itself in a very crucial way from all earlier periods: the cause of growth was no longer speculation; rather, it was based far more solidly on the production of immediately useful things that were directly entering the consumer market.[112]

On the basis of such insights, Marx and Engels carried out a full-fledged castling maneuver. In mid February 1851, Engels wrote to his friend:

A revolution is a purely natural phenomenon which is subject to physical laws rather than to the rules that determine the development of society in ordinary times. Or rather, in revolution these rules assume a much more physical character, the material force of necessity makes itself more strongly felt. And as soon as one steps forward as the representative of a party, one is dragged into this whirlpool of irresistible natural necessity. By the mere fact of keeping oneself independent, being in the nature of things more revolutionary than the others, one is able at least for a time to maintain one's independence from this whirlpool, although one does, of course, end up by being dragged into it. This is the position we can and must adopt on the next occasion. Not only no official government appointments but also, and for as long as possible, no official party appointments, no seat on committees, etc., no responsibility for jackasses, merciless

criticism of everyone, and, besides, that serenity of which all the con-
spiracies of blockheads cannot deprive us. And this much we are able
to do. We can always, in the nature of things, be more revolutionary
than the phrase-mongers because we have learnt our lesson and they
have not, because we know what we want and they do not, and *because, after what we have seen for at least three years, we shall take it a
great deal more coolly than anyone who has an interest in the business.*[113]

Upon a motion by Marx at the Rose and Crown Tavern in Soho[114]
on 12 November 1852, the Communist League was dissolved for the
reason that, even on the continent, its perpetuation was *no longer
expedient*.[115]

For the next twelve years Marx no longer belonged to any political organization. The period after the defeat of the revolution
witnessed the advent of realism in the arts, Realpolitik, positivism,
and—for Marx—so-called scientific socialism. Even the mythos of
the French Revolution lost some of its sheen for a while. Self-criti-
cally retrospective shortly before his death in 1895, Engels noted
that back then they had been completely blinded by the "memories
of the prototypes of 1789 and 1830," convincing themselves that
the "great decisive battle" had commenced, that it had to be waged
in a single and eventful revolutionary period, and that it could only
end with the final victory of the proletariat. History had not only
revealed their point of view to be an illusion but also completely
transformed the conditions under which the proletariat had to fight.
The mode of struggle was today obsolete in every respect. He now
also subjected the 1848/49 fantasies of world war to harsh criticism.
Especially given the modern industrial transformation of weapons
technology, a future world war, if it occurred, would be of "unprec-
edented cruelty and absolutely incalculable outcome."[116] Now, in
1895, Engels was promoting a new style of politics, namely, social
democracy, which—as demonstrated by the SPD's victories in the
Reichstag elections—indeed evidently promised more success.

He now saw that the Jacobins' legacy of terror had sided more
with the man who had fought against the revolution in 1848, subsequently achieving German imperial unity by force—with blood
and iron, through the deliberate, armed implementation of Jacobin
methods. "If there is to be a revolution, we would rather make it
than suffer it," Bismarck telegraphed to General Manteuffel in mid
August 1866.[117] During the war with Austria, Bismarck even toyed

with the idea of "releasing all the dogs that can bark" and inciting guerillas under Lajos Kossuth in Hungary and Giuseppe Garibaldi in Dalmatia against the Habsburg monarchy.[118] He went so far as to make advances to Marx, hoping to exploit his *great talents in the interests of the German people*.[119] "Have we perchance evoked the civil war of 1866?" Engels asked his readers. Or was it Bismarck—"Have we driven the King of Hanover, the Elector of Hessia, and the Duke of Nassau from their hereditary lawful domains and annexed these hereditary domains? And these overthrowers of the German Confederation and three crowns by the grace of God complain of overthrow! *Quis tulerit Gracchos de seditione querentes?*"[120]—who would allow the Gracchi to complain about an insurrection?

But there was a long way to go before reaching that point. During Marx's first years in London, the trauma of the unsuccessful revolution and exile prevailed. Lajos Kossuth was one of the most prominent continental revolutionary refugees there at the time. He was celebrated as a romantic hero, yet Marx and Engels's attitude to Kossuth had noticeably cooled. "Like the Apostle Paul," Engels wrote to Marx, "Mr. Kossuth is all things to all men," shouting *Vive la République* in Marseilles and *God save the Queen* in Southampton.[121] A few weeks later, Marx found himself amused by Kossuth's hankypanky with the Bavarian courtesan Lola Montez in London.[122] Even Mr. *Mazzini* fared little better in their judgment, as was also the case for the *more noteworthy* German *jackasses* who populated the community of exiles on the Thames—the democrats Kinkel, Hecker, Struve, Vogt, and Mr. *Ruge*, or the communist warhorse August von Willich,[123] who later, as a Union general, would participate in William Tecumseh Sherman's march on Atlanta, living long enough to see this redeem him in Marx's eyes. Together with Engels, Marx wrote a pamphlet—one just as misshapen as *The Holy Family* had been—that dealt exclusively with the shattered existences of the *Great Men of the Exile*.

Was this, considered psychologically, a defense? "The great men of the Germany of 1848," it said, "had been on the point of coming to a sticky end when the victory of 'tyrants' rescued them, swept them out of the country and made saints and martyrs of them. They were saved by the counter-revolution. The course of continental politics brought most of them to London which thus became their European centre."[124] But Marx and Engels wanted nothing to do with their *spurious activity*, their *imagined parties* and *imagined struggles*.

Then came the great industrial exhibition in London in 1851, with Joseph Paxton's architectonic miracle of the Crystal Palace of iron and glass. It attracted many tourists, even from Germany, who gladly met with the great men of exile on the exhibition grounds, hosted either by the publicans Schärttner at the Hanau or Göhringer at the Star. Having talked shop about German and Prussian politics over their beer, all parties wound up heading home *unsteadily but strengthened in the knowledge that they had made their contribution to the salvation of the fatherland*. The emigration, Marx and Engels noted caustically, was staging a self-satisfying comedy, *a history of its own, lying outside world history*.[125]

Engels had for some time been living in Manchester as an employee of his father's branch office and in any event had very little to do with the activity in London. But Marx deliberately distanced himself from the circle of exiles, insofar as it did not affect his closest friends. He valued his *authentic* isolation and was glad that the system of reciprocal concessions, half-measures tolerated for the sake of decorum, and the obligation to make oneself look ridiculous in public *in the party along with all these jackasses* had come to an end.[126] The research he was conducting was his own, far more important, contribution to world history. On occasion he was visited by scholars like John Stuart Mill, author of the *Principles of Political Economy*, which had appeared in 1848; and he preferred to receive Mill, as an acquaintance reported, not with compliments but rather with economic categories. After all, they shared common interests in this field.

In the year of London's Great Exhibition, Louis Bonaparte staged a coup in Paris, making himself a de facto dictator. In doing so, he deliberately chose the symbolic date of 2 December, the day on which his uncle had been crowned emperor in 1804 and, one year later, won the Battle of Austerlitz. "Hegel remarks somewhere that all great world-historic facts and personages appear, as it were, twice," commented Marx with respect to the event. "He forgot to add: the first time as tragedy, the second as farce." This pert formulation masks how hard put Marx and most of his contemporaries were to explain what appeared to be a completely irrational event. The constitution of 1848, he wrote, collapsed when it was touched by a hat—a three-cornered Napoleon hat, as Marx said. It was a seizure of power. But who was it that seized power, and in whose name?

On 10 December 1848, Bonaparte had been elected president of the Republic by an overwhelming majority consisting above all of the rural population but including, as Marx knew, many proletarians and petty bourgeoisie who by electing him sought to punish the bloodstained opposing candidate, Cavaignac. As far the bourgeoisie was concerned, Marx maintained, the revolution had shown that its *own interests* were best served by making sure that *its bourgeois parliament was laid to rest.* That was one of the foundations for Bonaparte's success; the other was his bohemian and corrupt populism. He had always dreamed of a state coup, yet when he finally carried it out one of his first measures was the reinstitution of universal voting rights, which the bourgeoisie-dominated National Assembly had abolished in the summer of 1850. "This is the complete and final triumph of socialism!" Guizot declared after 2 December. In actuality it was the definitive victory of Bonaparte's populist despotism, which remained in power by means of new plebiscitary instruments.

According to Marx, Bonaparte's rule was based on three *idées napoléoniennes:* the interests of the conservative smallholding peasants, the clergy, and the army. Basically, it was *executive authority which has made itself independent;* by no means was it pure class rule by the bourgeoisie but rather a dictatorship with populist traits that nonetheless understood its task as that of securing bourgeois order.[127] Engels, meanwhile, held that the entire secret of modern Bonapartism lay in the fact that the traditions associated with his name put Louis Napoléon in a position to safeguard the "the balance of the contending classes of French society."[128] Later he would make the claim that the bourgeoisie "is not cut out to rule directly" and that therefore the "Bonapartist semi-dictatorship is the *normal form*" of its class rule.[129] These were not very convincing theories. In any case, the peculiar entity at the Seine—which, following a plebiscite approving a new empire, crowned Louis Napoléon in November 1852—was evidently not a class state in the strictest sense of the theory of historical materialism. Almost eight million French citizens voted for the new emperor; only two hundred fifty thousand voted against. On 2 December 1852—again, a symbolic date for historical Bonapartism—he moved as the emperor to Paris and into the Tuileries.

Marx's treatment of the eighteenth Brumaire of Louis Bonaparte nonetheless constitutes an impressive piece of contemporary historical writing that reveals the talent of a great historiographer. Precisely crafted linguistically and dramaturgically, his narrative of the revolution's course to the point of this coup d'état is replete with accurately researched details and offers decidedly nuanced descriptions of the acting parties and factions. Among the frustrating results of his investigation was the finding that, in contrast to the 1789 revolution, the revolution of 1848 had found itself on a declining slope right from the outset.[130] Thus more than ever, the time was ripe to investigate the *causes that necessitated both the late outbreak and its defeat*, causes that were not to be sought in the accidental efforts, talents, faults, errors, or treacheries of certain leaders, but *in the general social state and conditions of existence* of each of the convulsed nations.[131] Thus it was all the more necessary to turn to researching the anatomy of bourgeois society, from which all political activity ultimately proceeded.

Marx sat in the reading room of the British Museum almost every day from nine o'clock in the morning to seven o'clock at night. He delved deeply into the writings of John Locke and David Hume, Adam Smith and David Ricardo, Henry Charles Carey, Thomas Robert Malthus, and other authors of the classical economic and political sciences. He acquired mountains of literature about precious metals, money, credit, banking, ground rent, factory systems, agriculture, colonial history, and technology. He worked through entire years of publications of *The Economist*, the blue books of the British factory inspectors (which he was the first to subject to scholarly analysis), the *Edinburgh Review*, the *Quarterly*, the *Westminster Review*, and a plethora of other sources, recording everything that appeared to be important in growing masses of notebooks. Yet his critique of the political economy, which at the time he thought he could quickly finish, did not progress. "The material I am working on is so damnably involved," he wrote to his friend Weydemeyer in mid 1851, and in addition there were always the *interruptions of a practical kind* that were "inevitable in the wretched circumstances in which we are vegetating here."[132]

Interruptions of a practical kind. That June, in the restricted confines of Dean Street, "Lenchen" Demuth gave birth to a son whose father most certainly was the paterfamilias Marx. For the sake of familial peace, Engels chivalrously assumed official responsibility for the paternity. Yet when Frederick Demuth's birth was registered in the civil registry at Somerset House, the name of the father was left blank. Admittedly, Jenny sensed a few things, but

she was certain of nothing. The child was immediately given to foster parents. During these days, Marx's situation looked, in his rather
euphemistic formulation, quite dismal.[133] Constant financial worries
plagued him as well. The *Politisch-Ökonomische Revue* was such a
complete financial failure that he often had to bring the silverware
of Jenny's noble Scottish forebears to a pawnbroker to bridge his
household's regular financial crises. But there were still other reasons
why his political economics did not make any progress. For one, he
could not find a publisher. Moreover, he often delved so deeply into
details that he came away having found nothing but excuses for not
finishing.

As Wilhelm Liebknecht described him, Marx "always worked
intensely, thoroughly."[134] And scrupulously, one might add, which
meant that writings he actually wanted to use to belligerently challenge the bourgeois world and deal a fatal blow to its futuristic op-
timism could, for personal reasons, drag on almost incessantly. His
Contribution to the Critique of Political Economy did not appear until
1859; the first volume of *Capital* was published in 1867. Apologiz-
ing for the delay, he wrote: "The enormous amount of material re-
lating to the history of political economy assembled in the British
Museum, the fact that London is a convenient vantage point for
the observation of bourgeois society, and finally the new stage of
development which this society seemed to have entered with the
discovery of gold in California and Australia, induced me to start
again from the very beginning and to work carefully through the
new material." His time had also been considerably curtailed by *the
imperative necessity of earning a living.*[135]

Marx was referring to his work as a correspondent for the *New
York Daily Tribune*. He had come to know its editor in chief, Charles
Anderson Dana, during the revolution in 1849 through Freiligrath
in Cologne. At the time, the *Tribune* was the most influential newspaper in the United States, presumably with the widest circulation
of any newspaper in the world, and Dana was a successful American businessman touched by socialist ideas. In 1841 he had become
a member of the Brook Farm communal settlement near Boston,
whose sympathizers included Nathaniel Hawthorne, Ralph Waldo
Emerson, and Henry David Thoreau, noteworthy intellectuals
whose influence on American culture and mentality can hardly be
overestimated. Brook Farm practiced alternative educational models and turned increasingly to experimentation inspired by Fourier.

After an effort to build a large phalanstery ended in a conflagration, the settlement was dissolved in 1847.[136] Since then Dana had worked for the *Tribune*. Fourier's ideas haunted its pages, but the newspaper campaigned above all against slavery, the death penalty, and the autocratic regimes in Europe.

In August 1851 Dana asked Marx to become one of the newspaper's eighteen foreign correspondents.[137] He was to receive one pound sterling for each weekly report. In 1853, the editor in chief raised this honorarium to two pounds sterling after learning that his London correspondent's contributions were very popular among his readers. In April 1857, Dana also asked Marx to compose articles for the planned *New American Cyclopedia*. The arrangement resulted in almost five hundred articles, some of which, however, stemmed from the pen of the ghostwriter Engels, who was always prepared to help. But then Marx raised his fees,[138] the orders from overseas subsided because of the Civil War, and the *Tribune* gradually lost its monopoly to the *New York Times*.[139] Still, during these years Marx kept American readers decidedly well informed, not only about conditions in Europe but also about social problems—for example, the enclosure movement in England and Scotland, the suffering in Ireland, the Chartist movement, and the movement for the ten hours bill. And they could feel that they were understood when he assured them that those damned in Europe had, to the extent possible, always found sanctuary in the United States of America.[140]

Many of the articles in 1853 dealt with issues in the East—more precisely, with the crisis that would ultimately lead to the Crimean War, giving Marx the opportunity to once again take aim at his archenemy, Russia. When the czar announced his claims to the Ottoman Danube principalities—and thus also to the Dardanelles—Marx warned in a severe tone about the *timidity of Western statesmen*[141] faced with the Russian threat. "To sum up the Eastern question in a few words," he wrote, explaining his view of the problem to the American readers,

> The Czar, vexed and dissatisfied at seeing his immense Empire confined to one sole port of export, and that even situated in a sea innavigable through one half of the year, and assailable by Englishmen through the other half, is pushing the design of his ancestors, to get access to the Mediterranean; he is separating, one after another, the remotest members of the Ottoman Empire from its main body, till at last Constantinople, the heart, must cease to beat.[142]

But Constantinople was the golden bridge between East and West, and Western civilization could not keep this bridge open *without a struggle with Russia*.[143]

Russian troops had occupied the Danube principalities in July 1853, and in October Sultan Abdülmecid I declared war against St. Petersburg. In early January 1854, after the Russian Black Sea fleet annihilated the Turkish navy at Sinop, England and France intervened in the war on the side of the Turks, bombarding the Russian coast, conducting landing operations, and laying siege to the Sevastopol fortress in the Crimea for almost a year. The war resulted in half a million dead. In the end, Russia had to fall in line and refrain from its ambition. Under the Peace of Paris, concluded on 30 March 1856, the czar lost his hegemonic position on the European continent forever. The Holy Alliance had shot itself in the head, which was actually good news for Marx: now Prussia and Austria might finally "be relieved from the control of Russia."[144]

The second piece of good news was the outbreak of the economic crisis of 1857. The revolution is marching forward, Marx reported to Engels in Manchester in mid July, *as shown by the march of the Crédit mobilier*.[145] And the onset of the American crisis in late October—*its outbreak in New York was forecast by us in the November 1850 Revue*—was downright *beautiful*.[146] As difficult as the frustrations of his finances were, *never, since 1849, have I felt so cosy as during this outbreak*.[147] Engels responded with almost identical euphoria, saying that since the swindle in New York had collapsed, he could hardly find any peace. He felt "tremendously cheerful" and noted that "in 1848 we were saying now our time is coming, and so in a certain sense it was, but this time it is coming properly; now it's a case of do or die."[148] In fact, the crisis of 1857 was the first to affect the entire world. In line with Marx's early diagnosis, it had *dimensions such as have never been seen before*,[149] and even King Friedrich Wilhelm IV feared that now "the revolution is stalking the world once more. May God have mercy!"[150] The worldwide crisis, caused by a stock market crash on New York's Wall Street after the collapse of the Ohio Life Insurance & Trust Company, suddenly led to panicked sell-offs. Worldwide, it gripped the financial system, industry, trade, and finally the agricultural sector, one after another. Marx was once again working *enormously*[151] on the elaboration of his economic principles. In light of the latest developments, he and Engels would need to report to the German public no later than the following spring to show *that we are still there as always, and always the same*.[152]

The *enormous* work was that of bringing the *Outlines of the Critique of Political Economy* to the page, and the reason for the feverish haste was that Marx definitely wanted to have it written prior to the *déluge*, the great flood of the expected worldwide crisis. He worked *like mad all night*[153] so that the details of the related aspects of what the world now faced would be clear, at least to him. The result was a preliminary rough draft of what he had taken on as his great life work—and what in the end he was able to realize only in part. Ultimately, the entire work was supposed to consist of six books: "1. On Capital. 2. Landed Property. 3. Wage Labour. 4. State. 5. International Trade. 6. World Market."[154] The *Outlines*, first published from his estate in 1939 and 1941 by the Moscow publisher for foreign-language literature, was essentially limited, however, to book one of the planned series—the analysis of capital in general. The subjects of landed property and wage labor were later included in the three volumes of *Capital* and the subsequent *Theories of Surplus Value*. The books on the state, international trade, and the world market would never exist, despite the fact that Marx never for a moment relinquished the intention of returning to these subjects. How the results would have looked remains a matter of speculation, but in terms of its basic assumptions the book about the state would presumably not have looked much different from the general theses on the subject that Marx had already formulated in the 1840s.

The books about the world market and international trade, however, would have given his theory about industrial cycles the unity that later would also be missing from the more comprehensive representations in the three volumes of *Capital*.[155] During the sleepless and smoke-filled nights when he put the *Outlines* on paper, he addressed this subject only sketchily, at various points in the manuscript. Marx saw the fundamental cause of modern cyclical crises in the development of the credit system. On the one hand, the credit system followed with a certain necessity from businesses' need to remain liquid even though investments had not yet been amortized through the sale of produced goods in the market. Capital, Marx maintained in the *Outlines*, thus developed the unavoidable need to achieve *circulation without circulation time*. Credit met this need. But on the other hand, out of intrinsic necessity the credit system itself developed a dangerous tendency toward *over-trading* and *over-speculation* because the real market conditions could first be determined only in retrospect. Briefly put, credit suspended the *barriers to the valorisation of capital* only by giving them their *most general form* and thus produced, in oscillation, *the period of overproduction and underproduction as two periods.*[156] It was a pure possibility theory.

Marx evidently intended to examine in detail the law of cyclical change between prosperity and crisis in his book about the world market.[157] It is impossible to know how his theory would have developed and whether it could even have existed, in a strict sense, as a scientific explanation of a complex phenomenon. In any case, this phenomenon became globally apparent for the first time in summer 1857, but—in defiance of Marx's and Engel's impatient expectations, and of what they had long wanted to believe—by the end of December 1857, the markets had noticeably calmed again. Even the second wave they had predicted failed to materialize. Evidently it was not a do or die situation.

Marx had originally planned to quickly establish the form of the *Outlines* as well as the plan for the entire six-book series, and to have the whole project appear in successive installments. But the work proceeded *very slowly*, above all because during his course of study continually revealed *new aspects* that needed to be *thought out further.*[158] When, after intense labor pains, it was actually published in 1859 by Franz Duncker in Berlin as a *Contribution to the Critique of Political Economy*, the half-finished text was not much more than a fragment. "Don't be bowled over by this," wrote Marx to Engels shortly before sending the manuscript to Duncker: "although entitled *Capital in General*, these instalments contain nothing as yet on the subject of capital, but only the two chapters: 1. *The Commodity*, 2. *Money* or *Simple Circulation*." If things went well, he thought, he could quickly follow up with the chapter on capital.[159] But things did not go well at all.

Wilhelm Liebknecht declared that no book had disappointed him more than this one. The decisive chapter about capital was in fact missing, so the book remained only an academic treatment of goods and money; it said nothing about Marx's central thesis about the basis of class antagonisms in modern relations of production. Despite a long and complicated foreword about historical materialism, it remained a scholarly and ultimately apolitical book, even if Engels maintained that it clearly revealed that "economics is not concerned with things but with relations between persons, and in the final analysis between classes."[160] Johannes Miquel, an old member of the Communist League, reported that he found "very little actually new" in the text.[161] As a future Berlin *Oberbürgermeister*, Prussian finance minister, and the architect of the principles of the German tax system that is still in force today, Miquel was someone who clearly understood something about the subject. By that time he had already become a liberal and a cofounder of the German National Association, but he was very familiar with the *Communist Manifesto* from their time together during the struggles. Miquel presumably expected more from his old friend Marx, especially with respect to information about the political core of his economic theory. The book went practically unnoticed by the public. There were other issues in Germany that Marx could hardly understand from the loneliness of his exile in London. The economy was flourishing again, and the so-called "New Era" in Prussia brought a phase of liberalization in public life that began overnight upon the incurably mentally ill Friedrich Wilhelm IV's departure from the throne at the end of 1858.

Marx was extremely frustrated. After all, the text contained the result of fifteen years of research, that is, *the best years of my life*.[162] In Germany, he told Liebknecht, he had expected everything, *attacks or criticism*, but not *complete ignoring*.[163] Engels's review—dictated in large parts by Marx himself—in the short-lived emigrant journal *Das Volk* did not change the book's reception at all. Marx, Engels disclosed to his readers, was the first since Hegel to attempt "to develop any branch of science in its specific inner coherence," but his "logical method" fundamentally distinguished him from the idealistic assumptions of speculative philosophy. To wit, Marx's science was based on a materialistic conception of history, and thus for him the logical method was nothing but "the historical method, only stripped of the historical form and of interfering contingencies." Engels concluded his review by stating that he would address the actual economic content of the book in a subsequent article[164]—which, however, never saw the light of day. Neither was there a continuation of the work itself.

Yet Marx had a faithful and reliable friend in Germany at this time: Ferdinand Lassalle. Lassalle's far-reaching connections and tireless string-pulling were also to thank for Marx's contact with Duncker and the fact that he ultimately received a book contract in which the publisher quoted a much higher honorarium than usual. In the early 1850s, next to Miquel, Lassalle was one of the few political thinkers in Germany who considered themselves Marx's party comrades. Miquel fell still farther under the influence of the zeitgeist's new liberal "Realpolitik," the principles of which were first formulated in 1853 by Ludwig August von Rochau, a former radical and participant in the charge on the Frankfurt guardhouse. The Revolution of 1848, according to Rochau, had failed because of insufficient insight into real power relations; therefore in the future one needed to learn to deal with realities rather than political fictions. In particular, the idea of a social revolution was nothing but a "figment of the imagination," at best a "violent act of politics" that unwittingly only played into the hands of incorrigible conservatives.[165] This was increasingly also the opinion of Miquel, who in his last letter to Marx observed that his hope of a revolution occurring soon in Germany had noticeably diminished in recent years.[166]

But ever since their first meeting in the fall of 1848, Lassalle had remained loyal to Marx. He had become a socialist very early and quite independently through his own interpretation of Hegel, Lorenz von Stein's writings on the history of the social movement in France, and a personal encounter with Pierre-Joseph Proudhon in Paris. On 17 September 1848, at the time of the Malmö cease-fire, he appeared together with Marx as a speaker at a mass rally under red flags on the Rhine meadow near Worringen.[167] He was rhetorically an extremely gifted speaker, and the influence he was able to exercise over the masses and the public would with time become one of the perhaps most difficult psychological problems that Marx faced during his life. Writing to Marx in June 1852, Lassalle noted that after the failed revolution he, like Marx, felt that in the future "no struggle would be successful in Europe anymore" if it was not "from the outset a pronounced purely socialist" struggle. He continued: "thus precisely during this apparently deathly quiet the real German workers' party is being born."[168] Marx was less certain. But in the correspondence of the early 1850s, Lassalle, who was years younger, was always someone who sought advice and forthrightly recognized Marx's authority in theoretical questions, even if he never developed into a real Marxist. For a time the correspondence ceased.

Lassalle resumed it again in 1857, when a book he published on the philosophy of Heraclitus the Obscure from Ephesus took the educated world of Berlin by storm. Suddenly celebrated as a wunderkind, he was honored at a banquet, in the presence of the Prussian minister president, by being granted membership in the Philosophical Society of Berlin. Varnhagen von Ense, Alexander von Humboldt, Richard Lepsius, and August Boeckh praised the work enthusiastically.[169] A copy was sent to Marx in London. He found the reconstruction of Heraclitus's system *brilliant*, he flattered Lassalle.[170] But in reality he felt that the *worthy Lassalle* was only poaching on the domain of others—all the more so since Marx himself had made a much more significant contribution with his own dissertation. For the rest, Marx felt that Lassalle was a sensationalist for whom being the talk of the town in Berlin was all that mattered: *This is the man who has written Heraclit*. Perhaps, noted Marx to Engels, *the laddie might be of some service to us in finding a publisher*.[171] Indeed, Lassalle arranged for his own publisher, namely Duncker, to take on Marx's *Critique of Political Economy* and shortly thereafter Engels's anonymously published *Po and Rhine*. Engels thanked him politely for his "bons offices"—his good services.[172]

This was not completely fair, nor did it mark the nadir of the relationship between the two exiled Church Fathers and their German admirer, whom they alternately mocked in their correspondence as *Baron Itzig, Ephraim Gescheit, Jüdel Braun, Polish Schmuhl*, and with other anti-Semitic invective. Jealousy played a significant role here. Lassalle's *Heraclitus* was the talk of the day; nobody wanted to hear anything about Marx's *Critique of Political Economy*. Lassalle moved in the best circles of Berlin society and simultaneously called out to his audience in the tradesman association of the Oranienburg suburbs that soon, when the workers too claimed their civil rights, the bourgeoisie would be crying "murder and death."[173] Meanwhile, Marx was researching and thinking on his own in London, *in great isolation*,[174] as he wrote to Lassalle.

A controversy regarding the Italian War of 1859 grew into a serious dispute. It concerned the question of how the German states were to behave in light of the pact for the liberation of northern Italy concluded by Louis Bonaparte and the prime minister of Piedmont-Sardinia Cavour. In his text *Po and Rhine*, Engels presented the view that Bonaparte's Italian ambitions could only be the prelude to developments in which he would ultimately also demand the Rhine border, since otherwise his coup d'état on the eighteenth Brumaire would not really be complete. If the Po was the "pretext" for Louis Napoléon, then under all circumstances, Engels maintained, the Rhine had to be his "ultimate goal." Nobody in Germany could therefore seriously think about giving up the Po without a fight, for ultimately that was the place to defend the Rhine.[175] Thus it was long believed amongst high-ranking military in Berlin that the anonymously published *Po and Rhine* had been written by a politicized Prussian general.[176] Additionally, Engels's ideas came awfully close to the majority opinion in Germany, which had been gripped by the most intense wave of anti-French nationalism since the Rhine crisis of 1840. Talk was of the "Empire's outside wall" along the Po, and the *Augsburger Allgemeine Zeitung* paraded before its readers the "lordly rights of the Germanic race" that ostensibly needed to be defended in northern Italy.[177] As little as Engels shared such positions, he was conversely just as convinced that nothing was a greater impediment to the revival of socialism in Europe than the new Bonapartism in Paris. Admittedly, he was no friend of the Habsburg "prison of nations," but nor was it any solution to have Austria vacate a position of power only for it to be occupied by a usurper. Once greater Germany was unified, it could safely abstain from all plundering in Italy.

Lassalle saw things somewhat differently. Again with Duncker, he published the polemic *The Italian War and the Task of Prussia: A Voice of Democracy*. As he saw it, Bonaparte was working indirectly for German unity, if he aimed to wrest northern Italy from Austria and force this reactionary state of many nations to step back toward its German heartlands. At such a time, he maintained, a man like Frederick the Great would have marched into Vienna and left it to the Habsburg monarchy to decide whether it could even assert its claims in its non-German territories anymore. Today, though, a comparable solution would not be in the interests of the democrats. Lassalle therefore suggested that the German states maintain neutrality in the Italian War and, parallel to Bonaparte's Italian intervention, liberate Schleswig-Holstein from Danish rule. Besides, Austria was the absolute embodiment of the reactionary principle in Europe, and thus a war against France would only strengthen the German people's identification with the divinely ordained crown. Moreover, he concluded, Bonaparte was in no position to think about conquests, not even in Italy.[178]

The result was precisely the last one. At the end of April 1859, the Austrians initiated hostilities, and on 20 June they suffered their final disaster at Solferino. Having conquered Lombardy, Louis Napoléon turned it over to Cavour in exchange for Nice and Savoy. Lassalle had perceived matters far more realistically than Engels, who was blinded by the caricature of Louis Bonaparte as the anti-revolutionary archenemy. Marx, however, considered Lassalle's *pamphlet* to be an *enormous blunder*. In the northern Italian crisis, and also given the threat of a French-Russian alliance against Austria, Germany could by no means remain neutral but was duty-bound to demonstrate that it was decidedly *patriotic*. With his headstrong views, Lassalle would in the future have to resign himself to being publicly disavowed by Marx and Engels. Especially now, it was necessary to maintain *party discipline, otherwise everything will be in the soup*.[179] What party? Marx, Engels—and Lassalle? Or that of the arrogated self-consciousness of history? Lassalle, however, did not regard the dispute as a party matter at all but simply a normal conflict of opinions.

In 1861 he proposed to Marx that they found a newspaper in Berlin. It was to be entirely in the tradition of the old *Neue Rheinische Zeitung*. Wilhelm I ("beautiful Wilhelm")—officially elevated to the throne from his position as regent after his brother's death—had announced a general amnesty. But this amnesty had limits with respect to refugees; moreover, as a stateless person Marx did not possess a passport. Nonetheless, he risked the trip. At the time he had just turned forty. In Zalt-Bommel near Nijmegen he stayed for two weeks with his uncle Lion Philips, one of the founding fathers of the Dutch Philips corporation, courting his cousin Antoinette, who would later be number one in the Dutch section of the First International.[180] When it suited him—and especially vis-à-vis this *cruel little witch*[181]—Marx could be quite charming.

On 17 March, he arrived in Berlin by train at approximately 7:00 A.M. and drove along the Bellevuestraße to meet with Lassalle, who lived *in a very beautiful house* in one of the best parts of the city. Everything was fully prepared for his reception; subsequently they visited Countess Hatzfeldt, Lassalle's eccentric life companion, for whom he had, as a lawyer, successfully conducted a multi-year inheritance dispute. The countess, Marx informed Antoinette, appeared to him to be a *very distinguished Lady, no blue-stocking*, strongly interested in the matters of the revolution, and above all displaying a pleasant *aristocratic laissez-aller*, something that he, who deeply hated all bourgeois trivialities, found especially pleasing. She also allowed herself to become easily enthused about a campaign against the brutal treatment of the French professional revolutionary Auguste Blanqui in his lonely fortress imprisonment. Lassalle's petition to the police president for the reinstatement of Marx's Prussian state citizenship, however, went nowhere.[182]

On occasion there was fellowship, theater, and ballet at the Royal Opera Unter den Linden, and above all a gala dinner arranged by Lassalle in honor of Marx's return to Germany. It was an illustrious company. The elderly General von Pfuel, who once openly admitted his homoerotic tendencies to Heinrich von Kleist, sat across from Marx. As governor of Berlin during the March revolution, he had courageously prevented a bloodbath. In the fall of 1849 he became the Prussian minister president, but he was soon dismissed because of his unmistakable constitutional leanings. Now the old warhorse was supposedly full of hope for the liberality of the new era. Marx sat between Countess Hatzfeldt and Ludmilla Assing, the niece of Varnhagen von Ense, who inundated him with her goodwill. Court Councilor Förster, who had known Hegel personally and was among the publishers of his writings, proposed a toast for the Fatherland's returning son.[183] For a while, Marx toyed with the idea of settling in Berlin.

The current situation in Prussia, he noted, was *ill-boding for the powers that be*, and all of the old parties were in a process of dissolution. This might actually be the appropriate moment to launch a newspaper in the Prussian capital.[184] So he remained for a while. He visited his friend Köppen from the days of the Berlin Doctor Club and found that he had hardly changed. As for Rutenberg, he learned that the former chief of the *Rheinische Zeitung* had had to leave the liberal *National-Zeitung* because he had become too reactionary. Bruno Bauer was collaborating on a *Staatslexikon* (political encyclopedia) and otherwise indulging in country life in Rixdorf.[185] For the most part, however, Marx was bored *stiff*.[186] There was no *haute politique*—high politics—here.[187] But he did not want to leave Berlin until the Prussian government had approved the reinstatement of his citizenship.[188]

The mood with Lassalle soured when they began speaking in binding terms about the composition of the future editorial office. Lassalle wanted himself and Marx to be equally responsible for directing the newspaper; if Engels were likewise to become a chief editor then by no means were both of them together to have more votes than he did. But Marx wrote confidentially to Engels that even if Lassalle provided the money, in the best case scenario, *if subjected to rigid discipline, Lassalle might be of service as one of the editors*. Otherwise they would make fools of themselves.[189] In the end, the project did not amount to anything. Neither did the effort to acquire citizenship. Germany, Marx wrote to Antoinette at a station along his return route, was such a beautiful country that it was best to live *outside its borders*.[190] Basically, he—the herald of the *real movement*—needed the ivory tower, where one did not have to besmirch oneself with the temptations, compromises, trivialities, and necessities of everyday political life. Perhaps he also feared—consciously or unconsciously—that in Prussia he might one day be caught in the maelstrom of Realpolitik, to which Miquel had already succumbed.

During the 1862 World Exhibition in South Kensington, which drew six million visitors, Lassalle stayed with Marx in London. Since 1856 the family had lived at Grafton Terrace near Hampstead Heath in a seven-room house with a small garden. An inheritance of Jenny's had enabled the move from the restricted confines on Dean Street, yet 1862 was once again a year of unmitigated financial straits. Lassalle, by contrast, was living it up. Marx could hardly bear it. Allowing his anger full rein in a letter to Engels, Marx wrote that the *baronized Jew* had actually lost five thousand Taler in a speculation; he would presumably rather throw the money into the dirt than lend it to a friend.[191] This was not quite the case: Lassalle had lent Marx fifteen pounds sterling and offered to extend him credit in any desired amount as long as Engels would secure the loan. Yet for Marx the matter remained an irritant. When Lassalle left London again, their correspondence ceased for the next two years.

A long-term political collaboration between Marx and Lassalle would hardly have been possible in any event. Lassalle was always more concerned with social issues than with socialism. In October 1862, three months after his return from London, he announced to Countess Hatzfeldt that he would establish a "collective labor association for all of Germany" headquartered in Berlin and put himself "at its head." As a response to the liberal Progress Party's tepid programs for solving social problems, he wanted the "fourth Estate" to develop as an independent political force with the prospects of civic recognition. His model consisted of state-funded productive organizations by which members of the working class, instead of being exploited, could become independent entrepreneurs.[192]

Lassalle never understood Marx. He always remained a Hegelian, especially with regard to the mediating role of the state. As opposed to Marx, he also had much more than unconditional intellectual leadership in mind; he wanted to become a real leader—in Marx's words, a *workers' dictator*.[193] On 23 May 1863, at the constituent meeting of the General German Workers' Association in Leipzig, Lassalle was elected to a five-year term as president with plenary powers. According to Isaiah Berlin, Lassalle in fact advocated the doctrine of personal dictatorship and—quite contrary to Marx, who once said that leadership is *never a pleasant thing*[194]—the romantic idea of a Führer principle. But according to Berlin, this was precisely what made Bismarck consider him capable of providing satisfaction.

In May 1863 the head of the Prussian regime summoned Lassalle to an initial secret meeting, to be followed by others over the next ten months. Bismarck felt that Lassalle was one of the "most clever and charming men" he had ever dealt with. After all, they had the same enemy in the liberal bourgeoisie.[195] Lassalle explained to Bismarck that the workers, despite their republican ethos, were fully prepared to see "the crown as a natural instrument of a social dictatorship" "rather than the egotism of the bourgeois class"—that is, if the crown changed from "a monarchy of the privileged classes" to a "social and revolutionary people's monarchy."[196] It was no coincidence that the idea of arranging these secret negotiations came from Bismarck's assistant Hermann Wagener, an admirer of the socially conservative Hegelian Lorenz von Stein.

After Lassalle's death in a duel in Geneva in August 1864, Marx noted that he had probably gone astray because in reality *he was, like Mr Miquel, a 'realistic politician', only on a larger scale and with grander aims, a Marquis Posa of the proletariat.*[197] His judgments were not always so severe. *Lassalle's misfortune*, Marx wrote to Engels in early September 1864, had *damnably preoccupied* him in recent days. It was hard to believe that such a loud and noisy person was now dead as a doornail, and he felt truly sorry that their relationship had become so clouded in recent years. After all, in Marx's eyes Lassalle still remained one of the *vieille souche* and the *foe of our foes*.[198] These words sound surprisingly noble, yet Isaiah Berlin is almost certainly correct to claim that, had he lived, Lassalle would certainly have developed into a first-rate obstacle for Marx.[199] Tellingly, when the leadership of the General German Workers' Association was offered to him, Marx refused it—and not only because Prussia, as before, refused to reinstate his citizenship, but above all because he wanted nothing to do with *royal Prussian governmental socialism*,[200] or with the *Tory-Chartist character*[201] of the Lassalle association, and because even Wilhelm Liebknecht, sent specially to Berlin, had been unable to purge the party of *the stench left behind by Lassalle*.[202]

Lost Illusions

For Marx, real world history took place in another way and at other places. On 28 September 1864, four weeks after Lassalle's death, the First International was raised from the baptismal font in London's St. Martin's Hall. The old music hall in Charles Street, not far from Covent Garden, had been reopened after a fire two years earlier. Usually there were concerts here, and on occasion also readings—for example, by Charles Dickens—and sometimes also political meetings. Two thousand participants showed up on this evening at the concert house lit by gaslight candelabras, which was densely occupied to the point of suffocation. Marx, too, was there. He was overwhelmed. *There is now evidently a revival of the working classes taking place*, he reported enthusiastically to Engels in Manchester. On this evening, it was resolved to found a Workingmen's International Association, with a general council in London and sections in Germany, Italy, France, and England.[203] The founders of the International, Marx wrote to his financially powerful but philanthropically inclined uncle Lion Philips, were the same people who had organized the grand reception of Giuseppe Garibaldi in London and, through an enormous meeting in St. James's Hall, prevented a war between England and the northern states of America—that is, they were *the real workers' leaders in London,* in particular the union leader George Odger. It was a *real movement* from the moment of its birth, and that was all that mattered to him.

The mood at the time was internationalist in a way that it had seldom been before, in many respects exceeding the euphoria of the Spring of Nations in 1830. For the first time, the meeting included transatlantic components, most clearly evident in the sympathy of the British workers' movement for Abraham Lincoln's war against slavery. This even gripped Marx. As he noted at the end of November 1864, *never has such a gigantic revolution occurred with such rapidity* as in America. Only three and a half years earlier Lincoln had proclaimed that no further concessions would be made to slave-holders, and now, his declared, and in part already accomplished, goal was the complete abolition of slavery.[204] In Abraham Lincoln, *the single-minded son of the working class*,[205] Marx saw a great revolutionary who did not shy from using armed force to bring down an entire societal system, in this case the slavery-based relations of production of the American South. Lincoln, for Marx, embodied a type of citizen completely different from the frightened subjects of the European monarchs. This example, Marx hoped, would in the future have *a highly beneficial influence on the whole world.*[206] Namely, the war against slavery unmistakably marked the beginning of *a new era of ascendancy for the working class.*[207] It was worldwide because the openly declared war against slavery could only be the prelude to a general struggle against all slavery, thus also wage slavery.[208] To the same extent that he wanted to see czarist Russia toppled into an abyss, Marx—unlike Lassalle, who as a Hegelian advocated the notion that the Americans were incapable of having their own ideas—admired the American dream, which at the time was still leavened with many socialist ideas.

Lincoln's friends on the other side of the Atlantic were not liberals like William Gladstone, who initially predicted (and for reasons of free trade in cotton, also desired) victory for the South—and who maintained, after the secession, that an entirely new nation had been created south of the Potomac. Rather, they were the European and especially the British workers, who, through large rallies in London, Manchester, and Sheffield against England's entry into the war on the side of the South, first made the public aware that the American situation concerned not only contracts for the British ship-building industry and the supply of cotton but also the question of the abolition or retention of the system of slavery. Marx was impressed above all by the *sound attitude of the British working classes.*[209] Even though supply failures of cotton caused by the war on the far side of the Atlantic led to a substantial crisis in the textile industry and to massive layoffs,[210] they took to the streets with admirable persistence for the sake of a political principle.[211]

A similar situation occurred in April 1864 during the reception of Giuseppe Garibaldi in London. The partisan leader and hero—a legend in his own lifetime—was cheered by hundreds of thousands of people who were clearly, as the *Times* reported, from the working class. The former carpenter and union leader George Potter rode picturesquely on a horse next to Garibaldi's wagon. Such highly romantic scenes would recur in similar fashion in other English towns. Marx viewed Garibaldi's national ambitions rather critically, but the fact that the British workers' movement's sympathies for the Italian freedom fighter were chiefly directed against the usurper Louis Napoléon, who still occupied Rome, might have allowed him to come to terms with this flaw. In an era of ascendant bourgeois national movements, the receptions for Garibaldi were festivals of proletarian internationalism—much like the previous year's large rallies in sympathy for Poland.

In late January 1863, a national uprising had broken out in Russian-occupied Congress Poland. "What do you think of the Polish business?" Marx wrote to Engels upon hearing the news. This much was certain: the *era of revolution* was once again *fairly opened in Europe.* In fact, Marx expected the uprising in Poland to start a revolutionary wave like that of 1848, in which *the lava will flow from East to West and not in the opposite direction.*[212] Revolutions in Poland, according to the dream, would be followed by the collapse of czarism and then, as an almost necessary consequence, a new German revolution. But the Polish uprising was brutally crushed and its leaders relentlessly punished with death penalties, forced labor, or deportation. The western states, whence the Polish insurgents had expected support, held themselves back; Prussia even found itself openly on the side of Russia. Massive protests, especially on the part of the trade unions, opposed these developments. In summer 1863, a delegation of French workers even traveled to London for a large sympathy rally for Poland.

The International grew out of this meeting for Poland. To this day it remains unclear who seized the initiative. The French who participated in the founding meeting in St. Martin's Hall later spread the version that it was a child born in France and breast-fed in London. In any case, French and English workers' representatives discussed the matter after the London meeting for Poland. Freemason connections might also have played a role.[213] Be that as it may. Secretary of the London Trades Council George Odger wrote an address to the workers of France, inviting them to an international congress slated for fall 1864 in London. Marx was anything but the initiator, and he was invited to St. Martin's Hall only at the last minute, but he would very quickly become the most important and significant voice of the International.

Marx's invitation was delivered by Victor Le Lubez, a French emigrant living in London, with the inquiry as to whether Marx wanted
to participate in the meeting "pour les ouvriers allemands"—for
the German workers. Though he had become accustomed to turning down such requests over the past ten years, Marx immediately
agreed. This time, he informed Engels, he had the clear feeling that
for the first time, *real powers* were in play on the sides of both London and Paris.[214] He did not say a word in St. Martin's Hall, but he
soon sat on the program commission that developed the principles
and statutes of the new association. Nobody there could match him
as a theoretician. A number of drafts were circulated and rejected,
until finally the commission met for further discussion at his house
on 20 October; in the end the matter was left in his hands alone.
As he informed Engels with great satisfaction, the general council
adopted his *Inaugural Address of the International Working Men's Association* with *great enthusiasm*.[215]

The *Inaugural Address* was not a new *Communist Manifesto*. The
composition of the International was too heterogeneous for that.
Anyway, Marx wrote to Engels, time must pass *before the revival of
the movement allows the old boldness of language to be used*.[216] But the
reticence he displayed tentatively also had other reasons, which
carefully tell a story of lost illusions. He had been preoccupied for
some time with the fact that the *almost childish enthusiasm* with
which they had greeted the revolutionary era prior to 1848 was a
thing of the past and now forever *gone to the devil*.[217] As the crisis
invoked by the American Civil War slowly ebbed in 1864, Engels
was even overcome with doubts about their old dogma concerning the relationship between crisis and revolution. It was really a
shame, he wrote to Marx, that "these things do not come to a proper
head."[218] Marx tried to calm him with the unfounded argument that
the crises of the future would replace what they *lost in intensity* with
what they *now gained in frequency*.[219] The Great Depression of 1873,
which marked the end of the Industrial Revolution in England, Germany, and Western Europe as a whole, was admittedly very intense.
In the meantime, however, such uncertainties regarding prophesies
of revolution and crises also bespoke a new realism on the part of
the International.

Marx did not attain his leadership position in the general council of this association as he had done in 1847 in the Communist
League, namely through his futuristic revolutionary models. Rather,

he did so as a dignified theorist of the need for union politics. In 1865 this question occasioned a controversy on the International's leadership committee. A member of the General Council, the former carpenter John Weston, publicly advocated the thesis that a general wage increase was of no use to workers and would only lead to an increase in prices. Weston, who in any event found himself in a minority position, argued that unions were therefore somewhat harmful. Weston was a supporter of the early socialist experimenter Robert Owen; like Lassalle, he saw the solution to social problems in the expansion of self-administrating productive cooperatives. Marx was asked to counter Weston. *We shall do our best,*[220] he said, and on 20 and 27 June 1865 he delivered a lecture entitled "Wages, Price, and Profit" to the General Council in London.

At heart it was about what determined the levels of wages. The starting point of the "iron law of wages," as put forth by Weston and Lassalle, could lead to totally different conclusions. One existed in the communist utopias advocated by both these men; the other, in Marx's own Jacobin theory of revolution that he himself—back then still supporting a form of the iron law of wages—had propounded in 1848. Now, however, he had changed his position on two decisive counts. To be sure, then as now, he held the view that the general tendency of capitalist production was to sink the average standard wage. But in determining the value of labor, which according to his theory was the basis of wage levels, he now included a variable quantity, one that was subject to historical change: namely, the *traditional standard of life* of a respective country. Incidentally, the level of wages had nothing to do with other market prices. High wages only reduced the profits of the capitalists, and the entire question ultimately resolved *into a question of the respective powers of the combatants,* thus of class struggle. With these explanations, Marx became the leading intellectual of the International. Basically, however, the controversy concerned the theory of a political economy of trade unions, which was how the General Council understood it as well, even if Marx closed his lecture with the remark that unions totally defeated their own purpose if they limited themselves to waging a guerilla war against the effects of the existing system *instead of simultaneously trying to change it.*[221]

Like Weston, Marx gave instruction to Lassalle's successor in the German Workers' Association, Johann Baptist von Schweitzer, who in any event already stood closer to the idea of unions than his predecessor. Coalitions with the unions that grew out of the working class, he wrote in a long letter to Schweitzer, were extremely important, and not only as a means of organizing that class. In Germany the right of association—to form coalitions—would also limit police rule and bureaucratism and tear up the *Gesindeordnung* (rules governing relations between masters and servants) in the countryside. In short, unions were an important *measure for making the subjects responsible*, whereas Lassalle's state-supported cooperative societies extended *the system of tutelage*. The honor of the workers' party thus urgently required that it reject such delusions. He ended his letter to Schweitzer, however, much more clearly than his lecture in London. The working class, Marx told him somewhat dramatically, is either *revolutionary* or it is *nothing*.[222]

Marx actually believed that the International would enable him to lead the European and even the American working class along such a path. *Les choses marchent*—things are moving forward—he gushed to Engels, and with the International they would have a powerful machine in their hands during the next revolution.[223] In barely over a year they had managed to draw the *only really big workers' organization*—the English trade unions that earlier had dealt only with questions of wages—*into the movement*.[224] What movement? In reality, the International Workers' Association was never at any point revolutionary. What was real for the association was something else—for example, the ten hours bill, which according to Marx was not only a practical success but also the *victory of a principle*. For the first time, through the statutory determination of the maximum length of the workday, *the political economy of the middle class* succumbed *to the political economy of the working class*.[225] This victory, Marx asserted in his polemic against Weston, would never have been achieved through a private agreement between workers and capitalists. It needed the *legislative interference* of the state, which, however, only came about because of the *working men's continuous pressure from without*.[226] From this perspective, then, one might ask, did the possibility not exist for other victories of the political economy of the proletariat, that is, victories within the existing conditions? During this period Marx's revolutionary prospects took on the appearance of a social democrat wearing a Jacobin hat. They became increasingly vague, even if he never admitted it.

The International itself was basically the product of a momentary alignment of various interests and moods. The latter should not be underestimated. The influence of the Methodist movement, for example, and its cult of worldwide brotherhood on the English working class was considerable and contributed significantly to the emotional character of the campaign against slavery and the support for the Italian and Polish struggles for freedom. It also promoted the readiness for international solidarity among workers, who all saw themselves as victims of the same exploitation. In terms of immediate interests, though, the British primarily wanted the network of the International to prevent the importation of strikebreakers and cheap labor from the continent.

In fact, the success of the 1866 strike by London's tailor apprentices could be traced back to the International Workers' Association and its activities. Conversely, in early 1867 the British helped the bronze workers of the French firm Bardedienne during their strike. The International collected funds for the striking workers, and the General Council turned to the trade unions, which immediately promised to provide all kinds of support and credit. The labor conflict ended on 24 March with the complete success of the bronze workers.[227] Workers in Basel who had been locked out, thrown out of their homes, and deprived of their credit line with food merchants were able to weather their lengthy strike from fall 1868 to spring 1869 only with the help of the International.[228] There were many actions of mutual solidarity during this period of conflict, in which employers engaged in extreme brutality, often with fatal consequences and frequently with the support of the police and state. The more effectively the International made itself felt in these affairs, the more its prestige increased in Europe. But, as Foreign Minister Lord Granville explained to worried foreign governments, the International always remained an organization that was primarily concerned with labor conflicts. Revolutionary plans, if they did exist, reflected perhaps the views of foreign members, but not those of the British workers.[229] In fact, they played hardly any role in the work of the International, and where they did appear Marx, as the mouthpiece of the *real movement*, fought them fiercely.

In England, the unions were the major field of activity for the International, and many of the tone-setting union leaders sat on its General Council. The *Bee-Hive*, the official organ of the trade unions directed by George Potter, functioned simultaneously as its mouthpiece.[230] On the continent, most of the International's initial support was in France, Belgium, and Switzerland. Later there were also members from Austria, the Netherlands, Spain, Italy, and the United States, including the National Labor Union with a million members. But it could barely find footing among the workers in heavy industry in northern England. Germany, too, was difficult, above all because of Lassalle's continuing influence. Not until the fall of 1868 did the German Workers' Association publicly commit itself to the International's principles. The International brought widely different currents together under its roof, welcoming British unionists, the positivist historian Beesley, Belgian freethinkers, Genevan clockmakers, republicans, democrats, French radicals, and even Proudhonists,[231] who suffered a decisive defeat in 1867 when, totally in keeping with Marx's political economy of the unions, the International Congress in Brussels declared that strikes were a legitimate weapon of the working class.[232] In 1868, the Congress recommended Marx's *Capital*, which had been published the previous year, to "the workers of all countries."[233] The Social Democratic Workers' Party, founded in Eisenach in 1869, committed itself from the outset to the principles of the International. Wilhelm Liebknecht ensured that its members joined the association as individuals because collective membership was prohibited by German law.

To Marx's dismay, in November 1868 the Alliance Internationale de la Démocratie Socialiste under the Russian anarchist Mikhail Bakunin also applied for membership. Marx knew Bakunin well from his days in Parisian exile, and when he saw him again in 1864 for the first time in sixteen years—Bakunin having escaped his Siberian banishment—he found that Bakunin was one of the few people *to have moved forwards and not backwards*.[234] Now, however, he feared—with some justification—that Bakunin wanted to use his alliance as an *instrument to disorganize the International*.[235] Thus Bakunin first had to officially dissolve his alliance and divide it into independent national sections. Even so, once the Russian, with his always impenetrable secret associations, began haunting the International, Marx was increasingly overcome by fears of a Bakunin plot, a *complete conspiracy*[236] of the *Bakunin gang*.[237] And in fact, Bakunin had made it a top priority to fight a merciless war against the "authoritarian communism of Marx" and the entire German school.[238]

Marx grew increasingly concerned about England as well. The influx of cheap Irish labor to the island, compelled by poverty, had led to a *profound antagonism between the Irish and English proletarians* and in a certain sense divided the working class into two classes.[239] These circumstances changed England's political landscape, and it was principally the "English workers' hatred of the Irish" that led to a clear Tory majority in the fall 1868 elections in industrialized Lancashire.[240] But in the scenario Marx envisioned, only England—the *metropolis of capital*[241]—because of its high level of industrialization, organized working class, and dominant position in the world market, could serve as *the lever for a serious economic revolution*.[242] He appeared already to be seeking reasons why this act of world theater would never be performed.

Thus the Franco-Prussian war of 1870 almost provided Marx with a sort of relief from the often small-minded routines of the International and his increasing doubts about the British workers' movement. Until shortly before the onset of hostilities, he adhered to his old idea from the 1840s that German unity could be achieved only through a German revolution *sweeping away the Prussian dynasty*.[243] But just one day after France declared war on Prussia and the South German states joined the North German Confederation, Marx was hoping that the Prussians would prevail. "The French deserve a good hiding," he wrote to Engels, just as convinced as the latter that the war could not be waged without the chauvinism of the French population at large.[244] If Prussia was victorious, then the centralization of state power would also ultimately lead to the centralization of the German working class, and the center of gravity of the western European workers' movement would shift from France to Germany. Marx put these thoughts to paper two weeks before the war actually entered its fighting phase with the storming of Weißenburg by Bavarian and Prussian troops on 4 August.

For Marx, the actions performed in the costumes of Grenadier and Cuirassier uniforms on the battlefields of Alsace and Lorraine were also evidently the secret work of the cunning of reason. If the Prussians won, he calculated, then the resulting predominance of the German working class over the French on the world stage would inevitably also lead to the *predominance of our theory over Proudhon's*.[245] As Engels maintained, ever since the war against Austria and the founding of the German Confederation in 1866, Bismarck had in any case done "a bit of our work, in his own way and without meaning to."[246] Now he was—again without knowing it—well on his way toward also finishing off Proudhon for good and ensuring Marx's unchallenged position in the international workers' movement.

After four weeks of fighting, the fortress of Sedan, having been bombarded by Krupp's cast steel artillery until it was ripe for attack, was forced to surrender on 2 September. Over a hundred thousand

French soldiers, including Louis Napoléon, were taken prisoner. "My Emperor, my Emperor is a captive!" mocked Engels in an allusion to a poem by Heinrich Heine.[247] But the war continued. Two days after the fall of Sedan, the Republic was proclaimed in the Paris Hôtel de Ville, and under the leadership of the young Léon Gambetta the call went out immediately for a national uprising of the people against the Germans. The Germans responded to this French populist uprising by terrorizing civilians, imposing requisitions, burning down entire villages, and shooting both alleged and actual guerillas. Marx saw this as a relapse into barbarism reminiscent of the Thirty Years' War, something he believed had long been overcome.[248] Additionally, with the appearance of the *lust for Alsace and Lorraine*, which he considered the *greatest misfortune* that could befall Europe and especially Germany,[249] he completely changed his mind about the war. A defensive war had turned into a war of conquest. "History will measure its retribution," he wrote on 9 September 1870 in the name of the General Council, "not by the extent of the square miles conquered from France, but by the intensity of the crime of reviving, in the second half of the 19th century, the policy of conquest!"[250]

As of 18 January 1871, a cease-fire prevailed. On 28 February, Adolphe Thiers, chief of the French Executive, who had always opposed the war, was forced to sign a preliminary peace treaty in Versailles, and on 1 March the National Assembly, which had moved to Bordeaux, ratified it. The Thiers government's policy of surrender was one of the reasons for the uprising of the Paris Commune. Marx had not desired this development, even though after the cease-fire was arranged he felt that France could perhaps be saved if it finally grasped that revolutionary measures and revolutionary energy were required in order to conduct a revolutionary war.[251] But that was not to be expected from a country under the leadership of Thiers and Jules Favre, *one of the most notorious tools of the reign of terror* of Cavaignac in 1848.[252] Moreover, Marx always rejected actions that were not carefully considered. As the French members of the International exiled in London set off for Paris after the capture of Louis Napoléon and the proclamation of the Republic, he feared they might commit *all sorts of follies there in the name of the International*, overthrow the provisional government, and seek to establish a *Commune de Paris*.[253] The French working class should not allow itself *to be deluded by the national souvenirs of 1792*, he insisted in the name of the General Council. Any attempt to topple the new regime while the enemy was practically pounding on the gates of Paris would be nothing but desperate folly. They would do better by looking forward and using the republican freedom to employ their *energies and wisdom* to build up the organization of their own class.[254] Thus Marx was advocating the actual position of the International.

Yet when, in the National Assembly elections of early February 1871, the majority of the French voted not for Gambetta's republicans and the continuation of the war but for the peace-seeking monarchists, Marx's mood instantly changed. He now characterized the representatives in this assembly of *Krautjunkers* (cabbage Junkers) as only the *rebellious slaveholders of Bordeaux*.[255] They were the actual secessionists from republican honor, like the Confederates in the American Civil War. To place the requisite emphasis on the historical-political parallels, Marx caricatured the French assembly's political leaders in garish colors, polemically in the style of George Grosz, who was no better a painter than Marx was consistently a serious historiographer in his text about the civil war in France. Not only had Thiers *proved his lying powers as an historian* prior to becoming a statesman and in the end possessed a brain *all the vitality of which had fled to the tongue;* he also, Marx claimed, had agitated for the war against Prussia—which was clearly untrue. Now the *Krautjunker* assembly had appointed Thiers its chief executive.

In contrast, the majority in Paris—besieged by the Prussians since September 1870—had voted republican and patriotically. The National Guard was under arms, and the first demands for the election of a Commune rang out by October. Revolutionary committees formed in the quarters of Paris and joined the National Guard to become a Central Committee. Thiers and Jules Favre, on the other hand, were in Marx's view nothing but reprobate creatures for whom appeasing the insurgent capital was opportune mainly because only after Paris was again at peace could they receive commission payments worth millions of francs for arranging state loans in the billions.[256] Only through a violent intervention, he maintained, presuming to have understood their motives, could the *appropriators of wealth* hope to shift the costs of a war that they brought about themselves onto the shoulders of the *producers of wealth*.[257] In his judgment, this conspiracy was the true secret of the *slaveholders' rebellion* in France.

In fact, however, the French had lost a war for which they had been poorly prepared. They had little recourse, apart from agree-

ing to the humiliating conditions of the peace treaty and, as impo-
tent spectators, enduring the proclamations of a German emperor
in the Hall of Mirrors in Versailles. Bismarck knew their weakness,
and he therefore refused to intervene in Paris. Instead he made a
mockery of the French. They were supposed to fulfill the stipulated
conditions of the peace treaty themselves, which was not possible
without the government's control of its own capital city. Bismarck
provided them with a battalion of released war prisoners to solve
the problem. The Commune of Paris was officially proclaimed on 29
March through the municipal assembly. On 1 May—as in 1793—a
Committee of Public Safety public was formed. At the end of May,
French government troops forced their way into the city at the Porte
de Saint-Cloud. The civil war in Paris lasted one week. According
to estimates by Marshal Mac-Mahon, the war resulted in seventeen
thousand dead on the side of the Commune, though presumably
there were many more. Ninety-three death sentences were issued;
two hundred fifty Communards were sentenced to forced labor; and
forty-five hundred were transported to New Caledonia.

Marx's text on the civil war in France was an obituary of this
drama, one that would finally make him a legend in Europe. The
Paris-Journal honored him in a headline as the "Grand Chef de
l'Internationale,"[258] and thereafter the title wound its way through
the European press. The text, which the General Council published
as an address, went through three editions in two months and was
translated into most European languages. Everyone believed that
the Paris Commune was the work of the International, which was
not the case. In reality, according to Benedetto Croce, it represented
a rebellion of the defeated and the armed, people who had not yet
given up and for whom a few federalist ideas were mixed up with the
tendencies of a socialist Republic.[259] In a surrounded, starved-out
city, Republicans, nostalgic old Jacobins, Blanquists, and Proudhonists belonging to the International (in whom Marx, incidentally,
had little confidence) came together—despite considerable differences—in an emergency situation under a red flag. They included
the painter Gustave Courbet; the author Jules Vallès, whose novel
Jacques Vingtras was one the most gripping depictions of the events;
and Eugène Pottier, author of the "Internationale," which later became the anthem of the worldwide communist movement.

The Commune ordered the separation of church and state, prohibited night work in bakeries, confiscated operations and factories

that had been abandoned by their owners, and encouraged the creation of associations with inalienable common capital and workers' self-administration. It absolved the petty bourgeoisie of its debts, ordered free schooling for boys and girls, introduced the principle of the election and recall of state officials, and abolished the division of powers, which Marx considered one of its most important measures.[260] France itself was supposed to be transformed, following the Parisian model, from a centralized state into a community-based federation of self-administered municipalities. To the extent that the Commune aligned itself according to any basic ideas, they were most likely drawn from Proudhon's *Du principe fédératif*. In this work written in 1863, Proudhon praised federalism as the universal key liberating humans from every kind of human enslavement and expected that the institution of federal, "mutualist" property would provide an escape from exploitation by capital and the domination of banks. "Whoever says republic says federation, or he says nothing," he maintained; also, "whoever says socialism says federation, or he says nothing."[261] Basically, however, the Commune was what Marx had feared from the start: the last act and swan song of the revolutionary years from 1792 to 1794. The myth of the revolution had raised its head one last time and was brutally drowned in blood.

In a certain way, thought Marx, who still wanted to discern in the events the hidden workings of reason, the Commune, too, remained an opaque *sphinx*[262] that did not understand itself. As Hegel interpreted the secret of the sphinx, it represented an "objective riddle," a larva awaiting unveiling through a spirited "know thyself."[263] What then was the Commune,[264] Marx asked—as had Oedipus, who toppled the sphinx from the cliff with the words the answer to the riddle is Man.[265] "Its true secret was this," came Marx's answer: "It was essentially a working class government, the product of the struggle of the producing against the appropriating class, *the political form at last discovered under which to work out the economical emancipation of labour.*"[266] Engels would later give Marx's theses a tangible form, maintaining that the Commune was the dictatorship of the proletariat in history.[267] In a conversation with Eduard Bernstein, however, he qualified that assessment, adding that such interpretations—including Marx's—wanted to give expression "more to the unconscious tendencies of the Commune than to its conscious plans."[268] The Commune did not follow any plan. In keeping with the doctrine of historical materialism, Marx saw it as a performance of the wisdom of history itself in the world-revolutionary drama he had already described, in his account of the eighteenth Brumaire of Louis Bonaparte, as a devouring and purifying purgatory.[269] Concluding the address by the General Council, he wrote: "Working men's Paris, with its Commune, will be forever celebrated as the glorious harbinger of a new society. Its martyrs are enshrined in the great heart of the working class. Its exterminators history has already nailed to that eternal pillory from which all the prayers of their priest will not avail to redeem them."[270]

With this obituary, Marx—the "Grand Chef de l' Internationale"—became overnight the *best calumniated and most menaced man of London*. The public attention *after a tedious twenty years' idyll in the backwoods* clearly did him well. The *Observer* even threatened him with legal prosecution.[271] In lead articles, the *Times, Telegraph, Standard, Spectator, Daily News*, and *Pall Mall Gazette* all commented on the text about the civil war in France, which caused more of a sensation than any previous address by the General Council. To the public, the International suddenly appeared as a great European power. The *Spectator* praised Marx's powerful language, and the *Examiner* even came out in support of the International.[272]

At the beginning of June 1871, Jules Favre sent a circular letter to the governments of Europe warning of the danger of the International. The Spanish government did the same. In France, a harsh emergency law was enacted against the International, but the British government was not very impressed by these frightening portrayals, and even Bismarck did not believe them. (However, in 1872 he used the specter of communism to create the so-called Three Emperors' League, a belated echo of the Holy Alliance.) Marx himself, in an extensive interview with the *New York World*, energetically denied that the International was trying to force a specific political form on any movement.[273] Yet in a certain sense that was precisely what he tried to do with his address on the civil war, especially with the claim that the Commune had shown that the working class *cannot simply lay hold of the ready-made state machinery*[274] but rather must destroy it. Later, Lenin and the Russian Bolsheviks presumably took this as the basic substance of Marx's state doctrine.[275]

With the collapse of the Paris Commune, the great period of the International approached its end. Two trade union leaders, Benjamin Lucraft and George Odger, who had sat on the association's General Council since its beginnings, announced their resignation in response to the address about the civil war in France. Earlier, they had refused to undersign the address with their names.[276] They were unwilling to be involved in a revolutionary radicalization of the International, now that it had issued an address on the civil war characterizing the Paris Communards as the *advanced guard of the modern proletariat*.[277] Their chief concern in the summer of 1871 was William Gladstone's Trade Union Act, which would legally recognize the right to strike and the legal protection of unions and their treasuries. Another issue on their agenda was the struggle for the nine-hour workday. A few months later the union leader John Hales, who until then had been the general secretary of the International, followed suit. The goals of the *real* workers' movement were different than Marx's, even if the trade unions did not likewise immediately jump ship.

On another front, Marx faced pressure from the Bakuninists. In this conflict, Marx, who initially envisioned his role in the International as the mouthpiece of a large movement, increasingly developed into a party unto himself. He considered Bakunin dangerous—as he did the Blanquists who had washed up in London with the masses of Communard refugees—because he did not want to see the International compromised by their actionism and ill-conceived attempts at coups d'état and revolutions. In 1872, Bakunin and his supporters were expelled at a congress of the International at The Hague—the first congress in which Marx personally took part. Then Engels made the motion to transfer the Central Committee to New York, a second strategic move that primarily targeted the Blanquists.[278] Marx and Engels wanted by any means to prevent the General Council from one day falling into the hands of these conspirators. But the time of the International was over anyway. It was dissolved on 15 July 1876 in Philadelphia,[279] and with that, Marx's career as a politician came to an end.

As early as 1874, in something like an anticipatory obituary, Friedrich Engels characterized the International as a typical product of the era of the second French monarchy—the expression of a naive cosmopolitanism of different factions that could not withstand the reality check of the Paris Commune's defeat and therefore inevitably disintegrated. He believed, however, that after Marx's writings had enjoyed some years of influence, the next International would be "directly Communist and will openly proclaim our principles."[280] Yet things turned out differently. "In fact, with the expulsion of anarchism," in the judgment of Benedetto Croce, "socialism was ex-punging from its midst, unconsciously, communism itself."[281] This remained valid for subsequent developments until the catastrophe of the First World War.

After the fall of the Commune, not even Marx still believed in a European revolution in the foreseeable future. His letters and publications from these years, incidentally, feature much about the quarrels with Bakuninists in the International, but hardly a word on the 1873 *Gründerkrise*—which was, after all, the greatest economic world economic crisis prior to 1929. He mentioned it only briefly in the afterword to the second edition of *Capital* in 1873 and again in a letter of mid June 1875.[282] This is noteworthy, for in the 1850s and 1860s an event of such secular significance, beginning with an epidemic of over-speculation and lasting many years before settling down, would still have produced great prophetic hopes. The crisis had resulted in a wave of anti-Semitism that Marx understood as little as he understood the nationalisms that in part were invoked by and also followed this wave. But more to the point, the economy underwent a complete transformation: the collapse revealed quick profits to be illusory, and soon everyone was talking about strategic thinking, the analysis of results, and systematic investment in indus-trial research and development. The days of the complete anarchy of primitive capitalism, which was a constant call for revolution, seemed to belong to the past. "No-one will speak of socialism again," Thiers maintained during these days, "and that is a good thing. We are rid of it."[283] Typical of Thiers, this was in any case a somewhat carelessly expressed instance of wishful thinking. But in fact, the myth of the tradition of 1792 had departed from Europe forever.

With the downfall of the Commune, the era of the nineteenth century's continental revolutions, into which Marx was born and which shaped him, was over. According to the judgment pro-nounced by Croce, all socialisms of the past now lived only in the sacred tales and golden legends of the party.[284] The new reality con-sisted in unions and interest groups, in the creation of political par-ties, in elective assemblies and parliamentary representations. In the years of the *Gründerzeit*, Europe became increasingly bourgeois. Even Marx—to end with an anecdote—was confronted with this fact in a surprising way. In mid August 1879 at the Waterloo station, he chanced to meet his old friend, the former radical Chartist Julian Harney, with whom he had founded the Universal Society of Revolutionary Communists in the 1850s. Both men were on their way to Jersey, that Channel Island where one spoke English and cooked French. The train arrived, and upon boarding they went separate ways to their compartments: while Harney had a first-class ticket, Marx's ticket was for second class.[285] In the socialist workers' movement of the bourgeois Fin de Siècle, Marx would once again move up to first class, but not the way he would have imagined.

Notes

1. Dolf Sternberger, *Panorama oder Ansichten vom 19. Jahrhundert* (Frankfurt am Main, 1974), 27.
2. Marx and Engels, *Manifesto of the Communist Party*, in MECW, vol. 6, 487, 489.
3. Marx, *Notebooks on Epicurean Philosophy*, Sixth Notebook, in MECW, vol. 1, 491.
4. Marx and Engels, *Manifesto of the Communist Party*, in MECW, vol. 6, 489f.
5. Marx, "Illustrations of the Latest Exercise in Cabinet Style of Frederick William IV," in MECW, vol. 3, 209.
6. Alfred Meißner, *Ich traf auch Heine in Paris: Unter Künstlern und Revolutionären in den Metropolen Europas* (Berlin, 1973), 103.
7. Marx, *Herr Vogt*, in MECW, vol. 17, 79.
8. Engels, "On the History of the Communist League," in MECW, vol. 26, 318.
9. Marx, "Critical Marginal Notes on the Article 'The King of Prussia and Social Reform: By a Prussian,'" in MECW, vol. 3, 201.
10. Waltraud Seidel-Höppner, *Wilhelm Weitling* (Berlin, 1961), 63 ff.
11. Engels, "On the History of the Communist League," in MECW, vol. 26, 319f.
12. Seidel-Höppner, *Wilhelm Weitling*, 71f.
13. McLellan, *Karl Marx*, 156.
14. Engels, "On the History of the Communist League," in MECW, vol. 26, 318f.
15. Marx to Proudhon, 5 May 1846, in MECW, vol. 38, 39.
16. McLellan, *Karl Marx*, 159.
17. Marx to Annenkow, 28 December 1846, in MECW, vol. 38, 96.
18. Gurvitch, *Dialektik und Soziologie*, 120.
19. Quoted in McLellan, *Karl Marx*, 92, 63.
20. Engels, "On the History of the Communist League," in MECW, vol. 26, 313.
21. Quoted in McLellan, *Karl Marx*, 170.
22. Marx, *Wage Labour and Capital*, in MECW, vol. 9, 213.
23. Engels, *The Condition of the Working Class in England*, in MECW, vol. 4, 581.
24. Engels, "On the History of the Communist League," in MECW, vol. 26, 321.
25. Friedrich Leßner, "Erinnerungen eines Arbeiters an Karl Marx," in *Erinnerungen an Karl Marx*, 174.

26. Marx and Engels, *Communist Manifesto*, in MECW, vol. 6, 481.
27. Marx, *The Poverty of Philosophy*, in MECW, vol. 6, 211.
28. Marx and Engels, *Communist Manifesto*, in MECW, vol. 6, 497, 518.
29. Hegel, *Encyclopaedia of the Philosophical Sciences*, §147, OUP, 208.
30. Marx and Engels, *Communist Manifesto*, in MECW, vol. 6, 495.
31. Sternberger, *Gerechtigkeit für das neunzehnte*, 79.
32. Engels, "The Movement of 1847," in MECW, vol. 6, 529.
33. Engels to Emil Blank, 28 March 1848, in MECW, vol. 38, 169.
34. Fanny Lewald, *Erinnerungen aus dem Jahre 1848* (Frankfurt am Main, 1969), 22f.
35. Croce, *History of Europe*, 168.
36. Marx, "Persecution of Foreigners in Brussels," in MECW, vol. 6, 567.
37. Marx to the Editor of La Réforme, in MECW, vol. 6, 565.
38. McLellan, *Marx*, S. 200
39. Marx, "Persecution of Foreigners in Brussels," in MECW, vol. 6, 568.
40. Marx and Engels, *Communist Manifesto*, in MECW, vol. 6, 493.
41. Engels to Marx, 8 March 1848, in MECW, vol. 38, 160.
42. Carl Friedrich Graf Vitzthum von Eckstädt to his mother, 5 March 1848, in *Revolutionsbriefe 1848/49*, ed. Rolf Weber (Leipzig, 1973), 40f.
43. Carl Friedrich Graf Vitzthum von Eckstädt to his mother, 13 March 1848, in Weber, *Revolutionsbriefe*, 52f.
44. Quoted in Wilhelm Blos, *Die Deutsche Revolution von 1848 bis 1849* (Berlin, 1923), 112; quotation translated by Bernard Heise.
45. Quoted in ibid., 128; quotation translated by Bernard Heise.
46. Rudolf Virchow to his father, 19 March 1848, in Weber, *Revolutionsbriefe*, 68; quotation translated by Bernard Heise.
47. Ibid., 70; quotation translated by Bernard Heise.
48. Adolph von Menzel to Carl Heinrich Arnold, 23 March 1848, Weber, *Revolutionsbriefe*, 77; quotation translated by Bernard Heise.
49. Ibid., 80; quotation translated by Bernard Heise.
50. Marx to Engels, 16 March 1848, in MECW, vol. 38, 162.
51. Engels, "On the History of the Communist League," in MECW, vol. 26, 323.
52. Engels to Marx, 25 April 1848, in MECW, vol. 38, 173.
53. G. Mallinckrodt to his son Gustav, 5 March 1848, in Weber, *Revolutionsbriefe*, 37ff.
54. Engels to Marx, 25 April 1848, in MECW, vol. 38, 172.
55. Otto Camphausen an W. Lenssen, 23 March 1848, in Weber, *Revolutionsbriefe*, 85; quotation translated by Bernard Heise.
56. Gustav Mevissen to David Hansemann, 21 March 1848, in Weber, *Revolutionsbriefe*, 75; quotation translated by Bernard Heise.
57. Marx and Engels, *Communist Manifesto*, in MECW, vol. 6, 518.
58. Mehring, *Karl Marx*, 185.
59. Jacques Droz, "Die Ursprünge der Sozialdemokratie in Deutschland," in Droz, *Geschichte des Sozialismus*, vol. 3, 20.
60. Engels, "On the History of the Communist League," in MECW, vol. 26, 325.
61. Stefan Born to Karl Marx, 11 May 1848, in Weber, *Revolutionsbriefe*, 144; quotation translated by Bernard Heise.
62. Marx, *Herr Vogt*, in MECW, vol. 17, 80.

63. Engels, "On the History of the Communist League," in MECW, vol. 26, 325f.
64. Marx and Engels, "The Programmes of the Radical-Democratic Party and of the Left at Frankfurt," in MECW, vol. 7, 49.
65. Marx and Engels, "The Democratic Party," in MECW, vol. 7, 27.
66. Marx and Engels, "The Crisis and the Counterrevolution," in MECW, vol. 7, 431.
67. Marx and Engels, "News from Paris," in MECW, vol. 7, 128.
68. Marx and Engels, "The 23rd of June," in MECW, vol. 7, 130.
69. Marx, "The Class Struggles in France 1848 to 1850," in MECW, vol. 10, 70.
70. Marx, The Eighteenth Brumaire of Louis Bonaparte, in MECW, vol. 11, 111.
71. Marx, "The Class Struggles in France 1848 to 1850," in MECW, vol. 10, 71.
72. Marx and Engels, "The 24th of June," in MECW, vol. 7, 138.
73. Hobsbawm, The Age of Revolution 1789–1848 (New York, 1996), 66.
74. Marx and Engels, "German Foreign Policy and the Latest Events in Prague," in MECW, vol. 7, 212.
75. Marx and Engels, "The Russian Note," in MECW, vol. 7, 308.
76. Marx and Engels, "The Victory of the Counter-revolution in Vienna," in MECW, vol.7, 505f.
77. Meißner, Ich traf auch Heine in Paris, 215.
78. Marx, "The Revolutionary Movement," in MECW, vol. 8, 214.
79. Ibid., 215.
80. Marx and Engels, "The Danish-Prussian Armistice," in MECW, vol 7, 421–423.
81. Wilhelm Ribhegge, Das Parlament als Nation: Die Frankfurter Nationalversammlung 1848/49 (Düsseldorf, 1998), 85ff.; quotation translated by Bernard Heise.
82. Hegel, Philosophy of History, 117.
83. Marx and Engels, "The Danish-Prussian Armistice," in MECW, vol. 7, 422.
84. Marx and Engels, "The Victory of the Counter-Revolution in Vienna," in MECW, vol. 7, 503.
85. Engels, "The Magyar Struggle," in MECW, vol. 8, 236.
86. Ibid., 238.
87. Engels, "Democratic Pan-Slavism," in MECW, vol. 8, 372.
88. Ibid., 378.
89. Engels, "Democratic Pan-Slavism," in MECW, vol. 8, 368.
90. Ibid., 365.
91. Ibid., 217f.
92. Friedrich Wilhelm IV of Prussia to Christian Carl Josia Bunsen, in Weber, Revolutionsbriefe, 331; quotation translated by Bernard Heise.
93. Marx, The Eighteenth Brumaire of Louis Bonaparte, in MECW, vol. 11, 107.
94. Engels, "Revolution and Counter-Revolution in Germany," in MECW, vol. 11, 5.
95. Marx to Engels, 23 August 1849, in MECW, vol. 38, 213.
96. Marx to Engels, 23 August 1849, in MECW, vol. 38, 212.
97. Engels to Harney, 5 October 1849, in MECW, vol. 38, 217.
98. Francois Bédarida, "Der englische Sozialismus von 1848 bis 1875," in Droz, Geschichte des Sozialismus, vol. 3, 133ff.
99. Marx and Engels, "Review (January–February 1850)," in MECW, vol. 10, 262f.

100. Marx and Engels, "Review (March–April 1850)," in *MECW*, vol. 10, 340.
101. Marx and Engels, "Universal Society of Revolutionary Communists," in *MECW*, vol. 10, 614f.
102. Marx and Engels, "Address to the Central Authority to the League, June 1850," in *MECW*, vol. 10, 377.
103. Marx to Weydemeyer, 19 December 1849, in *MECW*, vol. 38, 220.
104. Marx and Engels, appendices to the "Rules of the Communist League," in *MECW*, vol. 10, 634f.
105. Marx and Engels, "Address to the Central Authority to the League, June 1850," in *MECW*, vol. 10, 282.
106. Bédarida, "Der englische Sozialismus," 136.
107. Engels, introduction to Karl Marx's *The Class Struggles in France 1848 to 1850*, in *MECW*, vol. 27, 507.
108. Marx and Engels, "Review (May–October 1850)," in *MECW*, vol. 10, 490f., 510.
109. Marx and Engels, "Review (January–February 1850)," in *MECW*, vol. 10, 265f.
110. Ansprache der Zentralbehörde an den Bund, 6/22/1851, *MEW*, vol. 7, 562. Quotations translated by Bernard Heise.
111. Engels to Marx, 5 February 1851, in *MECW*, vol. 38, 280.
112. Marx and Engels, "Review (May–October 1850)," in *MECW*, vol. 10, 490ff.
113. Engels to Marx, 13 February 1851, in *MECW*, vol. 38, 290.
114. Marx, "Revelations Concerning the Communist Trial in Cologne," in *MECW*, vol. 11, 426.
115. Marx to Engels, 19 November 1852, in *MECW*, vol. 39, 247.
116. Engels, introduction to Marx, *The Class Struggles in France 1848 to 1850*, in *MECW*, vol. 27, 514.
117. Heinrich August Winkler, *Der lange Weg nach Westen: Deutsche Geschichte vom Ende des Alten Reiches bis zum Untergang der Weimarer Republik*, 2 vols. (Munich, 2000), vol. 1, 184.
118. Otto Pflanze, *Bismarck: Der Reichsgründer* (Munich, 1997), 314; quotation translated by Bernard Heise.
119. Marx to Engels, 24 April 1867, in *MECW*, vol. 42, 361.
120. Engels, Introduction to Marx, *The Class Struggles in France 1848 to 1850*, in *MECW*, vol. 27, 523.
121. Engels to Marx, 27 October 1857, in *MECW*, vol. 38, 488.
122. Marx to Engels, 24 November 1851, in *MECW*, vol. 38, 492.
123. Engels to Marx, 1 May 1852, in *MECW*, vol. 39, 98.
124. Marx and Engels, *The Great Men of the Exile*, vol. 8, S. 267
125. Marx and Engels, *The Great Men of the Exile*, in *MECW*, vol. 11, 259, 305, 311.
126. Marx to Engels, 11 February 1851, in *MECW*, vol. 38, 286.
127. Marx, *The Eighteenth Brumaire of Louis Bonaparte*, in *MECW*, vol. 11, 103, 142, 183, 140, 194.
128. Engels, "Real Causes Why the French Proletarians Remained Comparatively Inactive in December Last," in *MECW*, vol. 11, 215.
129. Engels to Marx, 13 April 1866, in *MECW*, vol. 42, 266.

130. Marx, *The Eighteenth Brumaire of Louis Bonaparte*, in MECW, vol. 11, 124.
131. Engels, *Revolution and Counter-Revolution in Germany*, in MECW, vol. 11, 6.
132. Marx to Weydemeyer, 27 June 1851, in MECW, vol. 38, 377.
133. Marx to Weydemeyer, 2 August 1851, in MECW, vol. 38, 402.
134. Wilhelm Liebknecht, *Karl Marx: Biographical Memoirs* (Chicago, 1908), 99.
135. Marx, preface to *A Contribution to the Critique of Political Economy*, in MECW, vol. 29, 265f.
136. Liselotte Ungers and Oswald Mathias Ungers, *Kommunen in der Neuen Welt* (Cologne, 1972), 61ff.
137. Marx to Engels, 8 August 1851, in MECW, vol. 38, 409.
138. Marx to Engels, 9 April 1859, in MECW, vol. 40, 412.
139. Marx to Engels, 23 January 1857, in MECW, vol. 40, 98.
140. Marx, "Elections – Financial Clouds – The Duchess of Sutherland and Slavery," MECW, vol. 11, 494.
141. Marx, "Russian Policy Against Turkey – Chartism," in MECW, vol. 12, 163.
142. Marx, "The War Question – Doings of Parliament – India," in MECW, vol. 12, 212.
143. Marx, "Financial Failure of Government – Cabs – Ireland – The Russian Question," in MECW, vol. 12, 231.
144. Engels, "The European War," in MECW, vol. 12, 556.
145. Marx to Engels, 11 July 1857, in MECW, vol. 40, 145.
146. Marx to Engels, 20 October 1857, in MECW, vol. 40, 191. (*Revue* refers to the *Neuen Rheinische Zeitung Revue* from November 1850.)
147. Marx to Engels, 13 November 1857, in MECW, vol. 40, 199.
148. Engels to Marx, 15 November 1857, in MECW, vol. 40, 201, 203.
149. Marx to Engels, 26 September 1856, in MECW, vol. 40, 72.
150. Friedrich Wilhelm IV to Groeben, 29 June 1857, in David Barclay, *Frederick William IV and the Prussian Monarchy 1840–1861* (Oxford, 1995), 277.
151. Marx to Engels, 18 December 1857, in MECW, vol. 40, 224.
152. Ibid.
153. Marx to Engels, 8 December 1857, in MECW, vol. 40, 217.
154. Marx to Engels, 2 April 1858, in MECW, vol. 40, 298.
155. Roman Rosdolsky, *Zur Entstehungsgeschichte des Marxschen "Kapital,"* 2 vols. (Frankfurt am Main, 1968), 28ff., 39.
156. Marx, *Outlines of the Critique of Political Economy*, in MECW, vol. 29, 49, 343; vol. 28, 12.
157. Roman Rosdolsky, *Zur Entstehungsgeschichte des Marxschen "Kapital,"* 2 vols. (Frankfurt am Main, 1968). 39.
158. Marx to Lassalle, 21 February 1858, in MECW, vol. 40, 270.
159. Marx to Engels, 13/15 January 1859, in MECW, vol. 40, 368.
160. Engels, "Karl Marx: A Contribution to the Critique of Political Economy," in MECW, vol. 16, 476.
161. Mehring, *Karl Marx*, 264.
162. Marx to Lassalle, 12 November 1858, in MECW, vol. 40, 354.
163. Quoted in McLellan, *Karl Marx*, 310.
164. Engels, "Karl Marx: A Contribution to the Critique of Political Economy," in MECW, vol. 16, 472, 474, 475.

165. Ludwig August von Rochau, *Grundsätze der Realpolitik. Angewendet auf die staatlichen Zustände Deutschlands* (Frankfurt am Main, 1972), 148, 146; quotations translated by Bernard Heise.
166. Gustav Mayer, *Friedrich Engels: Eine Biographie*, 2 vols. (Frankfurt am Main, 1975), vol. 2, 79.
167. Hans Peter Bleuel, *Ferdinand Lassalle* (Frankfurt am Main, 1982), 68ff., 93, 119, 192f.
168. Quoted ibid., 215, 220; quotation translated by Bernard Heise.
169. Ibid., 240.
170. Marx to Lassalle, 31 May 1858, in *MECW*, vol. 40, 317.
171. Marx to Engels, 22 December 1857, in *MECW*, vol. 40, 227.
172. Engels to Lassalle, 14 March 1859, in *MECW*, vol. 40, 402.
173. Quoted in Bleuel, *Lassalle*, 243f., 284; quotation translated by Bernard Heise.
174. Marx to Lassalle, 21 December 1857, in *MECW*, vol. 40, 226.
175. Engels, *Po and Rhine*, in *MECW*, vol. 16, 215.
176. Marx to Engels, 7 May 1861, in *MECW*, vol. 41, 280.
177. Lutz, *Zwischen Habsburg und Preußen*, 412.
178. Bleuel, *Lassalle*, 258ff.
179. Marx to Engels, 28 May 1859, in *MECW*, vol. 40, 435f.
180. Marx to Antoinette Philips, 18 March 1866, in *MECW*, vol. 42, 241f.
181. Marx to Antoinette Philips, 13 April 1861, in *MECW*, vol. 41, 274.
182. Marx to Antoinette Philips, 24 March 1861, in *MECW*, vol. 41, 270.
183. Ibid., 271.
184. Ibid.
185. Marx to Engels, 10 May 1861, in *MECW*, vol. 41, 288.
186. Marx to Carl Siebel, 2 April 1861, in *MECW*, vol. 41, 273.
187. Marx to Engels, 7 May 1861, in *MECW*, vol. 41, 280.
188. Marx to Carl Siebel, 2 April 1861, in *MECW*, vol. 41, 273.
189. Marx to Engels, 7 May 1861, in *MECW*, vol. 41, 281.
190. Marx to Antoinette Philips, 13 April 1861, in *MECW*, vol. 41, 275; trans. note: the words here are translated directly from the German version, *MEW*, vol. 30, 594.
191. Marx to Engels, 30 July 1862, in *MECW*, vol. 41, 389; trans. note: the words here are translated directly from the German version, *MEW*, vol. 30, 257.
192. Quoted in Bleuel, *Lassalle*, 312; quotations translated by Bernard Heise.
193. Marx to Kugelmann, 23 February 1865, in *MECW*, vol. 42, 102.
194. Marx to Antoinette Philips, 18 March 1866, in *MECW*, vol. 42, 243.
195. Quoted in Pflanze, *Bismarck*, 235; quotation translated by Bernard Heise.
196. Lassalle to Bismarck, 8 June 1863, quoted in Mehring, *Karl Marx*, 554.
197. Marx to Kugelmann, 23 February 1865, in *MECW*, vol. 42, 102f.
198. Marx to Engels, 7 September 1864, in *MECW*, vol. 41, 560.
199. Isaiah Berlin, *Karl Marx: His Life and Environment* (New York, 1978), 166.
200. Marx to Engels, 18 February 1865, in *MECW*, vol. 42, 97.
201. Engels to Marx, 13 February 1865, in *MECW*, vol. 42, 88.
202. Marx to Engels, 3 February 1865, in *MECW*, vol. 42, 77.
203. Marx to Engels, 4 November 1864, in *MECW*, vol. 42, 16.
204. Marx to Lion Philips, 29 November 1864, in *MECW*, vol. 42, 47, 48.

205. Marx, To Abraham Lincoln, President of the United States of America, in *MECW*, vol. 20, 20.
206. Marx to Lion Philips, 29 November 1864, in *MECW*, vol. 42, 48.
207. Marx, To Abraham Lincoln, President of the United States of America, *MECW*, vol. 20, 20.
208. Marx, preface to the first German edition of *Capital*, vol. 1, in *MECW*, vol. 35, 10f.
209. Marx, "English Public Opinion," in *MECW*, vol. 19, 138.
210. Marx, "The Crisis in England," in *MECW*, vol. 19, 53ff.
211. Marx, "A London Workers' Meeting," in *MECW*, vol. 19, 153f.
212. Marx to Engels, 13 February 1863, in *MECW*, vol. 41, 453.
213. Annie Kriegel, "Die Internationale Arbeiterassoziation (1864 bis 1876)," in Droz, *Geschichte des Sozialismus*, vol. 3, 187.
214. Marx to Engels, 4 November 1864, in *MECW*, vol. 42, 16; trans. note: the words here are translated directly from the German version, *MEW*, vol. 31, 13.
215. Ibid., 18.
216. Ibid., 18.
217. Marx to Engels, 13 February 1863, in *MECW*, vol. 41, 453; trans. note: the words here are translated directly from the German version, *MEW*, vol. 30, 324.
218. Engels to Marx, 2 November 1864, in *MECW*, vol. 42, 9.
219. Marx to Engels, 4 November 1864, in *MECW*, vol. 42, 19.
220. Marx to Engels, 20 May 1865, in *MECW*, vol. 42, 160.
221. Marx, "Value, Price and Profit," in *MECW*, vol. 20, 145, 146, 149.
222. Marx to Schweitzer, 13 February 1865, cited in Marx to Engels, 18 February 1865, in *MECW*, vol. 42, 95f.; trans. note: the words here are translated directly from the German version, *MEW*, vol. 31, 446.
223. Marx to Engels, 11 September 1867, in *MECW*, vol. 42, 424.
224. Marx to Kugelmann, 14 January 1866, in *MECW*, vol. 42, 221.
225. Marx, *Inaugural Address of the Working Men's International Association*, in *MECW*, vol. 20, 11.
226. Marx, "Value, Price and Profit," in *MECW*, vol. 20, 146.
227. Marx to Engels, 2 April 1867, in *MECW*, vol. 42, 351.
228. Marx, "Report of the General Council to the Fourth Annual Congress of the International Working Men's Association," in *MECW*, vol. 21, 70.
229. Mehring, *Karl Marx*, 459.
230. Marx, "Connections between the International Working Men's Association and English Working Men's Organisations," in *MECW*, vol. 21, 26.
231. Kriegel, "Die Internationale Arbeiterassoziation," 192ff.
232. Marx to Engels, 17 December 1869, in *MECW*, vol. 43, 405.
233. Jean Bruhat, "Das Kapital in der Geschichte des Sozialismus," in Droz, *Geschichte des Sozialismus*, vol. 3, 183.
234. Marx to Engels. 4 November 1864, in *MECW*, vol. 42, 19.
235. Marx, Confidential Communication, in *MECW*, vol. 21, 114.
236. Ibid., 115.
237. Marx to Engels, 10 February 1870, in *MECW*, vol. 43, 424.

238. Quoted in Mayer, *Engels*, vol. 2, 222; quotation translated by Bernard Heise.
239. Marx, Confidential Communication, in *MECW*, vol. 21, 120.
240. Engels to Marx, 20 November 1868, in *MECW*, vol. 43, 165.
241. Marx to Sigfried Meyer and August Vogt, 9 April 1870, in *MECW*, vol. 43, 475.
242. Marx, Confidential Communication, in *MECW*, vol. 21, 86.
243. Marx to Lafargue, 2 June 1869, in *MECW*, vol. 43, 288.
244. Marx to Engels, 20 July 1870, in *MECW*, vol. 44, 3.
245. Ibid., 4.
246. Engels to Marx, 15 August 1870, in *MECW*, vol. 44, 47.
247. Engels to Marx, 4 September 1870, in *MECW*, vol. 44, 61.
248. Marx to Kugelmann, 13 December 1870, in *MECW*, vol. 44, 92f.
249. Marx to Engels, 17 August 1870, in *MECW*, vol. 44, 51.
250. Marx, "Second Address of the General Council of the International Working Men's Association on the Franco-Prussian War," in *MECW*, vol. 22, 266.
251. Marx to Lafargue, 4 February 1871, in *MECW*, vol. 44, 114.
252. Marx to Hermann Jung, 18 January 1871, in *MECW*, vol. 44, 99.
253. Marx to Engels, 6 September 1870, in *MECW*, vol. 44, 64.
254. Marx, "Second Address of the General Council of the International Working Men's Association on the Franco-Prussian War," in *MECW*, vol. 22, 269.
255. Marx, *The Civil War in France*, *MECW*, vol. 22, 319, 322; trans. note: some of the words here are translated directly from the German version, *MEW*, vol. 17, 230.
256. Ibid., 314, 317, 320.
257. Ibid., 319.
258. Marx, To the Editorial Boards of the *Volksstaat* and the *Zukunft*, in *MECW*, vol. 22, 287.
259. Croce, *History of Europe*, 267.
260. Marx, *The Civil War in France*, *MECW*, vol. 22, 331.
261. Gurvitch, *Dialektik und Soziologie*, 133; quotations translated by Bernard Heise.
262. Marx, *The Civil War in France*, in *MECW*, vol. 22, 328.
263. Georg Wilhelm Friedrich Hegel, *Aesthetics: Lectures on Fine Art*, vol. 1, trans. T.M. Knox, electronic edition (Oxford, 2000), 361.
264. Marx, *The Civil War in France*, in *MECW*, vol. 22, 328.
265. Hegel, *Aesthetics*, vol. 1, 361. Hegel, Vorlesungen über die Philosophie der Geschichte, S. 272.
266. Marx, *The Civil War in France*, in *MECW*, vol. 22, 334.
267. Engels, introduction to Marx, *The Civil War in France*, in *MECW*, vol. 27, 191.
268. Quoted in Mayer, *Engels*, vol. 2, 228; quotation translated by Bernard Heise.
269. Marx, *The Eighteenth Brumaire of Louis Bonaparte*, in *MECW*, vol. 11, 106.
270. Marx, *The Civil War in France*, in *MECW*, vol. 22, 355.
271. Marx to Kugelmann, 18 June 1871, in *MECW*, vol. 44, 158.
272. Engels, "The Address *The Civil War in France* and the English Press," in *MECW*, vol. 22, 375.
273. McLellan, *Karl Marx*, 402.

274. Marx, *The Civil War in France*, in MECW, vol. 22, 328.
275. Lenin, *The State and Revolution* (Whitefish, MT, 2004), 32.
276. Kriegel, "Internationale Arbeiterassoziation," 215.
277. Marx, *The Civil War in France*, in MECW, vol. 22, 354.
278. Leßner, "Erinnerungen eines Arbeiters an Karl Marx," 181.
279. Kriegel, "Internationale Arbeiterassoziation," 213.
280. Engels to Friedrich Adolph Sorge, 12 September 1874, in MECW, vol. 45, 42.
281. Croce, *History of Europe*, 301.
282. Marx, afterword to the second German edition of *Capital*, vol. 1, in MECW, vol. 35, 20; Marx to Pyotr Lavrov, 18 June 1875, in MECW, vol. 45, 78.
283. Robert Schnerb, *Europa im 19. Jahrhundert: Europa als Weltmacht* (Munich, 1983), 437. Quotation translated by Bernard Heise.
284. Croce, *History of Europe*, 301.
285. Marx to Engels, 14 August 1879, in MECW, vol. 45, 370.

DISCOVERIES

The Terrible Missile

In 1879, at the request of the Hohenzollern Princess Victoria, the liberal Sir Mountstuart Elphinstone Grant Duff met Marx at the Devonshire Club at No. 50, St. James Street. Founded in 1874, the establishment was a favorite meeting spot for energetic, mostly younger Whigs. Grant Duff, as fully bearded as Marx, was supposed to provide the princess with an authentic portrayal of the former "Graand Chef" of the International, for the liberal daughter of the British king—married to Friedrich, the future heir apparent to the German throne—had political notions that were decidedly her own, running in some respects counter to Prussian traditions. After the meeting, the emissary of the Hohenzollern court wrote to the princess that his counterpart had impressed him as a "well informed, nay, learned man," who, in his opinion, advocated sound ideas when talking about the past and the present. But, according to Grant Duff, Marx became "unsatisfying when he turned to the future." Marx spoke extensively about the tremendous scale of the *Gründerkrise*, ongoing for over five years now. He expected, and in this respect agreed with Grant Duff, that inner political turbulence would soon lead to an overthrow in Russia, and both were worried about the increasing danger the arms race posed to Europe. Marx placed his hopes in a revolt against the Prussian military system once Russia had collapsed. Grant Duff, the perfect gentleman, did not follow his view completely and asked him politely how he would get from the expected republic to his final objective. The republic was just a step along the way, Marx replied: "all great movements are slow."[1]

Marx had become noticeably more cautious about his prognosis. Above all, he no longer expected the great crisis to have the same catalytic effect he had predicted earlier. In the best-case scenario of a Russian collapse, the crisis could increase dissatisfaction and lead to a republican situation—as actually would happen in a certain way in 1918. But he had evidently abandoned the hope that a crisis would reveal the capitalist system's inability to survive and thus immediately lead to a proletarian uprising; he now entertained vague prospects of a slow, growing movement.

But basically, demonstrating the necessary connection between crisis and revolution was the content of his entire life's work, which he continued now as he had before. Marx's lifetime coincided with the greatest transformation humanity had witnessed since the Neolithic period. Far more than other theoreticians before him, he was overwhelmed by the scope and speed of the Industrial Revolution's upending of an entire world in such a short time. Adam Smith's *Wealth of Nations* appeared in 1776, just prior to the Industrial Revolution; David Ricardo's *Principles of Political Economy* was published in 1817, when it was still in its infancy. Marx, whose *Capital* was also an intense engagement with both of these classical economists, was poised to become the most important theoretician of this secular transformation. To use the words of Immanuel Kant, he found himself in the middle of the fog instead of being able to view it from the outside. Grandiose sharp-sightedness was therefore almost inevitably accompanied by irrational expectations of redemption, especially since these, coming from other sources, were transferred to the mighty time machine that was seizing Europe and the world. His antinomic thinking misled him above all to declare contradictions that could have been resolved through trial and error to be fundamentally unsolvable. But this does not mean the contradictions Marx discovered in the modern world never existed.

Even enthusiastic visionaries can make lasting scientific discoveries. The most famous example is perhaps the hermetist Isaac Newton, who alongside his exacting studies always found himself searching for an alchemical doctrine regarding the general coherence of the whole, and whom alchemy frequently inspired to develop sustainable scientific hypotheses. Did the same also apply to

Marx? In the eyes of Joseph Schumpeter, for one, he was a first-rate economist, and in light of his considerable detailed economic research, the philosophical garb of his doctrine was something that could safely be ignored.[2] Thomas Nipperdey thought that his politically eschatological will was precisely what made him more clear-sighted than his contemporaries and predecessors.[3] Significantly, Marx was not a theorist of economic equilibrium or theologian of the market place—merits that the financial magnate George Soros, of all people, valued highly in him.[4] His most decisive economic discovery, according to Charles Taylor, was the identification of capitalism as the most innovative and creative economic system in human history—and simultaneously also the most destructive. But, Taylor maintained, he should have remained satisfied with this insight instead of losing himself in the hope that complex chaos could resolve itself into a new harmony and simplicity.[5] Richard Sennett supposed that Marx's vision of a fleeting modernity also had something to do with his origins in a world of Biedermeier tranquility and the nostalgic feeling for the ancient rhythms of the countryside that still lived within him,[6] as was especially vividly demonstrated by his familial Sunday excursions to the hills of Hampstead Heath, singing songs and reciting Shakespeare.[7]

By April 1864, two inheritances had enabled Marx to move from Grafton Terrace to a comparatively comfortable row house with a winter garden in Maitland Park between Camden Town and Hampstead Heath. His neighbor was the concierge of the House of Lords, Henry Goddard. Here, in a first-storey study with a picture window overlooking the park, the better part of his main work was born. Bookshelves stood on both sides of the fireplace and lined the walls, and in the middle of the room stood two tables crammed with papers, books, and newspapers. Next to his work desk was a leather sofa in which he occasionally relaxed. The wall over the fireplace was adorned with original wallpaper from the study of Leibniz, the great philosopher of the rationality of a world with inherently contradictory dynamics, with whom Marx incidentally shared an interest in calculus.[8] Enthroned on a mantel was a bust of Zeus from Otricoli. For the first time, Marx was working in an atmosphere befitting a private scholar.

But no sooner had he settled in than the room became a regular meeting place for commissions from the General Council of the International, which always interrupted his work on *Capital*. Over almost twenty years Marx had attempted many times to finish his work on economics. In 1866, a clean copy of the manuscript of the first volume of *Capital* was finally ready. He would be sending the first pages to his publisher in Hamburg next month,[9] he informed a friend in mid October; after it had gone into print, he wrote: "It is without question the most terrible missile that has yet been hurled at the heads of the bourgeoisie (landowners included)."[10] Using all scientific means, the *terrible missile* was supposed to prove to the bourgeoisie that its world order was finite and fleeting.

Without his precursors in the field of economics, Marx's thought was just as inconceivable as it would have been without Hegel or the theories of early communism and socialism. In this field, like everyone else of his era, he was a labor-value theorist. "The annual labour of every nation is the fund which originally supplies it with all the necessaries and conveniencies of life which it annually consumes," read the first sentence of Adam Smith's *Wealth of Nations*; and elsewhere Smith wrote: "Labour, therefore, it appears evidently, is the only universal, as well as the only accurate measure of value, or the only standard by which we can compare the values of different commodities, at all times, and at all places."[11] The engagement with Adam Smith comprises a large part of *Theories of Surplus Value*, sometimes referred to as the fourth volume of *Capital*, which was published from Marx's estate by Karl Kautsky between 1905 and 1910.

Marx accused Smith of theoretical inconsistencies and contradictions, but above all, by long habit, he treated him phenomenologically, as an unfinished step along the way to an actual self-awareness of the modern—the revealed *economic law of motion of modern society*[12] on which Marx was working. This also applied to David Ricardo, who likewise was among the labor-value theorists. They represented unfinished stages, due in part to the unfinished temporal stages in which they were produced, in part to the methodological limits of their theoretical approach, and in part—and, according to Marx, most importantly—the limitations of their bourgeois horizons. The crux of the matter for him was perhaps demonstrated most emphatically in a letter he wrote to a friend in Hanover:

> Every child knows that any nation that stopped working, not for a year, but let us say, just for a few weeks, would perish. And every child knows, too, that the amounts of products corresponding to the

differing amounts of needs demand differing and quantitatively determined amounts of society's aggregate labour. It is self-evident that
this necessity of the distribution of social labour in specific propor-
tions is certainly not abolished by the specific form of social production; it can only change its form of manifestation. Natural laws
cannot be abolished at all. The only thing that can change, under
historically differing conditions, is the form in which those laws assert themselves. And the form in which this proportional distribution of labour asserts itself in a state of society in which the intercon-
nection of social labour expresses itself as the private exchange of the
individual products of labour, is precisely the exchange value of these
products. Where science comes in is to show how the law of value
asserts itself.[13]

Neither Smith nor Ricardo had managed to do the latter because,
influenced by Isaac Newton's theory of causality, they were thinking
one-sidedly in terms of quantitative categories and fixed substances.[14]

Marx, however, was concerned with *the inner organisation of the
capitalist mode of production*, with the *analysis of capital in its basic
structure*,[15] and therefore with qualities, structures, and determined
social forms—with the life of the subject matter,[16] as he put it, following Hegel. The influence of Hegel's logic, especially his distinctions between inner causes, external requirements, and reciprocal
actions,[17] is noticeable throughout *Capital*. For Marx, the law of
value implemented an unconsciously unifying principle of societal
labor,[18] which guided the regulating mechanisms of the modern market[19] economy and was unique to that economy. It proceeded from
the simple assumption that value is added to available raw materials
only and exclusively through labor, and that nothing except this
added value can be allocated for distribution. Supply and demand
admittedly regulate prices, which sometimes deviate significantly
from value, but overall and in the long term they can only oscil-
late around the level of value—the "annual labor," in Adam Smith's
terms. Because that is the case, and because the regulating principle
functions unconsciously in the market economy, this level violently
reestablishes itself in periodical crises—which also represent corrections of value.

Marx's book is the representation of an ideal type, not an empirical description of capitalism. Moreover, it is not a treatise on
national economies but rather, according to its claims, a theory of
global economic relationships and their general principles. Marx

believed that this subject could be accomplished only with a theory that in all its details always maintained a view of the overall coherence. For him, as for Hegel, the truth was the whole, a *rich totality of many determinations and relations*.[20] This view determined his methodological approach. Here is a central quote:

> The 17th-century economists, for example, always started with the living whole, the population, the nation, the state, several States, etc., but analysis always led them in the end to the discovery of a few determining abstract, general relations, such as division of labour, money, value, etc. As soon as these individual moments had been more or less clearly deduced and abstracted, economic systems were evolved which from the simple [concepts], such as labour, division of labour, need, exchange value, advanced to the State, international exchange and the world market. The latter is obviously the correct scientific method. The concrete is concrete because it is a synthesis of many determinations, thus a unity of the diverse. In thinking, it therefore appears as a process of summing-up, as a result, not as the starting point, although it is the real starting point, and thus also the starting point of perception and conception. The first procedure attenuates the comprehensive visualisation to abstract determinations, the second leads from abstract determinations by way of thinking to the reproduction of the concrete.[21]

Marx thus did not begin his presentation in *Capital* with general concepts like population, division of labor, or production sectors, which in themselves, as he saw it, only represented a chaotic, unstructured, and therefore meaningless whole. Influenced by the discoveries of his era's modern biology, he focused first on what he felt represented—as in *microscopic anatomy*—the *cell form*[22] of modern reality: the commodity. At the first abstract level, capitalism represented a fully formed market economy that permeated the entire life of the society. Whereas his precursors had identified the commodity as something of a fixed entity, for Marx it represented the elementary embryonic form of the unity of all of the complexities and contradictions of capitalism. Its entire corresponding economic and social system could subsequently be appropriately explained, according to his central hypothesis, only on the basis of the immanent contradictions of the commodity and its development into money and capital.[23]

Marx's *Capital* contains three basic theses: (1) Hidden behind apparent objective economic conditions are actually social relationships; (2) the source of the acquisition of capital is the exploitation of labor; (3) the inner contradictions of capitalism lead to its collapse. On two and a half thousand pages in three volumes, he developed around these theses a widely ramified and richly detailed theory of the production, circulation, and distribution processes of capital. It was avowedly an economic theory that was simultaneously a social theory and a prognosis of historical development.

The commodity is not only a thing. The mystery of the commodity, according to Marx, lay in the fact that in the commodity, "the social character of men's labour appears to them as an objective character stamped upon the product of that labour; because the relation of the producers to the sum total of their own labour is presented to them as a social relation, existing not between themselves, but between the products of their labour."[24] This thought informs the whole of *Capital,* and leading to it was a straight path from the first theories of alienation and objectification of the early 1840s.[25] But now, as his program for a Copernican revolution of humanity had required in 1843, self-alienation in its *unholy form*[26] was exposed on the basis of what he saw as a developed positive science, based on empirical research. "As, in religion, man is governed by the products of his own brain," Marx wrote in the chapter about the general law of capitalist accumulation, "so in capitalistic production, he is governed by the products of his own hand."[27]

The critique of heaven had ultimately transformed into a critique of earth. Marx now stated that for a society of commodity producers, Christianity, with its cult of abstract humanity, was the appropriate form of religion. But for him, all this was only the expression of an inverted world in which social relations appeared as *material relations between persons and social relations between things.* With respect to people in a market economy, Marx wrote, "To them, their own social action takes the form of the action of objects, which rule the producers instead of being ruled by them."[28] In his view the capitalist market economy did not merely represent the delirium of an uncontrollable automatism; rather, precisely because it did, this market economy was above all a power relationship. And in contrast to earlier historical epochs like feudal societies in the Middle Ages or the slave-holding societies of the ancient world, which were based on relations of personal dependence, the capitalist market economy was a power relationship of objects over people. As a consequence, this also applied to the person of the capitalist himself. "But here individuals are dealt with only in so far as they are the personifications of economic categories, embodiments of particular class-relations and class-interests," wrote Marx in the preface to the first edition of *Capital*: "My standpoint, from which the evolution of the economic formation of society is viewed as a process of natural history, can less than any other make the individual responsible for relations whose creature he socially remains, however much he may subjectively raise himself above them."[29] Everything—at least everything essential for the functioning of the economic system—was, Marx held, determined not by individuals but instead by the inner organization and dynamic, the structure of the mode of production.[30] His analysis concerned only the *laws* themselves,[31] ignoring real-life psychological factors ranging from prudence and responsibility to greed and avarice, which for him were mere accidents. "Only as personified capital," Marx maintained, was the capitalist worthwhile for the scientific analysis of capitalism.[32] And as such, he was nothing but the incarnation of the material will of capitalistic relations. The actual object of his analysis was these relations, not the figure of the capitalist.

It was on this basis that Marx posed his question, in the first volume of *Capital*, about the origins of capital profit and its consequences for the dynamic of the system as a whole. Even Adam Smith had divided the value that workers added to material into two parts, one pertaining to wages and the other to profits.[33] Of all the contradictions that Smith otherwise entangled himself in, this was Marx's most groundbreaking realization, in particular because Smith had demonstrated that the "newly-created surplus-value in itself has nothing to do with the part of the capital which has been advanced (as materials and instruments)."[34] Smith thereby identified the problem, but he did not solve it, nor did David Ricardo. According to Marx, the ambiguous concept standing in the way of a solution was the *value of labour*.[35]

Left Ricardians of the 1820s like William Thompson and Thomas Hodgskin concluded from these theories that capital itself was wholly unproductive;[36] consequently they demanded the worker's full rights to the product of his work.[37] Marx, in contrast, held such talk about the unproductivity of capital to be complete nonsense,[38] with one significant limitation: "One can only speak of the productivity of capital," he stated, "if one regards capital as the embodiment of definite social relations of production"[39]—not, like Ricardo and his leftwing students, as *simple elements of every labour process*. For him, neither capital nor labor was productive in itself: it was rather capitalism that was productive. If Ricardo had spoken not of labor but rather of labor capacity or labor power, he would have discovered the key to the mystery of this system.[40]

The worker's labor power was the only product on the market that had the special quality of producing more value than it was worth itself.[41] Its own value—namely, that which was required to reproduce the worker himself—represented only part of the value that could be produced through the use of his labor power for a specific period of time. Marx used this division between the labor that was necessary to reproduce the worker and the surplus labor attained through the use of the worker's labor power to explain new profits—in his terminology, surplus value. This surplus value would increase with the length of the workday; it would also increase when gains in productivity reduced the cost of reproducing labor power and the amount of time needed to produce the product. Marx called the first absolute surplus value and the second relative surplus value. At the moment that a general labor market developed, the market economy—due to the unique nature of labor power as a commodity—became a relation of capitalist production, which paradoxically can be based on both the principle of fair exchange and exploitation at the same time.

Did Marx consider the appropriation of surplus labor theft? No, he said: considered purely in legal terms, there could be no objections. Neither could such objections be raised against the right of the worker, as the seller of his labor, to limit the workday to a standard length: "There is here, therefore, an antinomy, right against right, both equally bearing the seal of the law of exchanges."[42] But this applied only to the sphere of the market. The labor contract having been concluded, the worker discovered that he was not a free agent, "that the time for which he is free to sell his labour-power is the time for which he is forced to sell it."[43] In contrast to the market, the relation of production was a relation of exploitation that, with the progress of productivity, was also materialized in the labor process itself. "Being independent of each other, the labourers are isolated persons," Marx maintained, but as part of a productive mechanism they were only a particular mode of the existence of capital.[44] This development reached its zenith with the Industrial Revolution, for only machinery allowed it to become a technologically tangible reality, in which the power of capital over labor could also become materially complete.[45] "Capitalist production, therefore, under its aspect of a continuous connected process, of a process of reproduction," declared Marx in conclusion, "produces not only commodities, not only surplus value, but it also produces and reproduces the capitalist relation; on the one side the capitalist, on the other the wage labourer."[46] All this necessarily followed in a particular way from the explication of the inner contradictions of the commodity, which first—through the expansion of trade relations—produced money, then—as the accumulation of money—capital, and finally—through the emergence of the labor market—capitalism. Marx developed this genesis as a logical evolution on the basis of his theory of labor value.

Yet in a preliminary excerpt in 1844, he had already presented a theory of capitalism that entirely lacked the labor-value theory and the surplus-value theory based on the former, and that in principle would also have been compatible with a theory of marginal utility. Even prior to his reception of the classical labor-value theory, Marx had maintained that the relation of exchange resulted in labor becoming "directly labour to earn a living," leading to all the consequences that would basically also characterize his later theory.[47] Regardless, Marx's central argument—with or without labor-value theory—was that market relations cannot explain profit; rather, the explanation must be sought in the relations of production, for the market could distribute value but not create it.

But what happens to the profit? And what role do the owners of capital themselves play in the production process? During his studies of economics, when he was driven by the question of how capitalists calculate the part of their income that they themselves consume and do not invest, Marx had to pose these questions to his capitalist friend Engels in Manchester, who was experienced in such matters. "In commerce the merchant as a firm, as a producer of profits," Engels answered, "and the same merchant as a consumer are two entirely different people who confront one another as antagonists. The merchant as a firm means capital account and/or profit and loss account. The merchant as a guzzler, toper, householder and procreator means household expense account." In the balance sheet, the latter was actually a pure loss and must be "written off the profit."[48] And it was in fact the case, as John Maynard Keynes wrote after the First World War, that the nouveaux riches of the nineteenth century did not tend toward lavish expenditures, preferring the power they obtained through their investments over the amenities of immediate consumption.[49]

More important, however, was the question of whether Engels's calculation was in fact correct. Did not the owner of capital, insofar as he was active in his own operation, also perform socially necessary labor as planner, director, and organizer of the production process? "The labour of superintendence and management," Marx asserted, "is naturally required wherever the direct process of production assumes the form of a combined social process, and not of the isolated labour of independent producers." That, too, he maintained, was *a productive job, which must be performed in every combined mode of production.*[50] Marx was indeed not concerned with the individual capitalist but rather with the relation of capital, which remained a property and class relation even if by far the largest portion of the profit flowed into reinvestment. Marx was not a moralist.

Without a doubt, capitalism was and is unjust. Yet Marx directed all of his ambition precisely toward showing that things were being done in a rightful manner in modern class society. He saw surplus value and exploitation as dialectic categories, not moral ones. Never, Engels insisted in 1884, did Marx base his communist demands on an indictment of exploitation. "He says only," Engels noted tersely, "that surplus value consists of unpaid labour, which is a simple fact."[51] Marx's communist argument was much more that a system based on economic anarchy would, because of its exploitative character, encounter irresolvable contradictions and thus at some point collapse. He had to make this argument because his theory, according to its own claims, dealt with the *natural laws of capitalist production*[52] and not with moral indignation. These laws were the focus of the final chapter of the first volume of *Capital* and especially the chapter in the third volume about the tendency of profit rates to fall.

The individual capitalist in this great game, in Marx's assessment, was only a chess piece. His deployment was subject to pain of destruction, for competition dictated the immanent laws of capitalistic production as external coercive laws. "It compels him to keep constantly extending his capital, in order to preserve it, but extend it he cannot, except by means of progressive accumulation."[53] For Marx, this coercive mechanism was at the same time responsible for capitalism's revolutionary role in world history, namely, to create at all costs a *world of social wealth*.[54] Continuing technological innovation and increasing productive capacity of labor, as well as a concomitant increase in relative surplus value and the rate of exploitation, were the necessary consequences of this mechanism. In short, the colossal progress that he was able to observe in his lifetime had an *antagonistic character*.[55] "As the bourgeoisie develops, there develops in its bosom a new proletariat, a modern proletariat," he wrote as early as 1847 in *The Poverty of Philosophy*, directed against Proudhon. "From day to day it thus becomes clearer that the production relations in which the bourgeoisie moves have not a simple, uniform character, but a dual character; that in the selfsame relations in which wealth is produced, poverty is also produced."[56] The same antinomic ideas were also taken up twenty years later in the chapter on the general laws of capitalistic accumulation in the first volume of *Capital*. But they did not exactly conform to the facts of this same period. If, for the year 1850 in France, for example, one assumed an index of 100, then for 1870 the corresponding indices would be 358 for total profits, 175 for wages, and 123 for living expenses. Things looked similar in the other industrialized countries of Europe.[57] Profits had admittedly increased dramatically, but real wages had risen modestly as well. This corresponded to the figure of scissors, but hardly that of an antinomy.

In 1912, when Werner Sombart took stock of Germany's economic development in the nineteenth century, his results came as a surprise to many of his contemporaries. First, it was not true that the poor had grown increasingly poorer—not even those at the lowest levels of society who were commonly referred to as paupers. Second, the income of the middle classes had significantly increased. And third, it was not true that the number of the rich had increasingly shrunk—quite the opposite.[58] In many respects this contradicted Marx's prognosis, which along with the consolidation of wealth in an ever-decreasing number of hands also predicted the increasing proletarianization of the rest of the population.

To be sure, after the first great world economic crisis of 1857 and especially after the crisis of 1873—six years after the publication of the first volume of *Capital*—a significant concentration and centralization process was observable with respect to industrial enterprises and banks, and especially during the 1870s the formation of conglomerates, trusts, cartels, and syndicates increased. But even here, the developments did not take place so clearly in terms of polar opposites. The number of self-employed had in fact significantly declined during the second half of the nineteenth century, but while the trades were unable to maintain their position with respect to their share of total production, they managed to do so in terms of absolute numbers. In particular, metalworkers, construction workers, blacksmiths, locksmiths, plumbers, cabinetmakers, opticians, and also small business dealing with luxury goods proved quite capable of surviving.[59] In early July 1850 Marx himself stood fascinated in front of a model electric train on London's Regent Street, enthusiastic about the prospect that the "the electric spark" would in the future be even more revolutionary than "King Steam."[60] But he never considered the potential that would accrue in particular to small-scale industry and the trades through the development of serviceable three-phase motors.[61] He saw only what did not call his antinomic worldview into question.

Describing a central aspect of his general law of capitalist accumulation, Marx wrote:

> Accumulation, therefore, presents itself on the one hand as increasing concentration of the means of production, and of the command over labour; on the other, as repulsion of many individual capitals one from another. This splitting-up of the total social capital into many individual capitals or the repulsion of its fractions one from another, is counteracted by their attraction. This last does not mean that simple concentration of the means of production and of the command over labour, which is identical with accumulation. It is concentration of capitals already formed, destruction of their individual independence, expropriation of capitalist by capitalist, transformation of many small into few large capitals.[62]

Basically, the law was supposed to demonstrate that capital was well on its way toward passing a sentence of expropriation against itself, whereby a Hegelian figure of sublation would follow.[63] "One capitalist always kills many."[64] Marx was not so much describing a real, and actually observable, course of events during his time but rather the logical figure of a polarization: on the one hand, the expropriation of capital by capital led to growing concentration and centralization; on the other hand, the same process led to the downfall of the middle classes, the growth of the proletariat, and the mass of unemployed that Marx called the "industrial reserve army." "It follows therefore," he concluded, "that in proportion as capital accumulates, the lot of the labourer, be his payment high or low, must grow worse."[65] But growing along with "the mass of misery, oppression, slavery, degradation, exploitation," Marx reasoned on the basis of this antinomic coercive mechanism, was also the outrage of "the working class, a class always increasing in numbers, and disciplined, united, organized by the very mechanism of the process of capitalist production itself."[66]

Here his language suddenly acquired the violence of Old Testament prophets like Isaiah, who in his purifying judgment promised some that they would be "smoke in my nostrils" and others that the Lord would create for them "new heavens and a new earth."[67] "The knell of capitalist private property sounds," Marx announced at the end of the first volume in the tone of a punishing World Judge: "The expropriators are expropriated," for the capitalistic mode of production begot, *with the inexorability of a law of Nature, its own negation.* For Marx, this inversion meant a final *negation of negation*:[68] the riddle of history that he had pursued for a quarter of a century was also finally solved by means of positive science. In reality, however, this was just the explosive seduction of a logical antinomy laden with tremendous historical-theological emotions.

Crisis and End Times

Marx naturally saw himself as a scientific theoretician of social evolution who operated on a strictly empirical basis. "Darwin's work is most important and suits my purpose in that it provides a basis in natural science for the historical class struggle," he wrote to Lassalle in mid January 1861: "One does, of course, have to put up with the clumsy English style of argument. Despite all shortcomings, it is here that, for the first time, 'teleology' in natural science is not only dealt a mortal blow but its rational meaning is empirically explained."[69] He did not want to say that his theory bore similarities to Darwin's natural selection. But the idea that teleology could have a rational core had fascinated him ever since he thought he had discovered the rational core of absolute knowledge from Hegel's *Phenomenology of Spirit* in the communist sublation of the alienation of man.[70] The difference, though, was that Darwin did not make prognoses about the future of species. He had discovered in human anatomy the key to the anatomy of other species, but his view of evolution always remained retrospective. Had Marx actually been the one who, as Engels stated in a eulogy upon his friend's death in 1883, like Darwin recognized the "fundamental law according to which human history moves and develops itself,"[71] he would have contented himself with the role of Minerva's owl, which began its flight only with the fall of dusk. There are no scientific statements about the future of history, and if one seeks a general guiding criterion, at most it is the very indeterminate notion that the course of history is marked by increasing complexity.[72]

Even so, if one formulates the parameters as did Ernest Gellner, for example, who is beyond any suspicion of having Marxist sympathies, then historical materialism and the theory about modes of production were indeed discoveries. "The contention is," Gellner maintained, "that the economic or productive base does indeed determine our problems, but that it does not determine our solutions."[73] Capitalism is undoubtedly a problematic system, a fact that is revealed especially by its periodic outbreaks of crisis. Even today, with respect to this problem, the science of economics finds itself in a situation comparable to that of the geologist who very well knows the dangers of California's San Andreas Fault but does not know when the next earthquake will occur and how dangerous it could be for the city of San Francisco. In 1954, John Kenneth Galbraith wrote in his classical book about the Great Crash of 1929: "The causes of the Great Depression are still far from certain."[74] And Joan Robinson, a student of John Maynard Keynes, noted in 1966, shortly before a much less intense crisis: "It is impossible to understand the economic system in which we are living if we try to interpret it as a rational scheme."[75] Nothing about this has changed since then. As a leading theorist in America, Lester Thurow, once said, crises are "built into its [capitalism's] genetic code."[76]

Marx thought so too, and this insight was perhaps one of his most important discoveries. At the beginning of the nineteenth century, James Mill, the father of Marx's occasional visitor and discussion partner John Stuart Mill, had developed the thesis about the "metaphysical necessity" of market equilibrium, which was brought to the attention of the public by the Frenchman Jean-Baptiste Say[77] and has represented the creed of all market fundamentalists ever since. The view of the *tedious Say*, noted Marx, "that *overproduction* is not possible or at least that no *general glut of the market* is possible" is basically founded on nothing but the naive and simplistic illusion that in a developed market economy "*products* are exchanged *against products*."[78] Pure humbug, he wrote on this occasion: as if modern capitalism was simply barter trade that had existed for eons, but only on a far greater scale.

In contrast, the entire architectonics of Marx's great economic work, starting with the commodity as a "cell form"—the "genetic code" of the modern world—and going into many individual details, was a highly complex portrait of an economic system. Not only was it not based on a simple barter system, but together with the market, it had formed an entity—always endangered and contradictory—whose determining measure was the profitability of capital and not the consumer needs of market participants. In this system there was no metaphysical equilibrium; nor could there be, for the system consisted of too many contradictory elements. However, without equilibrium it was not viable in the long term. Whatever was not there therefore had always to reestablish itself, in the normal case through market fluctuations and in extreme cases through violent corrections, marking the moment of the outbreak of a crisis.

Hardly anyone has described the roots of this mechanism as precisely as Marx. His philosophical background, which elsewhere misled him into historical-theological speculation, served him well here. Making use of Hegel, Marx described capitalism as an identity of identity and non-identity,[79] thus a *unity of the different aspects*,[80] which, as a unity, must necessarily assert its inner contradictions at some point in the process of its development. As with the relation of capital itself, its periodic crises were also, for Marx, already founded in the form of the commodity. "No one can sell unless some one else purchases. But no one is forthwith bound to purchase, because he has just sold," it says in the first book of *Capital:*

> To say that these two independent and antithetical acts have an intrinsic unity, are essentially one, is the same as to say that this intrinsic oneness expresses itself in an external antithesis. If the interval in time between the two complementary phases of the complete metamorphosis of a commodity become too great, if the split between the sale and the purchase become too pronounced, the intimate connexion between them, their oneness, asserts itself by producing—a crisis.[81]

Marx posited these diverging trajectories of selling and buying as the most general cell form of the crisis, the *potential crisis* as he formulated it, but *without content, without a compelling motivating factor.*[82] They were, formulated in Hegelian fashion, its intrinsic potential form, which had to be complemented by a series of factors before it could turn into an actual crisis.

Like a hidden virus, this cell form could quickly produce a veritable outbreak of a disease once it no longer pertained merely to buying and selling but rather to the investment of capital. If such an investment became unprofitable or was even threatened with losses, accumulation faltered. The reasons for this varied, but as a rule they had something to do with general overproduction in relation to solvent demand,[83] which could be covered for a certain time through an expansion of credit.[84] Market disproportions could play a role in this, but the key factor was above all consumer power *based on antagonistic conditions of distribution*—that is, the buying potential of the working population, which was limited by the relation of capital itself.[85] At some point, the money lay fallow, and this phenomenon of idle capital, according to Marx, *usually precedes crises.*[86] It often found ways that only led faster to the outbreak of a crisis—for example, speculative transactions. John Kenneth Galbraith classically described this mechanism using the example of the Florida boom and other bubbles prior to the Great Crash of 1929. Marx observed it for the first time during the crisis of 1857. Uncommitted capital from trade and industry moved into the stock market, allowing stock prices to rise to completely unrealistic heights. This occurred chiefly with respect to railway stocks, even though, as Marx wrote to Engels, revenues had in places dropped dramatically by a quarter. It was, he maintained, nothing but *gambling in market*[87]—a game of pure chance that at some point would inevitably collapse.

In extreme conditions, a new *consonance* of the market, according to Marx, could be reached only by *passing through the most extreme dissonances.*[88] Basically, he viewed the crisis as empirical proof of the validity of the unconsciously asserted law of value: a de facto trial-and-error process that could strikingly prove the veracity of his theoretical deductions. "The world trade crises," he concluded, "must be regarded as the real concentration and forcible adjustment of all the contradictions of bourgeois economy."[89] There is little to object to here, even if Marx devoted only scant attention to the psychological factors that generally play a large role in overspeculation. An extreme early example of this was the Dutch tulip bubble of the 1630s, which burst after speculation had driven up the value of four black tulips to that of a house on the Grachtenring in the center of Amsterdam.[90] But this preindustrial though nonetheless capitalistic trade crisis did not affect the entire economy. And even extreme psychological irrationalities could come into play only in a system that revealed the capitalistic genetic code observed by Marx.

Even Marx's theory could hardly predict when, under what circumstances, and with what intensity a crisis would erupt. However, it is an undisputed fact that each *bust* to date has been followed by a *boom*. Marx did not see this any differently: "a crisis always forms the starting-point of large new investments," he maintained.[91] Periodic "crooked dealing" was virtually a prerequisite for "*respectable* trade and industry."[92] Marx regarded a large crisis as not merely a violent adjustment of disproportionalities that occurred at the moment when, in line with Hegelian logic, "all conditions"[93]—inner contradictions and external causes—required for its eruption were at hand. It also formed the privileged mechanism by which capitalism, in correcting its immanent destructive tendencies, secured its immediate survival. Apart from that, Marx held, the periodic devaluation of available capital through crises was a means—intrinsic to capitalism itself—to stop the fall of general profit rates and accelerate the accumulation of capital value through the creation of new capital.[94]

He did not invent this theory. Adam Smith had thought he could discern a trending decline in profit rates through the indicator of empirically rising interest rates, and David Ricardo observed that the pressure of a growing industrialized population on scarce natural resources necessarily then led to increasing food prices and rents. As a countermeasure, Smith recommended the expansion of international trade to increase profit rates; Ricardo promised similar results from free importation of cheap grain from overseas.[95] Marx could not accept such solutions, first of all because they were purely national-economic in nature. For an analysis of the global economy, which was his aim, they were not applicable because over time on a global scale their effects would disappear on their own. At heart, however, his criticism pertained to the fact that neither Smith nor Ricardo wanted to view the trend of falling rates of profit as an *inherent law* of capitalism. They stood before a phenomenon they admittedly perceived, but they could not explain it because they sought external causes for something that, according to Marx, could only be found in the inherent contradictions of the system itself. As Hegel once said, just as cold or wetness could hardly be the cause of a fever,[96] the reasons provided by Smith and Ricardo could hardly be the cause of the trend of falling rates of profit.

Marx saw profit as a different category from surplus value. The latter indicated the relation of the value of labor power to the value newly produced by that labor power within a certain period of time. In contrast, profit represented the actual gains of capital. It was calculated on the basis of total expenses, which included above all—apart from labor power—the amortization value of the technological facilities used. To be sure, these facilities in themselves did not produce any value, but they were the product of previous labor and in that respect represented a value. Marx therefore called them constant capital, as opposed to the variable capital of labor power, which produced new value. The development of technological innovation, however, engendered an always-changing relation between constant and variable capital in favor of constant capital—which in Marx's terminology was the equivalent of capital's increasing organic composition of value. In this *simple*-to-discover relationship, he thought he had now discovered *the mystery whose solution has been the goal of all political economy since Adam Smith.*

The *actual tendency of capitalist production,* according to Marx, produced namely "a progressive relative decrease of the variable capital as compared to the constant capital, and consequently a continuously rising organic composition of the total capital. The immediate result of this is that the rate of surplus value, at the same, or even a rising, degree of labour exploitation, is represented by a continually falling general rate of profit." The general profit rate's progressive tendency to fall, Marx continued, was only *an expression peculiar to the capitalist mode of production* of the progressive development of the social productivity of labor.[97] Sticking with Hegel's analogy, it was neither cold nor wetness that caused the fever, but rather the virus—the relation of capital itself—whose driving force was represented precisely by the profit rate. It was, for Marx, at once the driving force and the cause of disease for capitalism, and he assumed the actual cause of the English economists' anxiety over declining rates of profit lay in this inherent contradiction.[98] For Marx, meanwhile, the trend toward decline was for the same reason *the most important law of modern political economy*.[99] From his perspective, this law could decisively prove that the *real barrier of capitalist production is capital itself*.[100] For him it was another critical fulcrum of the scientific demonstration of an impending negation of the negation.

In any case, that was the trend. Considering the enormous development of productive powers during the past thirty years alone, Marx cautiously maintained in the third volume of *Capital*, instead of the previous difficulty of explaining the falling profit rate, the difficulty arose of explaining why this fall had not occurred faster and more severely. There must obviously be *counteracting influences at work, which cross and annul the effect of the general law, and which give it merely the characteristic of a tendency*.[101] Within the generally fragmentary third volume, the chapter on counteracting tendencies, written in manuscript in the mid 1860s, remained especially fragmentary—as if Marx had meanwhile been gripped by the same fear he had ascribed to Smith and Ricardo when formulating his general law. He identified the predominant factors as the increase in the degree of exploitation and the decline of wages below the value of labor power, international trade, and the declining cost and increased efficiency of technology. Apart from increased productivity in agriculture and consumer goods production, which he did not mention, the latter was actually the salient point. This namely shows, according to Marx, "that the same influences which tend to make the rate of profit fall, also moderate the effects of this tendency."[102] However, this in turn prompted the question whether technological progress actually had to lead necessarily to an increase in capital's organic composition of value.[103] Marx himself conceded that the mass of elements of constant capital could certainly increase while its value remained the same or even fell.[104] And in fact, since Marx's time capitalism's greatest progress has been the declining costs of production techniques. What could only have been seen as an exception during his time later became the rule in industrial and agricultural development.[105] For Marx, however, above all else, the *periodical depreciation of existing capital* during economic crises was the actual systemically inherent means to reduce the fall of profit rates.[106] Still, he believed, none of this would ultimately change the fact that the fall of profit rates, despite counteracting tendencies, ultimately had to lead to the collapse of capitalism. It could be no other way, without calling his entire theoretical construct into question.

At the beginning of the 1880s he arrived at the conviction that the old ten-year cycle was over, and that in future intermediate crises would make themselves felt at shorter intervals. Engels even saw this as evidence of the complete exhaustion of capitalism. "If, from being acute, the crises becomes chronic yet lose nothing of their intensity, what is likely to happen?" he wrote in 1886 to August Bebel: "We have entered a period which poses a far greater threat to the existence of the old state of society than did the period of ten-year crises."[107] In any event, Marx had long ago predicted the scenario that would be staged during these end times. Pronouncing his curse on the capitalistic market economy at the end of the 1850s, Marx wrote: "The growing discordance between the productive development of society and the relations of production hitherto characteristic of it, is expressed in acute contradictions, crises, convulsions. The violent destruction of capital as the condition for its self-preservation, and not because of external circumstances, is the most striking form in which it is advised to be gone and to give room to a higher state of social production."[108] As of yet there has been no collapse, and capitalism has survived wars, great catastrophes, and thereby also the hypothesis of falling profit rates. What actually occurs after severe crises has always been a new organization of capitalism at a more effective level.

But Marx only saw the antinomic alternative between a dubious metaphysical market equilibrium and the idea of *common, all-embracing and far-sighted control*[109] that would banished the chaos of crises, transition capitalism to common property, and at the same time, by abolishing the law of value, end the domination of profit rates. The solution he had in mind was very simple—indeed, in principle, insufficiently complex—if he believed that the situation could be mastered by suspending the *production relation itself which is expressed in the category of money*[110] and replacing it with a thoroughly planned *organization of labor.*[111] Apparently, in 1843, while Marx was working through Hegel's political law in Kreuznach, it occurred to him briefly that such models would necessarily develop new systemic contradictions. Every bureaucracy, he noted at the time, had a tendency to consider the entity of the state—and subsequently the state-analogous management of affairs that Marx had in mind as a future prospect after the "death of the state"—as its *private property,* and every bureaucrat was thus compelled to *deal with the actual state jesuitically.*[112] Yet he never came back to this idea.

Thereafter, for the rest of his life, enchanted by the inverted historical theology of his eleventh thesis on Feuerbach, Marx wanted to changed an inverted world by leveling complexities—instead of only interpreting the world and thereby perhaps making it controllable within limits. A proper interpretation of the contradictions of capitalism would, in any event, have secured important advantages. Every future policy of state (and global) regulation ultimately relies on how and to what extent policy makers properly interpret what is supposed to be regulated. Marx's theory provided important theoretical approaches and suggestions. Equally significantly, however, and in all of his writings from beginning to end, his description of a communist future was always an unsteady walk on thin ice.

Notes

1. Quoted in Melvin J. Lasky, *Utopia and Revolution: On the Origins of a Metaphor* (Chicago, 1976), 628, note 96.
2. Joseph Schumpeter, *Kapitalismus, Sozialismus und Demokratie* (Bern, 1950), 78, 12.
3. Nipperdey, *Deutsche Geschichte 1800–1866*, 525.
4. George Soros, *Die Krise des globalen Kapitalismus: Die offene Gesellschaft in Gefahr* (Frankfurt am Main, 2000), 27f.
5. Charles Taylor, "Kapitalismus ist unser faustischer Pakt," in *Fegefeuer des Marktes: Die Zukunft des Kapitalismus*, ed. Jens Jessen (Munich, 2006), 10f.
6. Richard Sennett, *Die Kultur des neuen Kapitalismus* (Berlin, 2007), 19.
7. Liebknecht, *Karl Marx*, 131.
8. Paul Lafargue, "Karl Marx, Persönliche Erinngerungen," in *Mohr und General: Erinnerungen an Marx und Engels* (Berlin, 1985), 318.
9. Marx to Kugelmann, 13 October 1866, in *MECW*, vol. 42, 328.
10. Marx to Johann Philipp Becker, 17 April 1867, in *MECW*, vol. 42, 358.
11. Smith, Adam, *An Inquiry Into the Nature and Causes of the Wealth of Nations*, vol. 2, *The Glasgow Edition of the Works and Correspondence of Adam Smith*, 6 vols., electronic edition (InteLex 2002), vol.1, 54.
12. Marx, preface to the first German edition of *Capital*, vol. 1., in *MECW*, vol. 35, 10.
13. Marx to Ludwig Kugelmann, 11 July 1868, in *MECW*, vol. 43, 68.
14. Jindrich Zeleny, *Die Wissenschaftslogik und 'Das Kapital'* (Frankfurt am Main, 1968), 23ff.
15. Marx, *Capital*, vol. 3, in *MECW*, vol. 37, 818, 266.
16. Marx, afterword to the second German edition of *Capital*, vol. 1, in *MECW*, vol. 35, 19.

17. Georg Wilhelm Friedrich Hegel, *Hegel's Doctrine of Formal Logic*, in *G.W.F. Hegel: The Oxford University Press Translations*, 117ff.
18. Helmut Reichelt, *Zur logischen Struktur des Kapitalbegriffs bei Karl Marx* (Frankfurt am Main, 1970), 144.
19. Jürgen Habermas, *Zur Rekonstruktion des Historischen Materialismus* (Frankfurt am Main, 1976), 115.
20. Marx, *Outlines of the Critique of Political Economy*, in *MECW*, vol. 28, 37.
21. Ibid., 37f.
22. Marx, preface to the first German edition of *Capital*, vol. 1, in *MECW*, vol. 35, 8.
23. Zeleny, *Die Wissenschaftslogik und "Das Kapital,"* 53, 136.
24. Marx, *Capital*, vol. 1, in *MECW*, vol. 35, 83.
25. Reichelt, *Zur logischen Struktur des Kapitalbegriffs bei Karl Marx*, 137.
26. Marx, *Contribution to the Critique of Hegel's Philosophy of Law*, in *MECW*, vol. 3, 176.
27. Marx, *Capital*, vol. 1, in *MECW*, vol. 35, 616.
28. Ibid., 85.
29. Ibid.,10f.
30. Louis Althusser and Etienne Balibar, *Das Kapital lesen*, 2 vols. (Reinbek, 1972), vol. 2, 247.
31. Marx, *Capital*, vol. 1, in *MECW*, vol. 35, 9.
32. Ibid., 588.
33. Marx, *Theories of Surplus Value*, in *MECW*, vol. 30, 385.
34. Ibid., 387.
35. Marx, *Theories of Surplus Value*, in *MECW*, vol. 31, 252.
36. Ibid., vol. 32, 397.
37. Bedarida, "Der Sozialismus in England bis 1848," 54ff.
38. Marx, *Theories of Surplus Value*, in *MECW*, vol. 32, 404f.
39. Ibid., 398.
40. Ibid., 37.
41. Engels, introduction to Marx, *Wage Labour and Capital*, in *MECW*, vol. 27, 200.
42. Marx, *Capital*, vol. 1, in *MECW*, vol. 5, 243.
43. Ibid., 306.
44. Ibid., 338.
45. Ibid., 426.
46. Ibid., 577.
47. Marx, "Comments on James Mill, Élémens D'économie Politique, 1844," in *MECW*, vol. 3, 219.
48. Engels to Marx, 3 April 1851, *MECW*, vol. 38, 327.
49. Joan Robinson, *Economics: An Awkward Corner* (New York, 1967), 3.
50. Marx, *Capital*, vol. 3, in *MECW*, vol. 37, 381.
51. Engels, preface to the first German edition of Marx, *The Poverty of Philosophy*, in *MECW*, vol. 26, 282.
52. Marx, *Capital*, vol. 1, in *MECW*, vol. 35, 9.
53. Ibid., 588.
54. Ibid.

55. Marx, *Capital*, vol. 1, in *MECW*, vol. 35, 640.
56. Marx, *Poverty of Philosophy*, in *MECW*, vol. 6, 175.
57. Schnerb, *Europa im 19. Jahrhundert*, 322.
58. Werner Sombart, *Die deutsche Volkswirtschaft im 19. Jahrhundert*, quoted in Michael Stürmer, *Das ruhelose Reich: Deutschland 1866–1918* (Munich, 2004), 65.
59. Michael North, ed., *Deutsche Wirtschaftsgeschichte* (Munich, 2000), 228.
60. Liebknecht, *Karl Marx; Biographical Memoirs*, 57.
61. North, *Deutsche Wirtschaftsgeschichte*, 243.
62. Marx, *Capital*, vol. 1, in *MECW*, vol. 35, 621.
63. "The repulsion therefore has an equal right to be called Attraction; and the exclusive One, or Being-for-self, suppresses itself": Georg Wilhelm Friedrich Hegel, "The Science of Logic," in Hegel, *Encyclopaedia of the Philosophical Sciences*, §84, OUP Translation, 143.
64. Marx, *Capital*, vol. 1, in *MECW*, vol. 35, 750.
65. Ibid., 639.
66. Ibid., 750.
67. Isa. 65: 5 and 17.
68. Marx, *Capital*, vol. 1, in *MECW*, vol. 35, 750.
69. Marx to Lassalle, 16 January 1861, in *MECW*, vol. 41, 246f.
70. Marx, *Economic and Philosophic Manuscripts of 1844*, in *MECW*, vol. 3, 331.
71. Engels, draft of a speech at the graveside of Karl Marx, published in the newspaper *La Justice*, 20 March 1883, in *MECW*, vol. 24, 463.
72. Habermas, *Zur Rekonstruktion des Historischen Materialismus*, 155.
73. Ernest Gellner, *Plough, Sword and Book* (Chicago, 1988), 19.
74. John Kenneth Galbraith, *The Great Crash 1929* (New York, 2009), 171.
75. Robinson, *Economics: An Awkward Corner*, 3.
76. Lester C. Thurow, *Fortune Favors the Bold: What We Must Do to Build A Long and Lasting Global Property* (New York, 2003), 90.
77. Marx, A Contribution to the Critique of Political Economy, in *MECW*, vol. 29, 333.
78. Marx, *Theories of Surplus Value*, in *MECW*, vol. 32, 124.
79. Georg Wilhelm Friedrich Hegel, *The Difference between Fichte's and Schelling's System of Philosophy* (Albany, 1977), 156.
80. Marx, *Theories of Surplus Value*, in *MECW*, vol. 32, 131.
81. Marx, *Capital*, vol. 1, in *MECW*, vol. 35, 123.
82. Marx, *Theories of Surplus Value*, in *MECW*, vol. 32, 140.
83. Ibid., 137.
84. Engels to Marx, 11 December 1857, in *MECW*, vol. 40, 220.
85. Marx, *Capital*, vol. 3, in *MECW*, vol. 37, 243.
86. Marx, *Theories of Surplus Value*, in *MECW*, vol. 32, 126.
87. Marx to Engels, 25 December 1857, in *MECW*, vol. 40, 231; translator's note: the words here are translated directly from the German version, *MEW*, vol. 29, 237f.
88. Marx, *Outlines of the Critique of Political Economy*, in *MECW*, vol. 28, 86.
89. Marx, *Theories of Surplus Value*, in *MECW*, vol. 32, 140.
90. Thurow, *Fortune Favors the Bold*, 50.

91. Marx, Capital, vol. 2, in MECW, vol. 36, 188.
92. Marx to Engels, 8 December 1857, in MECW, vol. 40, 216.
93. Quoted in Zeleny, Die Wissenschaftslogik und "Das Kapital," 3; quotation translated by Bernard Heise.
94. Marx, Capital, vol. 3, in MECW, vol. 37, 248.
95. Joseph M. Gillman, Das Gesetz des tendenziellen Falls der Profitrate (Frankfurt am Main, 1969), 9ff.
96. Georg Wilhelm Friedrich Hegel, Wissenschaft der Logik, vol. 2, Werke in zwanzig Bänden, ed. Eva Moldenhauer, 20 vols. (Frankfurt am Main, 1969–1971), vol. 6, 228.
97. Marx, Capital, vol. 3, in MECW, vol. 37, 211.
98. Ibid., 257f.
99. Marx, Outlines of the Critique of Political Economy, in MECW, vol. 29, 133.
100. Marx, Capital, vol. 3, in MECW, vol. 37, 248.
101. Ibid., 230.
102. Marx, Capital, vol. 3, in MECW, vol. 37, 234; Marx, Theories of Surplus Value, in MECW, vol. 32, 542.
103. Gillman, Das Gesetz des tendenziellen Falls der Profitrate, 29.
104. Marx, Capital, vol. 3, in MECW, vol. 37, 234.
105. Gillman, Das Gesetz des tendenziellen Falls der Profitrate, 35.
106. Marx, Capital, vol. 3, in MECW, vol. 37, 248.
107. Engels to August Bebel, 20–23 January 1886, in MECW, vol. 47, 390.
108. Marx, Outlines of the Critique of Political Economy, in MECW, vol. 29, 134.
109. Marx, Capital, vol. 3, in MECW, vol. 37, 121.
110. Marx, Outlines of the Critique of Political Economy, in MECW, vol. 28, 61.
111. Ibid., 108; translator's note: the words here are translated directly from the German version, Karl Marx, Grundrisse der Kritik der Politischen Ökonomie (Berlin, 1953), 42.
112. Marx, Contribution to the Critique of Hegel's Philosophy of Law, in MECW, vol. 3, 47; see also Daniel Bell, Die nachindustrielle Gesellschaft (Frankfurt am Main, 1979).

CONSEQUENCES

To the Sun, to Freedom

Thus, with a certain degree of inevitability, Marx's political effect was subject to the law of unintended consequences. The history of the International had already shown that Marx's greatest success came when he acted as a theoretician of union struggle, and that it surpassed its zenith the moment he wanted to proclaim his old chiliastic message of salvation after the Paris Commune. The history of German social democracy would stage anew this struggle between heaven and earth. Even during the 1848 revolution, Stefan Born's Workers' Brotherhood—at the time the most important workers' organization on the continent—was already marked by a "revisionist" softening of communist principles. "We are not conspiring against the existing regime," Born maintained during the revolutionary days, when he was still a member of the Communist League: "We only want to be allowed our own place in the common Fatherland."[1] The *real* workers' movement, as Marx was forced to learn with frustration, always revealed such traits of pragmatic softening bound up with the desire for civic recognition. The same problem would reappear with Lassalle and the British trade unions. Marx therefore watched German social democracy like a hawk.

Its history began with Lassalle's German Workers' Association, and over the course of time the Social Democratic Party became the first party in the world to explicitly invoke Marx. Above all it was a political entity that kept alive a wide range of traditions from 1848 in a counter-world that withdrew from the official world of the Kaiserreich.

The Socialist Workers' Party of Germany was established in 1875 in Gotha through the amalgamation of Ferdinand Lassalle's German Workers' Association, founded in 1863, and the Social Democratic Workers' Party that Wilhelm Liebknecht and August Bebel founded in Eisenach in 1868. Increasingly under suspicion in the new empire of being *vaterlandslose Gesellen* (journeymen without a fatherland), party members found strength in Marx's confidence in history, and especially in the comforting certainty that in the end they would stand with the victors, since developments would inevitably have to proceed along a trajectory in favor of the workers' movement. Marxism established itself on solid ground as a kind of secular religion of redemption; it was revolutionary only within limits, but Bismarck would be powerless against it in the long run. And through futuristic dreams popularized by best sellers like August Bebel's *Woman and Socialism*, it seduced hundreds of thousands readers with the consolation that the future held a better world where, after the expropriation of capitalists, a central plan would allow for a workday of only two or three hours, and where, once exploitation had disappeared, all crime would vanish as well. First published in 1879, Bebel's book had gone through fifty editions by 1909.[2] It contained much about a futuristic world along the lines of Fourier—something that could excite even bourgeois teenagers of the *Gründerzeit* with its faith in science—and a little Marx.

Capital found its readers much less easily. It took four years to sell the first thousand copies of the first edition. A French and Russian translation appeared in 1872. The latter in particular went through considerably more editions than the German version. Nikolai Ivanovich Sieber at the University of Kiev praised the book as an important further development of the theories of Adam Smith and David Ricardo, which very much flattered Marx.[3] But Sieber was basically a social liberal who—like the so-called Russian legal Marxists Mikhail Tugan-Baranovsky, Peter Struve, and Sergei Bulgakov—took from *Capital* above all the historical necessity of the capitalistic development of Russia. Ferdinand Freiligrath, who referred to himself as an *economist by instinct*, thought that many merchants and factory owners along the Rhine would be enthusiastic about the book, and that within these circles it would also fulfill its actual purpose. But the *terrible missile* occasionally had difficulty reaching its actual readers.

However, Arnold Ruge, Marx's erstwhile comrade-in-arms and later opponent during his time in Paris, conceded without envy that *Capital* was an "epoch-defining work," and that particularly the argument regarding surplus value through unpaid labor and the impending expropriation of the expropriators was classically successful.[4] Johann Baptist von Schweitzer reviewed the book in the *Social-Democrat*, as did the former tanner and autodidact Joseph Dietzgen in the *Demokratische Wochenblatt*.[5] Within Germany's social democratic movement, Liebknecht and Bebel admittedly considered themselves supporters of Marx, but this essentially pertained to only a couple fundamental programmatic points. Liebknecht felt that workers basically needed to clearly understand three things: first, that labor was the source of all value; second, that capital exploited the workers; and third, that in a social-democratic state wage labor needed to be replaced by an association. Anyone with a scholarly interest beyond that could, naturally, read *Capital*.[6] But Liebknecht himself had practical problems to solve. As he categorically informed Engels, Liebknecht was anyway of the opinion that theory and praxis were "two very different things."[7] He let Marx know that he would allow himself to be instructed on theoretical matters but that in the field of practice, compared to the Church Fathers in London, he was "somewhat more proficient."[8]

After the unification of the Reich in 1871, the two German workers' parties had found themselves under increasing pressure from above. Bismarck was gripped by a growing fear of "enemies of the Reich." At the end of March 1872, Bebel and Liebknecht were sentenced to two years in prison because of their negative attitude to the Franco-Prussian War and their sympathies for the Paris Commune. After crisis broke out in 1873, the situation grew more severe. In 1874, the General German Workers' Association was banned in Prussia. During the Reichstag election of the same year, however, Lassallean and Eisenach supporters of Marx campaigned successfully on shared electoral lists. Within the Reich as a whole they obtained only 6.5 percent of the votes, but regionally their successes were significantly higher in some places. In Hamburg they had 40.7 percent of the vote; in Saxony, 36.2 percent; in Schleswig-Holstein, 32.5 percent; and in Lübeck, 32.4 percent.[9] The ban in Prussia, the electoral successes, and the challenges of the crisis encouraged a unifying mood in both parties. The Lassalleans made an initial offer to the committee of Eisenachers sitting in Hamburg in fall 1874. On 22 May 1875, the party congress for unification took place in Gotha. One hundred twenty-seven delegates represented 29,659 members, the majority of whom were Lassalleans. Even so, Wilhelm Liebknecht was offered the office for dealing with program issues, and he could hardly manage to formulate anything beyond the previously negotiated pragmatic compromise.

Ever since the early 1850s when, exiled in London, he frequented Marx's home, Liebknecht had been a kind of confidant to the two heads of the movement in Germany. "He was my teacher," he said of Marx, who sometimes, according to Liebknecht, could destroy his enemies with the "aroused seriousness of Tacitus."[10] This aroused seriousness was now directed at him, after the appearance, without the Londoners' prior knowledge, of a jointly written program draft in the party press in early March 1875. Marx thought that such a *reprehensible program that demoralizes the Party*, which Liebknecht wanted to present in Gotha and from which Marx and Engels would remain *altogether remote*, could under no circumstances be recognized through diplomatic silence. It contained nothing but a blatant *canonization of the Lassallean articles of faith*, and the momentary success of unification was thus purchased far too dearly.[11] "Our party could hardly demean itself further," wrote Engels shortly thereafter, directing his anger at Bebel. "Neither Liebknecht nor anyone else has let us have any kind of information." Engels suspected that Liebknecht had allowed himself to be bamboozled by the Lassalleans. If the program was accepted, he threatened, he and Marx could "never recognise a new party set up on that basis." Hardly a word in this "insipidly written" program, he maintained, could withstand a serious critique.[12]

Marx composed comprehensive "Marginal Notes to the Programme of the German Workers' Party" and, even prior to the party congress, sent them to Germany. They were a scathing critique of the Gotha program, which in Marx's eyes did not reject a single one of the slogans once coined by Lassalle. He was especially annoyed by the formulation of the future "free basis of the state." Which state, he asked, noting that the freedom of the state basically only existed in raising itself above society, so no other state was as free as the despotic state in Russia. The question regarding the transformation of the state into a communist society, in contrast, could *only be answered scientifically*, the way Marx believed he had already done at the beginning of the 1850s. "Between capitalist and communist society," Marx continued in a final denunciation of Lassalle's phrasing, "there lies the period of the revolutionary transformation of the one into the other. Corresponding to this is also a political transition period in which the state can be nothing but the *revolutionary dictatorship of the proletariat*."[13] It was his last attempt to intervene in German politics. But it went largely unnoticed.

Liebknecht prudently kept the text under lock and key, thus assuring that only a very small circle of comrades were familiar with Marx's "Marginal Notes." If "the International had not created such a shameful fiasco," he shot back somewhat angrily at Engels, the unification would have taken place without problems, and it would have been easy to come together and agree upon the program of the International.[14] The latter was in any event, in contrast to Marx's irate drafts, not really a revolutionary program, as they both knew. Marx's concept of a revolutionary transition period of a proletarian dictatorship would never play a role in social democracy. His "Marginal Notes" simply disappeared amongst the files and were first published in 1891, not for political but rather antiquarian purposes—as a document from a bygone era in the history of the Social Democratic Party.[15] Only with Lenin and Bolshevism did the *Critique of the Gotha Programme* acquire the status of a fundamental revolutionary text. August Bebel took a very long time to respond to Engels's vehement accusations. He essentially agreed with Engels's critique of the draft of the program, Bebel wrote to London in September 1875, and he reproached Liebknecht harshly for his willingness to make concessions. But in general, he wrote, "we can be quite satisfied with the course of the party," placatingly invoking the mantle of history.[16] Marx would never again attempt with such severity to influence German social democracy.

Quite the contrary, in fact: he apparently came to terms with the old doctrines, namely that any real movement was better than a dozen programs.[17] "The muster-roll of the Social-Democratic party in Germany on the occasion of the general elections," he wrote enthusiastically in the beginning of 1877, "has rudely alarmed, not only our amiable German philistine, but also *les classes dominantes* in England and France." There was indeed a pleasant contrast between the *melodramatic fits and starts of the French* and the *businesslike way of proceeding of the German socialists*.[18] Apart from that, with social democratic workers' parties not only in Germany but also in other countries, he now felt that "instead of dying out, the International did only pass from its first period of incubation to a higher one where its already original tendencies have in part become realities."[19] Any new revolutionary spark ignited in the course of their sober, day-to-day business would probably concern the outbreak of revolution in Russia, which Marx once again feverishly expected in the wake of the Eastern Crisis of 1877. In this case, however, the *Social-Democratic legions at home* would be available in Germany and would very quickly convince the cultural philistines that there *are more important things in the world than Richard Wagner's music of the future.*[20] Marx was never quite able to decide between heaven and earth. Neither did he need to, at this point in time, for the Eastern Crisis ended anyhow with a compromise at the Berlin Congress.

Incidentally, as before, the *Social-Democratic legions* were a heterogeneous mass that hardly stood especially close to Marx's theories. The change was more or less the result of coincidence, having something to do with the sudden popularity of the writings of the blind and eccentric independent lecturer Eugen Dühring. Dühring gave lectures outside the university about his concept of a "socialistic" (*sozialitär*) transformation of the economy and his ethic of natural piety and courageously facing life; hordes of students with socialist inclinations and nonconformists streamed to these lectures as if they were revelations.[21] His voice was soft and his judgments were downright crude. He irreverently referred to Goethe as the *Kötchen* (little shit) and to Helmholtz as *Helmklotz* (helmet klutz); he called Gaussian mathematics a "geometry of stupidity." Shortly thereafter, Dühring also drew attention to himself as a militant anti-Semite when, in his book about the "Jewish question," he referred to the Jews as an "inner Carthage" "whose power must be broken by the modern nations [Völker] so that they do not themselves have to suffer the destruction by [this Carthage] of their moral and material foundations."[22] But that was in 1880. In the mid 1870s, the doctrines of this "new Communist" impressed even Bebel, no less so than they did the young bank employee Eduard Bernstein.

But when Dühring also took aim at Marx, calling him a "scientific portrait of misery" (*wissenschaftliche Jammergestalt*), Liebknecht boiled over, especially since he had just received an article written for *Vorwärts* that celebrated Dühring as a "fighter for science." He pressured London for a "sharp reckoning," but Engels, who was occupied with studies for his *Dialectics of Nature*, took his time making up his mind to do it. Marx was not available anyway, because Engels—who incidentally had been residing in London since 1870—was insisting that he complete the two subsequent volumes of *Capital*. Engels was "pestered ... dreadfully," as he noted in late November 1876, until he had undertaken the "disagreeable task"—"disagreeable because the man is blind so that the contest is unequal."[23] "Anti-Dühring" initially appeared as a series of articles in *Vorwärts* from January 1877 to July 1878 and then, shortly before the decree of the Anti-Socialist Laws, also as a book entitled *Herr Eugen Dühring's Revolution in Science*, published by Dietz in Stuttgart.

This book did more than anything else to spread Marxism throughout continental social democracy. Only after reading Engels's popular text about the "superiority of the Marx-Engels theory over all other justifications of socialism" did Bebel and Bernstein appeared to be convinced.[24] It was no different for Karl Kautsky, who was later the keeper of Grail of Marxism within social democracy, the exiled Russians Georgi Plekhanov and Pavel Axelrod, and the Italian Antonio Labriola. "Only now," wrote Engels's biographer Gustav Mayer, "did an actual Marxist school and tradition take form on the continent."[25] In 1889, this development led to the founding of the Second International of social democratic parties on an increasingly Marxist basis.[26] Marx became a very well-known figure even among European workers. At the beginning of the 1890s, Engels observed during a trip on the continent that Paris was virtually teeming with Marx medallions, and Germany, Austria, and Switzerland abounded with plaster busts of Marx.[27]

Engels's text against Dühring (Marx contributed substantially to its chapters on economics)[28] achieved its great popularity chiefly because it claimed to provide, within three hundred pages of clearly comprehensible language, a "more comprehensive view of the world." It explained what would later be called dialectical materialism—in the words of Engels, an "exact representation of the universe, of its evolution, of the development of mankind, and of the reflection of this evolution in the minds of men," and thus of nature, history, and thought. Such a representation, Engels continued, was only possible with the help of dialectics, which "comprehends things and their representations, ideas, in their essential connection, concatenation, motion, origin, and ending." Even the speculative figure of the negation of the negation became thus for Engels an "extremely general—and for this reason extremely far-reaching and important—law of development of nature, history, and thought." [29] Engels's text basically represented an attempt, in the form of a polemic against Dühring, to introduce a materialist version of Hegel's *Encyclopedia of the Philosophical Sciences* that, in terms of its construct, completely mimicked its Hegelian model. Like Hegel's text, it began with nature and, after a dialectical progressive movement, finished with socialism, which in the Hegelian original corresponded to Absolute Spirit. It struck a vital nerve in the zeitgeist of an epoch that craved a simple approach to the solution of all of the world's riddles.

Especially among freethinkers, "scientific worldview" was then an increasingly popular buzzword, and Engels was not the only one who opposed the closed worldview of theology and idealistic philosophy with a materialistic monism. But Engels considered himself, as a dialectician, vastly superior to authors like Ludwig Büchner, Ernst Haeckel, or Jacob Moleschott, whom he characterized as vulgar materialists. Additionally, he saw himself as the mouthpiece of the workers' movement, which, as he wrote a few years later, was the only legitimate "inheritor of German classical philosophy" and the only place where the "German aptitude for theory" remained unimpaired, whereas bourgeois science had long since regressed to "inane eclecticism."[30] Engels was the consequential founder of dialectical materialism and so-called proletarian science, which, however, would first come to full fruition during Stalin's real socialism.

For the time being, and especially after the promulgation of the Anti-Socialist Laws, it served social democrats, who were partially forced underground, as a kind of comforting philosophy. Bismarck won an initial battle when he finally managed to railroad a ban on the Social Democratic Party through the Reichstag on 18 October 1878. Two assassination attempts against the Kaiser in late spring that year had provided both the pretext and the required votes. Crown Prince Friedrich opposed the ban because he feared, quite rightly, that Bismarck's "war of annihilation" against Social Democrats would ultimately also affect the Liberals,[31] which would have been the reason his wife, Victoria, charged Grant Duff with learning more about Marx. The liberal crown prince, however, did not prevail. Forty-five social democratic newspapers, 1,300 print publications, and over 300 workers' organizations were banned, and

900 evictions were carried out from areas where the government declared a so-called small state of siege. Around 1,500 people ended up in prison.

But despite the prohibitions, arrests, evictions, and ruined lives, social democracy could not be erased from Germany's political life, especially since the prohibition applied to the party organization but not to the fraction in the Reichstag. During the twelve-year period in which it was banned, the number of social democratic voters increased fourfold. As Gordon A. Craig once noted, in an act of a conservative denial of reality Bismarck had completely underestimated the power of the social transformation.[32] He also underestimated the vitality of social democracy itself. Basically, Engels thought, Bismarck was once again working unwittingly "for us."[33] In 1879, a new party newspaper created in Zurich, the *Social Democrat*, spread throughout the Reich via an illegal postal service and was able to reestablish the connections between the party leadership and the individual party organizations. The first party congress of the Social Democrats in exile, which took place in 1880 at the Wyden castle in Switzerland, sided all the more strongly with Marx's ideas.

After the passing of Bismarck era, the Anti-Socialist Laws were abolished at the end of September 1890. At no time were the masses more aware of the class-based character of state and society than during the almost twelve-year duration of the emergency laws, Bebel reported on this day. Bebel had been shaping the party at least since the 1887 party congress in St. Gallen, and his prognosis about the inevitable "large unholy mess" (*großer Kladderadatsch*)—that is, the final crisis of the bourgeois world, which in the not-too-distant future would be replaced by a socialist "state of the future"—played a role here as well. In light of the *Gründerkrise*, which had already lasted longer than ten years, Bebel's expectation felt very immediate, like something that could happen at any time, almost overnight.[34] But the life of day-to-day politics suddenly gained increasing significance, inserting itself between the hopes for historical automatism and the utopia of a future state. The Erfurt Program of the SPD, resolved in 1891, made this apparent. It was the result of a cooperative effort by Karl Kautsky, the editor of the social democratic theory journal *Neue Zeit*, and Eduard Bernstein, who during the last two years of the Anti-Socialist Laws published the weekly journal *Sozialdemokrat* in London under Engels's wing.

Wholly in the tradition of Marx, Kautsky swore by capital's process of concentration and the system's susceptibility to crisis, concluding from this that

> Only the transformation of the capitalist private ownership of the means of production—land and soil, pits and mines, raw materials, tools, machines, means of transportation—into social property and the transformation of the production of goods into socialist production carried on by and for society can cause the large enterprise and the constantly growing productivity of social labor to change for the hitherto exploited classes from a source of misery and oppression into a source of the greatest welfare and universal, harmonious perfection.[35]

Shortly thereafter Kautsky wrote in *Neue Zeit* that the Social Democratic Party was admittedly "a revolutionary, but not a revolution-creating party," invoking this distinction to counter any possible rumors of an overthrow. Kautsky saw the revolution as something like a natural law of history that proceeded toward the collapse of capitalism.

But the second part of the Social Democrats' program, formulated by Bernstein, revealed an unabashed reform-oriented attitude. Bernstein believed less and less in the collapse of capitalism. The part of the program for which he was responsible dealt above all with numerous aspects of democratic reform: universal direct and secret voting rights for men and women; direct legislation by the people; a citizens' militia rather than a standing army; the guarantee of the right to the free expression of opinion, freedom of association, and freedom of assembly; the abolishment of all laws that contributed to the discrimination of women; the designation of religion as a private matter; the secularization of schools; free education and learning materials; free medical care and judicial administration; the election of judges by the people; the abolishment of the death penalty; and the reform of the tax code. For the protection of workers in particular, the following was demanded: the legal implementation of the eight-hour day; the prohibition of the gainful employment of children; an extensive ban on night work; guaranteed minimum rest periods; making the legal status of agricultural workers and servants equal to that of workers in commerce and industry; securing coalition rights for workers.[36] Engels thought that the theoretical portion of the Program was presentable, but that the practical demands could perhaps do with some corrections.[37] He apparently failed to notice that the Program featured the collision of two worlds that did not fit together.

Strangely enough, the Erfurt Program's combination of the prognosis of a *Kladderadatsch* and concrete democratic and social demands was precisely what captivated workers struggling for better economic conditions, social security, social recognition, and civic equality. This contradiction would define the social democratic movement until it could finally free itself from its counterworld milieu to become an integrated part of the society and state. The Erfurt Program continued to point the way for decades.

Its two authors, however, developed along different political lines: while Kautsky became one of the most influential interpreters of Marxist orthodoxy, Bernstein advocated increasingly openly for a revision of the Marxist understanding of socialism. He was ultimately successful, even if Rosa Luxemburg, on the Left within the party, accused him of wanting to transform social democracy into a democratic-socialist reform party and demanded his exclusion from the party.[38] "If the triumph of socialism is supposed to be an immanent economic necessity," Bernstein wrote in *Vorwärts* in late March 1899, "then it must be based on the proof of the inevitability of the economic collapse of the present society. This proof has not been provided and it cannot be provided."[39] Bernstein wanted social democracy to have its own Immanuel Kant, someone who would critically view the inherited Marxist theoretical system and "reveal where its apparent materialism [was] the highest and therefore most easily misleading ideology," because "the contempt of the ideal, the elevation of material factors to omnipotent powers of development" was nothing but a self-deception "that was and is exposed as such by the actions at every opportunity of the people who proclaim it."[40] In the future, a values- and reform-oriented political praxis would become the central element of social democratic politics, even though the language of revolution continued to dominate the social democratic milieu for a long time.

Was this a result that arose from Marx, subject to the law of unintended consequences? In a certain way, yes, for he always called for concrete steps in the struggle of the political economy of the proletariat against the political economy of the bourgeoisie and basically thought revolution possible only in exceptional circumstances. But if revolution did not occur, then the development toward social democratic reformism was simply a necessary realignment in accordance with reality that set in with capitalism's new phase of prosperity in the mid 1890s—which was no coincidence. Other realignments would at some point be due as well. "Those who create proletarians also create Social Democrats," Engels called out to his audience at a meeting in Berlin in late September 1893.[41] He sincerely believed that, according to the law of linear progression, if the party continued to grow at its previous rate "we shall have a majority between the years 1900 and 1910."[42] But this would never be the case. First, society would never be as polarized as Marx had predicted; second, not all workers were automatically social democrats. Thus, like social democrats in the rest of Europe who had joined the Second International, the party that had been created on the basis of Marx either had to become one among many democratic forces capable of forming coalitions or lapse into the status of a political sect. Marx always considered the latter to be the worst-case scenario. Only he had assessed the course of the *real movement*, to which he attached such great importance, differently and wrongly—resulting in consequences for civil society that, though unintended, were highly beneficial.

Salvation from the East

If social democracy developed as a critique of the Marxist heaven of ideas from an earthly perspective, then Bolshevism, in contrast, reinstated the unconditional dominion of that heaven. It was the second unintended consequence of Marx, who did not invent it. But in his old age, he saw Russia become a screen for the projection of almost messianic expectations—even though a phobia of Russia had previously been one of the most constant components of his worldview. Regarding the czarist regime as the most dangerous bulwark of the European Reaction, he had therefore called repeatedly for a revolutionary world war against Russia. Yet he also judged Alexander Herzen's and Mikhail Bakunin's faith in Russia's socialist calling to be nothing but a fanatical pan-Slavic conspiracy against civilization, going so far as to temporarily ally himself with the eccentric conservative David Urquhart simply because Urquhart publicly referred to Lord Palmerston—who during the Ottoman-Russian conflict stood on the side of Petersburg—as a paid agent of the czar.[43] At the beginning of the 1870s, however, his image of Russia began to change. Marx learned Russian[44] and immersed himself in the study of Russian agricultural conditions.[45]

During this period he let his Russian translator of *Capital* know that in the following volumes he would deal in detail with ground rents in their Russian form. Apart from that, he became interested in Nikolay Chernyshevsky and intended to write an article that would "create some interest in him in the West."[46] Nothing became of either of these intentions, but the *great Russian scholar and critic* Chernyshevsky rated honorable mention in the afterword to the second edition of *Capital* of 1873.[47] Chernyshevsky, Marx maintained, had written noteworthy articles on the question "whether Russia should start, as its liberal economists wish, by destroying the rural community in order to pass to a capitalist system or whether, on the contrary, it can acquire all the fruits of this system without suffering its torments, by developing its own historical conditions." Namely, if Russia, in its agricultural economy, continued to pursue the course of capitalism initiated by the Emancipation Reform of 1861 and the associated liberation of the peasants, it would *miss the finest chance that history has ever offered to a nation* and instead lose itself in the vicissitudes of capitalism.[48]

Chernyshevsky's name was closely associated with the movement of radical intelligentsia in the 1860s in Russia. A man with a German education, he had studied Hegel and, like Marx, had gained his materialistic worldview by way of Feuerbach, a worldview he first presented in his 1860 work *The Anthropological Principle in Philosophy*. Like many of his intellectual contemporaries, Chernyshevsky was deeply disillusioned with the results of the Emancipation Reform that Alexander II saw himself forced to undertake after the Crimean disaster. He became a socialist. From prison in 1862/63, he wrote his most famous work, the novel *What Is to Be Done?* Here he described life in a cooperative where a circle of conspiratorial political activists operated in the background; their leader, Rakhmetov, an ascetic and battle-hardened professional revolutionary, would later capture Lenin's imagination.[49] But Marx was more interested in Chernyshevsky's theoretical writings about the future of the Russian village community.

Chernyshevsky first mentioned the thesis that it was possible in Russia—and only in Russia—to bypass the phase of capitalistic development in order to arrive at socialism in an essay entitled "Critique of Philosophical Prejudices Against Communal Ownership." He was not an outspoken romantic and by Russian standards was something of a "Westerner" unopposed to the technological and scientific progress of capitalism. But he felt that in Russia, it was possible for modernization to operate on a communist basis from the outset by taking the common property of the village community as its point of departure. This, according to Chernyshevsky, would be a negation of the negation of archaic collectivism without the intermediate stage of capitalism.[50] Marx was so taken by this idea that he appropriated its figure of thought in almost all of its details. *Alone in Europe*, he claimed a few years later, the Russian community was *still the predominant organic form of rural life throughout an immense empire*. He continued:

> The common ownership of land provides it with the natural basis for collective appropriation, and its historical setting, its contemporaneity with capitalist production, lends it—fully developed—the material conditions for cooperative labour organised on a vast scale. It can thus incorporate the positive acquisitions devised by the capitalist system without passing through its Caudine Forks. It can gradually replace parcel farming with combined agriculture assisted by machines, which the physical lie of the land in Russia invites. Having been first restored to a normal footing in its present form, it may become the *direct starting point* for the economic system towards which modern society tends and turn over a new leaf without beginning by committing suicide.[51]

Russia might even display here an *element of superiority over the countries still enslaved by the capitalist regime*, Marx observed, if—and only if —*revolution comes at the opportune moment*. Faced with such prospects, Marx's ruminations rose to a height of pathos that sometimes verged on toppling over into unintentional sentimentalism. Even in *the district of Trier, in my native country*, he recalled with the long-term memory typical of a man his age, relics still existed of this archaic communal property, but only in Russia was it preserved extensively and without adulteration. It was as if these childhood memories and the associated romantic atavism had always been the unconscious springs that animated his utopia and were suddenly erupting again to assume authority by donning the garb of science.

In any case—with or without western capitalism's fall from grace—the historical agenda featured the *return of modern societies to the 'archaic' type of communal property, but in a superior form.*[52] As he maintained at the same time to refute Bakunin, Marx was still convinced that *a radical social revolution is bound up with certain definite historical conditions of economic development.*[53] But he believed that Russia, *thanks to a unique combination of circumstances*—above all because of its *contemporaneity with capitalist production*[54]—could avoid the mistakes of the West. This transfer of modernity to the East could take place only if the Revolution was also victorious in the West.

On the other hand, according to Marx's vision, a revolution in Russia could inspire the West. Just as his depiction of czarism as the center of the European Reaction was always larger than life, so too would be the consequences of its collapse.[55] "Russia, I believe, will play the most important part in the near future," his friend Engels wrote during the Eastern Crisis at the beginning of 1878:

> Whatever the outcome of the war, the Russian revolution is ready and it will break out soon, perhaps this year; it will begin, contrary to Bakunin's predictions, from above, in the palace, in the heart of the impoverished and *frondeuse* nobility. But once set in motion, it will sweep over the peasants, and you will then witness scenes in comparison with which those of '93 will pall. Once Russia has been pushed into revolution, the whole face of Europe will change.[56]

The *Bulgarian Horrors*—the Turkish massacre of an insurgent Bulgarian civilian population, which moved the British Liberal William Gladstone to launch a publicly effective protest and led to an early form of foreign policy based on human rights—was the immediate cause of the Eastern Crisis and Russia's intervention in the Balkans. Marx, however, saw only a Slavophile conspiracy at work here and in fall 1877 praised the *gallant Turks* for the severe *thrashing* they had given the Russians, which had initiated a *turning point in European history* by accelerating the erosion of czarism by years.[57] But shortly thereafter the Russian army was at the gates of Constantinople, and Sultan Abdülhamid II had to submit to the humiliating Treaty of San Stefano (today Yesilköy). "Things took a different course," conceded Marx, somewhat irritated.[58] Yet the hope for salvation from the East did not abandon him.

In late August 1879, the executive committee of the revolutionary Russian secret organization Narodnaya Volya—"People's Will"—sentenced Czar Alexander II to death for "crimes against the people." On 1 March 1881, they blew him sky-high with a bomb as he rode along a scenic embankment in his carriage.[59] Marx situated the *terrorist central committee* among those circles in Russia "where *Capital* is more read and appreciated than anywhere else,"[60] but this was not the only reason he showed sympathy for the assassination. In his eyes, the larger-than-life magnitude of czarist despotism necessarily required extraordinary action, *which no more lends itself to moralising—for or against—than does the earthquake in Chios*. He characterized the Petersburg assassins as *sterling chaps through and through, sans pose mélodramatique, simple, matter-of-fact, heroic*.[61] They had executed the will of the world.

Marx was not the only one to render such judgments. Even the *Social Democrat* maintained that in a country where there prevailed a tyranny like that in Russia, even poison and daggers, revolvers and dynamite must be regarded as permitted means to put an end to blood-soaked despotism.[62] Not even a staunch monarchist like Fyodor Dostoevsky could bring himself to condemn the assassin Vera Zasulich, who in late January 1878 severely wounded the governor of St. Petersburg, General Trepov, with a shot from a revolver. Punishing this woman, the author of *Demons* maintained, would be "inappropriate and superfluous."

Zasulich was in fact acquitted by a jury court.[63] She immigrated to Switzerland and in February 1881 turned inquisitively to Marx with her question about the future of the Russian village community. Those among the Russian emigrants who regarded these villages as having been sentenced to extinction "call themselves your disciples *par excellence*," she wrote to him.[64] Zasulich wanted his authentic opinion, and Marx replied that the analysis provided in *Capital* admittedly included no evidence whatsoever either for or against the viability of the village community; however, having engaged in *a special study* of the matter that included the use of original sources, he had become convinced *that this commune is the fulcrum of social regeneration in Russia*.[65]

This was not necessarily the view of the Marx supporters in Swiss exile whom Zasulich referred to, meaning in the first instance Georgi Plekhanov. He advocated the view that Russia by no means occupied a special place in the world: in his homeland as in others, the path to socialism was by way of capitalism, and to that extent the old peasant communities were sentenced to extinction.[66] Plekhanov held that a revolution that invoked socialism without fulfilling the necessary requirements would inevitably be a "political monster," a "tsarist despotism disguised in communist colors."[67] In principle, this kind of prognosis made Plekhanov the more rigorous Marxist, comparatively speaking.

In taking his position, Marx had in a certain sense even sided in favor of the romantic peasant socialism of the so-called ethnic traditionalists of the Narodnaya Volya party,[68] thus opening a viable path to the Bolshevist synthesis of the ethnic traditionalist movement and Marxism—which the social democrat Plekhanov decisively rejected. "If the Russian Revolution becomes the signal for a proletarian revolution in the West, so that the two complement each other," Marx wrote in the foreword to the second Russian edition of the *Communist Manifesto*, "the present Russian common ownership of land may serve as the starting point for communist development."[69] In this form, as Ernest Gellner once noted, Marxism appeared to be tailor-made for the Russian soul. It also resolved an apparently insurmountable Russian contradiction by reconciling the coercive tension between Russia's westernizing tendencies and its mystical, messianic, and populist inclinations to produce a unified vision.[70]

It was during the period of the Anti-Socialist Laws that Marx was suddenly gripped by his old revolutionary fever. The sooner czarism collapsed, he maintained, the sooner Bismarck's repressive policies would come to an end, and the wave of terror that beset Russia at the time seemed to herald its impending burial.[71] Plekhanov had spoken out quite clearly against terrorism; the immediate result of the czar's murder was the declaration of a state of emergency in many provinces in the Russian empire. It did not ignite a revolution, if only because the population remained indifferent in light of the assassination, whereas the terror increasingly took on an aimless life of its own.[72] Perhaps Marx was only infected by a brief flare-up of old-age radicalism, particularly since during the last years of his life his house increasingly became a meeting place for young Russian supporters and admirers. Not all of them were terrorists or revolutionaries; among them were people like Maxim Kovalevsky, a liberal opponent of czarism who after 1905 taught at Petersburg University and still, as an old man, considered Marx his beloved teacher. Also included was the young German Lopatin, who had vainly attempted to liberate Nikolay Chernyshevsky from his banishment in Siberia and had also, together with Nikolai Danielson, translated *Capital* into Russian.

But above all it was Russians like Plekhanov, Axelrod, Lev Deutsch, and finally also Vera Zasulich who were the first to officially call themselves "Marxists."[73] After Marx died on 14 March 1883, his burial in London's Highgate Cemetery was attended by scarcely more than a dozen close acquaintances, among them Wilhelm Liebknecht. Engels gave the eulogy. In Russia, however, Marx's death became a publicly recognized event. Students at the Petrovsky Agricultural Academy in Moscow sent a telegram expressly asking Engels to lay a wreath at his grave in their name.[74] "The Russian socialists," stated an address to the mourners from exiled groups in Paris, "bow before the grave of the man who sympathised with their strivings in all the fluctuations of their terrible struggle, a struggle which they shall continue until the final victory of the principles of the social revolution."[75] Much more so than in Germany and Western Europe, the doctrine of Marxism had gained a secure footing among the intelligentsia in Russia.

Here, too, was where it underwent its most radical revision and consequential reformulation. In 1902, Lenin—an aristocratic lawyer from Simbirsk on the Volga, already a second-generation Marxist, whose real name was Vladimir Ulyanov—wrote the foundational Bolshevik text *What Is to Be Done?* It was no coincidence that he borrowed the title from the Chernyshevsky novel featuring the character of the professional revolutionary Rakhmetov. In this text, Lenin called for an avant-garde party consisting of professional revolutionaries that, like a military formation, was to function according to the principle of central discipline. On the one hand, here Lenin was operating within the framework of Russian ethnic traditionalism, insofar as he reignited debate over an organizational model that Pyotr Tkachev, the first actual theoretician of the Russian revolution, had called for as early as 1874.[76] This was the pragmatic Russian characteristic of his plan.

On the other hand, however, he also sought a theoretical response to the Western European workers' movement's shift into so-called revisionism. Targeting a general problem in Marx's doctrine, Lenin wrote:

> The history of all countries shows that the working class, exclusively by its own effort, is able to develop only trade union consciousness, i.e., it may itself realize the necessity for combining in unions, for fighting against the employers, and for striving to compel the govern-

ment to pass necessary labor legislation, etc. The theory of socialism, however, grew out of the philosophic, historical, and economic theories that were elaborated by the educated representatives of the propertied classes, the intellectuals.[77]

Consequently, according to Lenin, political class consciousness could be brought to the workers "only from without"[78]—through the political mission of his envisioned organization of professional revolutionaries. Basically, he thereby said that the *real movement* that had always been held aloft by Marx inevitably had to undergo the reformist developments observable in Western European social democracy. Conversely, if one wanted to retain the original goals of communism, one had to decide against the *real movement*. Lenin corrected Marx by pulling the rug out from under his historical materialism.

The dilemma itself, however, was the result of a fundamental mistake by Marx. In 1845 he had written, and basically never questioned, the following:

> It is not a question of what this or that proletarian, or even the whole proletariat, at the moment *regards* as its aim. It is a question of *what the proletariat is,* and what, in accordance with this *being,* it will historically be compelled to do. Its aim and historical action is visibly and irrevocably foreshadowed in its own life situation as well as in the whole organisation of bourgeois society today.[79]

As Heinrich August Winkler once noted, Marx had succumbed to a historical fallacy when he tried to envision the future history of the modern proletariat in the role of a new universal class according to the model of the French Revolution of 1789.[80] The proletariat was—in contrast to its existence as a metaphysical assumption that was based on nothing—a sociological fact of modernity, not a world-historical class that could take the impulse of the storming of the Bastille to a higher level. Without openly saying so, Lenin saw things this way as well and thus had to either accept this fact or create a surrogate. Notoriously, he decided for the latter. Like a medieval order of knights, the Bolshevik party was to assert through violence this principle that had no equivalent in real historical development and civil life.

The results are well known. The rape of the earth led to the utopia of purges described by Gerd Koenen[81] and the domination of the surreal analyzed by Martin Malia,[82] which silently came to an end in autumn 1989. In the meantime the associated megalomania of the ability to create history claimed millions of victims. Are these to be blamed on Marx? Yes and no. Whoever stood by his conviction that communism was the *necessary* result of history then needed to produce it through violence, if Marx's prognoses proved unrealistic. In the end, the communist experiment failed due to a lack of the profane,[83] to a quasi-religious overloading of all real spheres of life. This fatal tendency, however, was already embedded in the materialistic eschatology of Marx's early writings. The landmark events of 1989 made it a profane year: human interests triumphed over what had long ago become an infirm, spiritless industrial variant of belief and redemption, and they did so without facing any resistance worth mentioning, running through doors that the Communist state powers had left open toward a freedom that had within seconds suddenly become possible. A clearer refutation of Marx's fundamental fallacies can hardly be imagined. However, this applies primarily to the political and historical-theological Marx.

For the same reason, during the Cold War Marx, as a theoretician of capitalism and historical evolution, had resided in a political ghetto; thus, with all of his fragmentary insights and contradictions, he remains to be discovered through impartial inquiry. It would be best, Richard Rorty once noted, if a higher knowledge of the forces that guide history were attainable without prophecies and demands. But even if today Marx seems somewhat dated in many respects, he formulated—in a manner that is still admirable—an important lesson learned in light of untrammeled industrial capitalism: the overthrow of authoritarian regimes and the creation of constitutional democracies is not enough to ensure equality and decency among human beings.[84]

What concerns us today—more so than his apocalyptic answers, attributable to the restless zeitgeist of the nineteenth century—are rather Marx's still-vexatious questions, through which he contemplated the unstable circumstances and self-destructive tendencies of our modern world. We have learned to mistrust prophesies, even those that, after the silent disappearance of communism, once again rashly predicted the end of history and have since been overthrown by the very spirits who proclaimed them.

Notes

1. Quoted in Jacques Droz, "Die Ursprünge der Sozialdemokratie in Deutschland," in Droz, *Geschichte des Sozialismus*, vol. 3, 20; quotation translated by Bernard Heise.
2. Brigitte Seebacher-Brandt, *Bebel: Künder und Kärrner im Kaiserreich* (Bonn, 1988), 157ff.
3. Marx, afterword to the second German edition of *Capital*, vol. 1, in MECW, vol. 35, 17.
4. Mehring, *Karl Marx*, 384.
5. Ibid., 382.
6. Seebacher-Brandt, *Bebel*, 144.
7. Liebknecht to Engels, 17 February 1865, in Wolfgang Schieder, *Karl Marx als Politiker* (Munich, 1991), 115; quotation translated by Bernard Heise.
8. Liebknecht to Marx, 13 May 1879, in Schieder, *Karl Marx als Politiker*, 115; quotation translated by Bernard Heise.
9. Joseph Rovan, *Geschichte der deutschen Sozialdemokratie* (Frankfurt am Main, 1980), 36.
10. Liebknecht, *Karl Marx*, 66 and 76.
11. Marx to Bracke, 5 May 1875, in MECW, vol. 45, 70; translator's note: the words here are translated directly from the German, Marx to Bracke, 5 May 1875, in MEW, vol. 34, 137.
12. Engels to Bebel, 18–28 March 1875, in MECW, vol. 24, 70, 67, 71,
13. Marx, "Marginal Notes on the Programme of the German Workers' Party," in MECW, vol. 24, 95f.
14. Quoted in Mayer, *Friedrich Engels*, vol. 2, 277; quotation translated by Bernard Heise.
15. Engels, preface to *Critique of the Gotha Programme* by Karl Marx, in MECW, vol. 27, 92f.
16. August Bebel, *Aus meinem Leben* (Berlin, 1988), 425f.; quotation translated by Bernard Heise.
17. Marx to Bracke, 5 May 1875, in MECW, vol. 45, 70.
18. Marx to Ferdinand Fleckles, 21 January 1877, in MECW, vol. 45, 190.
19. Marx, "Mr. George Howell's History of the International Working-Men's Association," in MECW, vol. 24, 239.
20. Marx to Wilhelm Alexander Freund, 21 January 1877, in MECW, vol. 45, 192.
21. Mayer, *Friedrich Engels*, vol. 2, 282.
22. Winkler, *Der lange Weg nach Westen*, vol. 1, 235; quotation translated by Bernard Heise.
23. Engels to Becker, 20 November 1876, in MECW, vol. 45, 174f.
24. Seebacher-Brandt, *Bebel*, 183; quotation translated by Bernard Heise.
25. Mayer, *Friedrich Engels*, vol. 2, 285; quotation translated by Bernard Heise.
26. Jacques Droz, introduction to Droz, *Geschichte des Sozialismus*, vol. 4, 14.
27. Engels to Turati, 16 August 1894, in MEW, vol. 39, 288.
28. Marx to Engels, 5 March 1877, in MECW, vol. 45, 205f.

29. Engels, *Anti-Dühring: Herr Eugen Dühring's Revolution in Science*, in MECW, vol. 25, 125, 23, 131.
30. Engels, *Ludwig Feuerbach and the End of Classical German Philosophy*, in MECW, vol. 26, 397.
31. Stürmer, *Das ruhelose Reich*, 217.
32. Gordon Craig, *Germany, 1866–1945* (Oxford, 1978), 143.
33. Engels to Lawrow, 10 August 1879, in MEW, vol. 34, 337; quotation translated by Bernard Heise.
34. Mayer, *Friedrich Engels*, vol. 2, 348.
35. "The Erfurt Program of 1891," in *From Revolutionary to Governing Party: Adjusting Political Programs: Selected Programs of German Social Democracy*, ed. Friedrich Ebert Stiftung (Manila, 2009), 7.
36. Winkler, *Der lange Weg nach Westen*, vol. 1, 288.
37. Engels to Kautsky, 3 December 1891, in MEW, vol. 38, 234.
38. Rosa Luxemburg, *Reform oder Revolution*, in *Gesammelte Werke*, 5 vols. (Berlin, 1970), vol. 1/1, 445.
39. *Vorwärts*, 26 March 1899; quotation translated by Bernard Heise.
40. Eduard Bernstein, *Die Voraussetzungen des Sozialismus und die Aufgaben der Sozialdemokratie* (Reinbek, 1969), 217; quotation translated by Bernard Heise.
41. Engels, "Speech at a Social-Democratic Meeting in Berlin on September 22, 1893," in MECW, vol. 27, 410.
42. "Interview of Frederick Engels by the *Daily Chronicle* Correspondent at the End of June 1893," in MECW, vol. 27, 553.
43. Engels to Marx, 10 March 1853, in MECW, vol. 39, 284.
44. Marx, Letter to *Otechestvenniye Zapiski*, in MECW, vol. 24, 199.
45. Marx, "Notizen zur Reform von 1861 und der damit verbundenen Entwicklung in Russland," in MEW, vol. 19, 407–424.
46. Marx to Nicolai Danielson, 12 December 1872, in MECW, vol. 44, 457.
47. Marx, afterword to the second German edition, *Capital*, vol. 1, in MECW, vol. 35, 15.
48. Marx, Letter to *Otechestvenniye Zapiski*, in MECW, vol. 24, 199.
49. Geoffrey Hosking, *Russia: People and Empire, 1552–1917* (London, 1997), 346f., 363f.
50. Nikolai G. Tschernyschewski, *Ausgewählte philosophische Schriften* (Moscow, 1953), 45ff.
51. Marx, Letter to Vera Zasulich, third draft, in MECW, vol. 24, 368.
52. Marx, Letter to Vera Zasulich, first draft, in MECW, vol. 24, 349, 360, 350.
53. Marx, "Notes on Bakunin's Book *Statehood and Anarchy*," in MECW, vol. 24, 518.
54. Marx, Letter to Vera Zasulich, first draft, in MECW, vol. 24, 349.
55. Gerd Koenen, "Ein deutscher Russland-Komplex? Elemente einer longue durée gegenseitiger Wahrnehmungen und projektiver Besetzungen," unpublished manuscript.
56. Engels, "On the Socialist Movement in Germany, France, the United States and Russia," in MECW, vol. 24, 205.
57. Marx to Sorge, 27 September 1877, in MECW, vol. 45, 278.
58. Marx to Liebknecht, 4 February 1878, in MECW, vol. 45, 296.

59. Hosking, *Russia*, 358.
60. Marx to Sorge, 5 November 1880, in *MECW*, vol. 46, 45.
61. Marx to Jenny Longuet, 11 April 1881, in *MECW*, vol. 46, 83.
62. Koenen, "Ein deutscher Russland-Komplex," 68.
63. Quoted in Hosking, *Russia*, 336.
64. Quoted in McLellan, *Karl Marx*, 441.
65. Marx to Zasulich, 8 March 1881, in *MECW*, vol. 46, 71.
66. Hosking, *Russia*, 361.
67. Hélène Carrère d'Encausse, *Lenin* (London, 2001), 32.
68. Koenen, "Ein deutscher Russland-Komplex," 67.
69. Marx and Engels, preface to the second Russian edition of the *Manifesto of the Communist Party*, in *MECW*, vol. 24, 426.
70. Ernest Gellner, *Bedingungen der Freiheit: Die Zivilgesellschaft und ihre Rivalen* (Stuttgart, 1995), 45.
71. Carrère d'Encausse, *Lenin*, 31.
72. Hosking, *Russia*, 358ff.
73. Carrère d'Encausse, *Lenin*, 32.
74. Engels to Lawrow, 24 March 1883, in *MECW*, vol. 46, 464.
75. Engels, "Karl Marx's Funeral," in *MECW*, vol. 24, 469.
76. Carrère d'Encausse, *Lenin*, 51.
77. Vladimir Ill'ich Lenin, *Essential Works of Lenin: "What Is to Be Done?" and Other Writings* (New York, 1966), 74.
78. Ibid., 112.
79. Marx and Engels, *The Holy Family*, in *MECW*, vol. 4, 37.
80. Heinrich August Winkler, "Die unwiederholbare Revolution," in *Streitfragen der deutschen Geschichte*, ed. Heinrich August Winkler (Munich, 1997), 9–30.
81. Gerd Koenen, *Utopie der Säuberungen: Was war der Kommunismus?* (Frankfurt am Main, 2000).
82. Martin Malia, *Vollstreckter Wahn: Sowjetunion 1917–1991* (Berlin, 1998).
83. Gellner, *Bedingungen der Freiheit*, 49.
84. Richard Rorty, *Das Kommunistische Manifest: 150 Jahre danach* (Frankfurt am Main, 1998), 29, 20.

BIBLIOGRAPHY

Akademie der Wissenschaften der DDR, Zentralinstitut für Literaturgeschichte and Centre d'Histoire et d'Analyse des Manuscrits Modernes am Centre National de la Recherche Scientifique, eds. *Heinrich Heine und die Zeitgenossen: Geschichtliche und literarische Befunde*. East Berlin, 1979.

Althusser, Louis, and Etienne Balibar. *Das Kapital lessen*. 2 vols. Reinbek, 1972.

Barclay, David. *Frederick William IV and the Prussian Monarchy 1840–1861*. Oxford, 1995.

Bauer, Bruno. *Feldzüge der reinen Kritik*. Frankfurt am Main, 1968.

Bebel, August. *Aus meinem Leben*. Berlin, 1988.

Bell, Daniel. *Die nachindustrielle Gesellschaft*. Frankfurt am Main, 1979.

Berlin, Isaiah. *Karl Marx: His Life and Environment*. New York, 1978.

Bernstein, Eduard. *Die Voraussetzungen des Sozialismus und die Aufgaben der Sozialdemokratie*. Reinbek, 1969.

Blanqui, Louis-Auguste. *Schriften zur Revolution, Nationalökonomie und Sozialkritik*. Reinbek, 1971.

Bleuel, Hans Peter. *Ferdinand Lassalle*. Frankfurt am Main, 1982.

Blos, Wilhelm. *Die Deutsche Revolution von 1848 bis 1849*. Berlin, 1923.

Buchheim, Christoph. *Industrielle Revolutionen*. Munich, 1994.

Busch, Günter. *Eugène Delacroix: Die Freiheit auf den Barrikaden*. Stuttgart, 1960.

Butler, Eliza Marian. *The Saint-Simonian Religion in Germany*. New York, 1960.

Carrère d'Encausse, Hélène. *Lenin*. London, 2001.

Clark, Christopher. *Preußen: Aufstieg und Niedergang 1600–1947*. Munich, 2007.

Craig, Gordon. *Germany, 1866–1945*. Oxford, 1978.

Croce, Benedetto. *History of Europe in the Nineteenth Century*. Translated by Henry Furst. New York, 1933.

Droz, Jacques, ed. *Geschichte des Sozialismus*. 4 vols. Frankfurt am Main, 1974.

Erinnerungen an Karl Marx. Berlin, 1953.

Fauvel, John et al., eds. *Newtons Werk: Die Begründung der modernen Naturwissenschaft*. Berlin, 1993.

Feuerbach, Ludwig. *Philosophische Kritiken und Grundsätze*. Leipzig, 1969.

Fourier, Charles. *Ökonomisch-philosophische Schriften*. Berlin, 1980.

Friedenthal, Richard. *Karl Marx: Sein Leben und seine Zeit*. Munich, 1983.

Friedrich Ebert Stiftung, ed. *From Revolutionary to Governing Party: Adjusting Political Programs: Selected Programs of German Social Democracy*. Manila, 2009.

Galbraith, John Kenneth. *The Great Crash 1929*. New York, 2009.

Gans, Eduard. *Philosophische Schriften*. Edited by Horst Schröder. Berlin, 1971.

Gellner, Ernest. *Bedingungen der Freiheit: Die Zivilgesellschaft und ihre Rivalen*. Stuttgart, 1995.

Gellner, Ernest. *Plough, Sword and Book*. Chicago, 1988.

Gillman, Joseph M. *Das Gesetz des tendenziellen Falls der Profitrate*. Frankfurt am Main, 1969.

Guizot, François Pierre Guillaume. *Die Demokratie in Frankreich*. Grimma, 1849.

Gurvitch, Georges. *Dialektik und Soziologie*. Berlin, 1965.

Gutzkow, Karl. *Wally, die Zweiflerin*. Frankfurt am Main, 1974.

Habermas, Jürgen. *Zur Rekonstruktion des Historischen Materialismus*. Frankfurt am Main, 1976.

Habermas, Jürgen. *Der philosophische Diskurs der Moderne*. Frankfurt am Main, 1988.

Hahn, Manfred, ed. *Vormarxistischer Sozialismus*. Frankfurt am Main, 1974.

Hardtwig, Wolfgang. *Vormärz: Der monarchische Staat und das Bürgertum*. Munich, 1998.

Hazard, Paul. *Die Krise des europäischen Geistes 1680–1715*. Hamburg, 1939.

Hegel, Georg Wilhelm Friedrich. *Briefe von und an Hegel*. Edited by Johannes Hoffmeister. 4 vols. Hamburg, 1954.

Hegel, Georg Wilhelm Friedrich. *Werke in zwanzig Bänden*. Edited by Eva Moldenhauer and Karl M. Michel. 20 vols. Frankfurt am Main, 1969–1971.

Hegel, Georg Wilhelm Friedrich. *The Difference between Fichte's and Schelling's System of Philosophy*. Albany, 1977.

Hegel, Georg Wilhelm Friedrich. *Hegel's Doctrine of Formal Logic*, in *G.W.F. Hegel: The Oxford University Press Translations*. Electronic edition. Oxford, 2000.

Hegel, *Encyclopaedia of the Philosophical Sciences*, §147, OUP, 208.

Hegel, Georg Wilhelm Friedrich. *G.W.F. Hegel: The Oxford University Press Translations*. Electronic edition. Oxford, 2000.

Hegel, Georg Wilhelm Friedrich. *The Philosophy of History*. Translated by J. Sibree. Kitchener, Ontario, 2001.

Heine, Heinrich. *The Poems of Heine*. Translated by Edgar Alfred Bowring. London, 1866.

Heinrich Heine, *Sämtliche Schriften in zwölf Bänden*. Edited by Klaus Briegleb. 12 vols. Munich, 1976.

Heine, Heinrich. *The Works of Heinrich Heine*. 20 vols. Translated by Charles Godfrey Leland. London, 1893.

Herrnstadt, Rudolf. *Die Entdeckung der Klassen*. Berlin, 1965.

Herwegh, Georg. *Werke in einem Band*. East Berlin, 1975.

Herwegh, Georg, ed. *Einundzwanzig Bogen aus der Schweiz* [1843]. Leipzig, 1989.

Hess, Moses. *The Holy History of Mankind and Other Writings*. Translated and edited with an introduction by Shlomo Avineri. Cambridge, 2004.

Hobsbawm, Eric. *The Age of Revolution 1789–1848*. New York, 1996.

Höppner, Joachim, and Waltraud Seidel-Höppner. *Von Babeuf bis Blanqui: Französischer Sozialismus vor Marx*. 2 vols. Leipzig, 1976.

Hosfeld, Rolf. "Massendemokratie oder Erziehungsdiktatur? Überlegungen zur politischen Form der Diktatur des Proletariats bei Marx." In *Eurokommunismus und Theorie der Politik*, ed. Hans Werner Franz et al. Berlin, 1979.

Hosfeld, Rolf. *Die Welt als Füllhorn: Heine: Das neunzehnte Jahrhundert zwischen Romantik und Moderne*. Berlin, 1984.

Hosfeld, Rolf. *Georg Wilhelm Friedrich Hegel*. Berlin, 1988.

Hosfeld, Rolf, and Hermann Pölking. *Die Deutschen 1815–1918: Fürstenherrlichkeit und Bürgerwelten*. Munich, 2007.

Hosking, Geoffrey. *Russia: People and Empire, 1552–1917*. London, 1997.

Immermann, Karl. *Werke*. Edited by Harry Maync. Vol. 3. Leipzig, n.d.

Jessen, Jens, ed. *Fegefeuer des Marktes: Die Zukunft des Kapitalismus*. Munich, 2006.

Koenen, Gerd. "Ein deutscher Russland-Komplex? Elemente einer longue durée gegenseitiger Wahrnehmungen und projektiver Besetzungen." Unpublished manuscript.

Koenen, Gerd. *Utopie der Säuberung: Was war der Kommunismus?* Frankfurt am Main, 2000.

Kojéve, Alexandre. *Hegel: Kommentar zur Phänomenologie des Geistes*. Frankfurt am Main, 1975.

Kool, Frits, and Werner Krause, eds. *Die frühen Sozialisten*. 2 vols. Munich, 1972.

Kosellek, Reinhart. *Preußen zwischen Reform und Revolution*. Stuttgart, 1987.

Lasky, Melvin J. *Utopia and Revolution: On the Origins of a Metaphor*. Chicago, 1976.

Lenin, Vladimir Ill'ich. *Essential Works of Lenin: "What Is to Be Done?" and Other Writings*. New York, 1966.

Lenin, Vladimir Ill'ich. *The State and Revolution*. Whitefish, MT, 2004.

Lenk, Kurt. *Deutscher Konservatismus*. Frankfurt am Main, 1989.

Lewald, Fanny. *Erinnerungen aus dem Jahre 1848*. Frankfurt am Main, 1969.

Liebknecht, Wilhelm. *Karl Marx: Biographical Memoirs*. Chicago, 1908.

Löwith, Karl. *Von Hegel zu Nietzsche: Der revolutionäre Bruch im Denken des neunzehnten Jahrhunderts*. Frankfurt am Main, 1969.

Löwith, Karl. *Der Mensch inmitten der Geschichte: Philosophische Bilanz des 20. Jahrhunderts*. Stuttgart, 1990.

Löwith, Karl. *Weltgeschichte und Heilsgeschehen: Die theologischen Voraussetzungen der Geschichtsphilosophie*. Stuttgart, 2004.

Lübbe, Hermann. *Politische Philosophie in Deutschland*. Munich, 1974.

Lutz, Heinrich. *Zwischen Habsburg und Preußen: Deutschland 1815–1866*. Berlin, 1985.

Luxemburg, Rosa. *Reform oder Revolution*, vol. 1/1, *Gesammelte Werke*, 5 vols. Berlin, 1970.

Malia, Martin. *The Soviet Tragedy – A History of Socialism in Russia 1917-1991*. Free Press, New York, 1994.

Mann, Golo. *Friedrich von Gentz: Geschichte eines europäischen Staatsmannes*. Frankfurt am Main, 1972.

Marcuse, Herbert. *Reason and Revolution: Hegel and the Rise of Social Theory*. Humanities Press, New York, 2nd Ed., 1954.

Marx, Karl. *Grundrisse der Kritik der Politischen Ökonomie*. Berlin, 1953.

Marx, Karl, and Friedrich Engels. *Werke (MEW)*. 39 vols. and 2 supplementary vols. Berlin, 1956–1990.

Marx, Karl, and Frederick Engels. *The Collected Works of Marx and Engels (MECW)*. Electronic Edition. InteLex: 2003.

Mayer, Gustav. *Friedrich Engels: Eine Biographie*. 2 vols. Frankfurt am Main, 1975.

McLellan, David. *The Young Hegelians and Karl Marx*. London, 1969.

McLellan, David. *Die Junghegelianer und Karl Marx*. Munich, 1974.

McLellan, David. *Karl Marx: His Life and Thought*. Bristol, 1973.

McLellan, David. *Karl Marx: Leben und Werk*. Munich, 1974.

Mehring, Franz. *Karl Marx: The Story of His Life*. London, 2003.

Meißner, Alfred. *Ich traf auch Heine in Paris: Unter Künstlern und Revolutionären in den Metropolen Europas*. Berlin, 1973.

Mignet, François Auguste. *Geschichte der Französischen Revolution von 1789 bis 1814*. Leipzig, 1975.

Mohr und General: Erinnerungen an Marx und Engels. Berlin, 1985.

Nietzsche, Friedrich. *Thus Spoke Zarathustra: A Book for All and None*. Translated by Adrian Del Caro. Cambridge, 2006.

Nipperdey, Thomas. *Deutsche Geschichte 1800–1866: Bürgerwelt und starker Staat*. Munich, 1983.

Nipperdey, Thomas. *Deutsche Geschichte 1866–1918: Arbeitswelt und Bürgergeist*. Munich, 1994.

North, Michael, ed. *Deutsche Wirtschaftsgeschichte*. Munich, 2000.

Pepperle, Ingrid. *Junghegelianische Geschichtsphilosophie und Kunsttheorie*. Berlin, 1978.

Pepperle, Heinz, and Ingrid Pepperle, eds. *Die Hegelsche Linke: Dokumente zu Philosophie und Politik im deutschen Vormärz*. Leipzig, 1985.

Peters, Heinz Frederick. *Die rote Jenny: Ein Leben mit Karl Marx*. Munich, 1984.

Pflanze, Otto. *Bismarck: Der Reichsgründer*. Munich, 1997.

Proudhon, Pierre-Joseph. *Bekenntnisse eines Revolutionärs*. Reinbek, 1969.

Raddatz, Fritz J. *Karl Marx: Eine politische Biographie*. Hamburg, 1975.

Reichelt, Helmut. *Zur logischen Struktur des Kapitalbegriffs bei Karl Marx*. Frankfurt am Main, 1970.

Reissner, Hanns-Günter. *Eduard Gans: Ein Leben im Vormärz*. Tübingen, 1965.

Ribhegge, Wilhelm. *Das Parlament als Nation: Die Frankfurter Nationalversammlung 1848/49*. Düsseldorf, 1998.

Ribhegge, Wilhelm. *Konservative Politik in Deutschland: Von der Französischen Revolution bis zur Gegenwart*. Darmstadt, 1992.

Riedel, Manfred, ed. *Materialien zu Hegels Rechtsphilosophie*. 2 vols. Frankfurt am Main, 1975.

Robinson, Joan. *Economics: An Awkward Corner*. New York, 1967.

Rochau, Ludwig August von. *Grundsätze der Realpolitik: Angewendet auf die staatlichen Zustände Deutschlands*. Frankfurt am Main, 1972.

Rorty, Richard. *Das Kommunistische Manifest: 150 Jahre danach*. Frankfurt am Main, 1998.

Rosdolsky, Roman. *Zur Entstehungsgeschichte des Marxschen "Kapital."* 2 vols. Frankfurt am Main, 1968.

Rousseau, Jean-Jacques. *Emile*. Teddington, 2007.

Rovan, Joseph. *Geschichte der deutschen Sozialdemokratie*. Frankfurt am Main, 1980.

Ruge, Arnold, and Karl Marx, eds. *Deutsch-Französische Jahrbücher* [1844]. Frankfurt am Main, 1973.

Salomon-Delatour, Gottfried, ed. *Die Lehre Saint-Simons*. Neuwied, 1962.

Schieder, Wolfgang. *Karl Marx als Politiker*. Munich, 1991.

Schmidt, Alfred. *Emanzipatorische Sinnlichkeit: Ludwig Feuerbachs anthropologischer Materialismus*. Munich, 1973.

Schneider, Michael. *Kleine Geschichte der Gewerkschaften: Ihre Entwicklung in Deutschland von den Anfängen bis heute*. Bonn, 2000.

Schnerb, Robert. *Europa im 19. Jahrhundert: Europa als Weltmacht*. Munich, 1983.

Schuffenhauer, Werner. *Feuerbach und der junge Marx*. Berlin, 1972.

Schumpeter, Joseph. *Kapitalismus, Sozialismus und Demokratie*. Bern, 1950.

Schunck, Peter. *Geschichte Frankreichs von Heinrich IV. bis zur Gegenwart*. Munich, 1994.

Schweitzer, Albert. *Geschichte der Leben-Jesu-Forschung*. Tübingen, 1933.

Seebacher-Brandt, Brigitte. *Bebel. Künder und Kärrner im Kaiserreich*. Bonn, 1988.

Seidel-Höppner, Waltraud. *Wilhelm Weitling*. Berlin, 1961.

Sengle, Friedrich. *Biedermeierzeit: Deutsche Literatur im Spannungsfeld zwischen Restauration und Revolution 1817–1848*. Vol. 1. Stuttgart, 1971.

Sennett, Richard. *Die Kultur des neuen Kapitalismus*. Berlin, 2007.

Siemann, Wolfram. *Die deutsche Revolution von 1848/49*. Frankfurt am Main, 1985.

Siemann, Wolfram. *Vom Staatenbund zum Nationalstaat: Deutschland 1806–1871*. Munich, 1995.

Smith, Adam. *An Inquiry Into the Nature and Causes of the Wealth of Nations: The Glasgow Edition of the Works and Correspondence of Adam Smith*. Electronic edition. InteLex: 2002.

Soros, George. *Die Krise des globalen Kapitalismus: Die offene Gesellschaft in Gefahr*. Frankfurt am Main, 2000.

Stein, Lorenz von. *Die industrielle Gesellschaft: Der Sozialismus und Kommunismus Frankreichs von 1830 bis 1848*. Munich, 1921.

Sternberger, Dolf. *Panorama oder Ansichten vom 19. Jahrhundert*. Frankfurt am Main, 1974.

Sternberger, Dolf. *Gerechtigkeit für das neunzehnte Jahrhundert*. Frankfurt am Main, 1975.

Steussloff, Hans, ed. *Die Junghegelianer: Ausgewählte Texte*. Berlin, 1963.

Stürmer, Michael. *Das ruhelose Reich. Deutschland 1866–1918*. Munich, 2004.

Taylor, Charles. *Hegel*. Frankfurt am Main, 1983.

Thurow, Lester C. *Fortune Favors the Bold: What We Must Do to Build A Long and Lasting Global Prosperity*. New York, 2003.

Tiliette, Xavier. *Schelling: Biographie*. Stuttgart, 2004.

Tschernyschewski, Nikolai G. *Ausgewählte philosophische Schriften*. Moscow, 1953.

Ungers, Liselotte, and Oswald Mathias Ungers. *Kommunen in der Neuen Welt*. Cologne, 1972.

Varnhagen von Ense, Karl August. *Kommentare zum Zeitgeschehen*. Leipzig, 1984.

Warschauer, Otto. *Saint-Simon und der Saint-Simonismus*. Leipzig, 1892.

Weber, Rolf, ed. *Revolutionsbriefe 1848/49*. Leipzig, 1973.

Wehler, Hans-Ulrich. *Deutsche Gesellschaftsgeschichte*. Vol. 2. Munich, 1996.

Weigel, Siegfried. *Der negative Marx: Marx im Urteil seiner Zeitgenossen*. Stuttgart, 1976.

Wheen, Francis. *Karl Marx: Das Kapital*. Munich, 2008.

Winkler, Heinrich August. *Der lange Weg nach Westen: Deutsche Geschichte vom Ende des Alten Reiches bis zum Untergang der Weimarer Republik*. Munich, 2000.

Winkler, Heinrich August, ed. *Streitfragen der deutschen Geschichte*. Munich, 1997.

Zeleny, Jindrich. *Die Wissenschaftslogik und "Das Kapital."* 2 vols. Frankfurt am Main, 1968.

INDEX OF NAMES